Online Communication

Linking Technology, Identity, and Culture

LEA'S COMMUNICATION SERIES

Jennings Bryant / Dolf Zillmann, General Editors

For a complete list of titles in LEA's Communication Series, please contact Lawrence Erlbaum Associates, Publishers, at www.erlbaum.com.

Online Communication

Linking Technology, Identity, and Culture

Second Edition

Andrew F. Wood
San José State University

Matthew J. Smith
Wittenberg University

2005 LAWRENCE ERLBAUM ASSOCIATES, PUBLISHERS
Mahwah, New Jersey   London

Senior Acquisitions Editor:	Linda Bathgate
Assistant Editor:	Karin Wittig Bates
Textbook Production Manager:	Paul Smolenski
Full-Service Compositor:	TechBooks
Text and Cover Printer:	Hamilton Printing Company

This book was typeset in 10/12 pt. Palatino Roman, Bold, Italic.
The heads were typeset in Stone Sans, Bold, Italic, and Bold Italic.

Cover design by Kathryn Houghtaling Lacey, based on an original design by Andrew Wood

Lawrence Erlbaum Associates, Inc., Publishers
10 Industrial Avenue
Mahwah, NJ 07430
www.erlbaum.com

Library of Congress Cataloging-in-Publication Data

Wood, Andrew F.
    Online communication : linking technology, identity, and culture / Andrew F. Wood, Matthew J. Smith. – 2nd ed.
        p.   cm. – (LEA's communication series)
    Includes bibliographical references and index.
    ISBN 0-8058-4849-5 (pbk. : alk. paper)
        1. Information technology—Social aspects.   2. Communication and technology.
    3. Communication—Social aspects.   I. Smith, Matthew J., 1971-   II. Title   III. Series.
    HM851 .W66 2005
    303.48'33—dc22

                                                                        2004013812

Books published by Lawrence Erlbaum Associates are printed on acid-free paper, and their bindings are chosen for strength and durability.

Printed in the United States of America
10 9 8 7 6 5 4 3 2

For my wife and daughter,
Jenny and Vienna,
my family in the valley and over the hill . . .
—ANDY

For my family,
Susan, Trevor, and Kent,
my links to reality . . .
—MATT

BRIEF CONTENTS

DETAILED CONTENTS

Part II: The Self Among Others

When someone says, "I'm going online," where are they going? Early in the 21st century, when so much of the globe is mapped and so much geography charted, is there really a new place to be visited on the World Wide Web? We think so. Considering online communication as a metaphorical journey involves adopting many of the same words and images that we use in other excursions. We borrow ideas from our physical interactions to make sense of communication through computer networks. Using the Internet, we *send* mail, we *visit* libraries, we even *surf*. Yet these words alone limit our understanding of online communication, so we must employ new ones. *Uploading, downloading, pinging, networking*—these relatively new words hint at a new world of human interaction that emerged with the popularization of the Internet. As you can guess, hundreds of books promise to make sense of this new world. The problem is that most of these books try to explore online communication as merely a site of new technologies. Few attempt the synthesis of technology, identity, and culture that we feel can place the Internet in human perspective. This book is our attempt to fill that void.

Online Communication aims to help you conceptualize the human uses of the Internet by examining the emerging theories that offer explanations for what people are doing with this technology, socially and communicatively. Now, for some people, *theory* is a dirty word. It suggests lofty and vague treatises, far beyond the grasp of the average person. Theory, however, has gotten a bad rap. When explained with accessible language and concrete examples, as we have tried to do here, theory helps us to see how processes tend to function in a variety of occurrences rather than in just one case. The value to using theory when approaching the Internet is this: Understanding how communication processes function in general will allow you to apply them to recognizing specific instances of these occurrences in your own life.

Over the last several years, a great deal has been written about the effects of computers on human communication. Journalists have made it the focus of their human interest stories, critics have cited it as the root cause of declines in society, and scholars have examined its effects on everything from the way we think to the way we relate to others. In order to establish some sense of coherence in addressing this body of information, we have organized this book into three general sections with 10 specifically themed chapters. What follows, then, is a brief overview of those sections and chapters and other key features you will encounter in reading *Online Communication*.

Part I of this book includes two chapters that serve as introductions to both the technologies of the Internet Age and their social implications. Beginning with chapter 1, we introduce computer-mediated communication (CMC) as a subject of academic research and a fascinating site where we may examine contemporary trends in society.

We examine CMC as a blurring of two types of interaction, immediacy and media-tion, in order to challenge the assumption that communication aided by computer networks is necessarily less personal and less powerful than traditional modes of human discourse. We then identify the technological and social features that distin-guish five common forms of CMC: electronic mail (e-mail), bulletin boards systems (BBS), Internet relay chat (IRC), multiuser domains (MUDs), and the World Wide Web (WWW). We conclude this chapter with an in-depth examination of the domi-nant metaphor used in conjunction with the Internet, *cyberspace*, and we consider the origins and implications of this frequently invoked term.

In chapter 2, we focus our attention further on the technology of online commu-nication, including a brief history of network computer technology as a social force. Starting with 19th-century thinking machines, we cover the modern evolution of cy-bernetic devices that influence our interaction with people and the environment. We provide specific insight on the Internet's evolution from a military command and con-trol network to the Web as a kind of cybernetic organism. We then address the essential characteristics that distinguish the Internet from other interpersonal and mass com-munication contexts by reviewing five key features setting it apart: packet-switching, multimedia, interactivity, synchronicity, and hypertextuality.

Part II of the book considers issues of online identity, taking into account how people construct presentations of self within a social environment. We begin with the construction of online identity in chapter 3. This chapter opens with a discussion of the phenomenon of *telepresence*, that is, the degree of realism one perceives through a given medium. We then turn to the role of theatrical metaphors in several scholarly studies of Internet usage and explain how qualities of role-taking and play are evident in online interactions. We also examine the degree to which online identities can be anonymous, and we raise warnings that the Information Age presents dangers to one's individual identity, online and in real life, in the forms of shadow identities and identity fraud, respectively.

Because personal identity affects interpersonal communication, we turn to ques-tions of establishing online relationships in chapter 4. Scholarly arguments contend that there are three distinct perspectives here: One asserts that CMC fosters an imper-sonal environment that is hostile to relationships; another says that CMC can sustain interpersonal relationships that are comparable to those negotiated face to face; and yet another suggests that CMC presents a hyperpersonal context in which people uncomfortable or unsuccessful in other contexts can excel at relating. In addition to a variety of theories associated with each of these perspectives, we also deal with relationship issues such as the online conflicts known as *flame wars* and infidelity in the form of *cyberaffairs*.

Our consideration of identity continues in chapter 5, where we consider how people address their own well-being through computer-mediated channels. Herein, we con-sider the controversial concept of Internet Addiction Disorder, presenting the cases for and against the existence of this communication-based problem. Thereafter, we also discuss ways in which people seek the aid of others in various forms of online ther-apy, such as virtual support groups. Accordingly, we review the types of messages that people typically exchange in these venues and pause to consider the possible shortfalls of these mediated dialogues as well.

The last chapter in this section on creating the self among others, chapter 6, re-flects on the growth of the social aggregate itself, the so-called virtual community. We examine several historical precedents for today's virtual communities, including the imagined communities created by the mass media and fan communities. We define the virtual community in terms of essential qualities and its attraction to participants and examine what standards and sanctions are in place to regulate the social behavior of good Internet citizens, or *netizens*.

Our third and final section, Part III, addresses issues of how the Internet has affected our culture and how people have responded to those changes with critiques. For example, in chapter 7, we turn to the corporate side of online communication and its impact on the information economy. Initially, we focus on the use of computer networks to enforce corporate discipline. We then turn our attention to methods in which corporations employ online communication to survey and influence the behaviors of consumers with techniques such as "cookies," voluntary data submission, and data mining. Along with discipline, we study the diffusion of innovation through computer technology in corporate environments, paying particular attention to the roles of interaction and diversity as factors that influence the pace of computer-mediated change at work. Finally, we evaluate the trend of corporate convergence and the creation of megamedia whose embrace of online communication promises to change fundamentally the ways in which we entertain and educate ourselves. We conclude this chapter with a discussion of the rise, fall, and potential rebirth of the Internet economy.

Chapter 8 addresses another question of culture shift, and the critiques that accompany it, when it examines the question of whether a digital divide exists beyond the media hype. We examine this divide along demographic dimensions such as gender, race, and class. We then turn to governmental and community-based efforts to close the digital divide before exploring recent critiques of the digital divide as an artificial problem that obscures more significant concerns. We conclude with a reminder that the theorized gap between information haves and have-nots may be debatable in the United States, but this divide is undeniable around the world.

Chapter 9 offers a response to the argument that online communication merely provides another site where the same old powers-that-be exercise control over our lives. To explore this possibility, we discuss the notion of discursive resistance through which individuals and groups employ online communication to critique economic and social systems while proposing new ones. This notion challenges us to theorize cyber*space* as a site to challenge dominant *places* of power. Although we offer case studies of ways in which online communication provides disenfranchised folks a chance to gain a voice in public life, we also note the rise of Web-based hate groups that employ the same freedoms for more insidious goals.

Chapter 10 concludes the volume with a study of the ways in which popular culture artifacts such as books and films attempt to make sense of the increasing role computer technologies play in our lives. This analysis begins with the "cyberpunk" movement and its literary antecedents dating back to Mary Shelley's *Frankenstein*. Studying cyberpunk, we reveal consistently appearing themes in literary evaluations of computer technology including fears that human beings may become obsolete in comparison with the machine. Turning to film, we see similar trends in movies ranging from Lang's (1926) *Metropolis* to the Wachowski brothers' *Matrix* trilogy. Although books and films may not represent "high" culture, they do manage to provide powerful insight into the ways in which we struggle to make sense of online communication.

In addition to the contents of the chapters themselves, three special components of *Online Communication* merit special attention: These fall under the labels Hyperlink, Ethical Inquiry, and Online Communication and the Law. Throughout this text, you will find material that has been set apart from the text in a stylized box and labeled a Hyperlink. If you are familiar with the Web, then you know that a hyperlink is a specially marked symbol (in the form of either words or images on the computer screen) that when clicked with a mouse will "jump" to another site on the Web. Clicking a hyperlink is like following a tangent, a line of thought that is related to but somewhat "off course" from the direction of a conversation. As you will see, our Hyperlinks perform a similar function in that they present information and indicate topics related to but not explored in as much depth as those themes addressed in each chapter. However, we hope that the insights presented in these asides will serve as bases for discussion in your classroom, around your dinner table, in a chat room, and wherever else you might find your own conversations "jumping," as it were, to online communication.

Along with Hyperlinks, boxes also set off an Ethical Inquiry in each chapter. Reviewers of the first edition of *Online Communication* asked for even more consideration of how people are using their communication tools and talents in responsible and respectful manners. In response, we offer questions about the nature of human communication conduct online. Rather than prescribe codes for ethical conduct per se, we hope that these interludes serve to spark discussion, within the reader, among classmates, or even involving people not reading this text. Our aim is to prompt discussion about the ethical challenges people face as they originate their new communication behaviors and translate some of their old communication behaviors into the online environment. Our hope is to spur readers on to reconsider, if not reaffirm, their positions as ethical communicators by weighing the choices and consequences they may well face, such as those in the brief queries presented here.

Additionally, we have placed a section entitled Online Communication and the Law at the conclusion of each chapter. Although this book is not geared for prelaw students, we have found that our attempt to provide a synthesis of technology, identity, and culture demanded some attention to the legal ramifications of the issues raised in this text. The belief by many Internet advocates that "information wants to be free"— illustrated by the fierce debate inspired by the Napster case—has met fierce response by artists seeking to protect their labor, corporations seeking to protect their profits, and parents seeking to protect their children. Similarly, the belief of many Internet observers that this medium should be regulated and taxed raises troubling questions: Who has the authority to monitor online content and seek revenue from Internet-based sales? The city, the state, the nation, or some other entity? Given that the Internet is not "based" in any locality, it is hard to imagine where it may be defined as a legal entity. These are good times to be an Internet lawyer! Thus, we tackle thorny legal issues that emerge from our chapters' topics such as one's right to "flame" other Internet users to recent efforts by the recording industry to flame peer-to-peer music sharers. If any of these topics seem entirely new to you, don't worry. They won't be for long. Ideally, the introduction of these special sections—Hyperlinks, Ethical Inquiries, and Online Communication and the Law—will provoke some stimulating conversations among your colleagues.

ACKNOWLEDGMENTS

In getting to the point where we could share our perspective of this material, we had considerable help along the way. We would like to thank our respective universities, San José State University and Wittenberg University, as well as our colleagues at each institution for their support while we were drafting this text. Second, we are grateful to several anonymous reviewers and colleagues teaching computer-mediated communication around the United States whose insights helped us to refine our prose. Third, we owe our gratitude to our editor, Linda Bathgate, and the staff of Lawrence Erlbaum Associates for their confidence in this project. Fourth, we express our appreciation to Joanne Bowser and her team of professionals at TechBooks for their superb editing skills. Fifth, we want to acknowledge the faculty of our alma mater, Ohio University, who helped encourage our scholarly efforts by guiding, challenging, and mentoring us through many intellectual, personal, and professional obstacles. Finally, we thank our students who offered critical advice to draft versions of this book. Our students guide us and inspire us to try great things. We hope this volume does the same for them.

—Andy and Matt

PART I

THE INTERNET AS SOCIAL TECHNOLOGY

The growing impact that the Internet has on our lives is increasingly difficult to ignore. Even those who might claim to be "computer illiterate" are likely to encounter the direct or indirect effects that the Internet has had on the society in which we live. For example, pick up *The Wall Street Journal* and you are likely to see that the stock market has risen or fallen in correspondence with the successes and failures of Internet-based companies. Begin a term project by doing some research, and you are likely to find that the campus library has all but abandoned card catalogs in favor of a quicker, more space-efficient electronic system, one that is probably accessible from your dorm room or home. Turn to your classmates and ask if they or someone they know has ever made friends or had a date with someone they met online, and they will probably cite an acquaintance or two. Without having to look much farther than the world around you, you are likely to find the ever-increasing influence of the Internet in the realms of economics, academics, and personal relationships, among many others.

Despite its pervasiveness in our lives, however, how well do you really understand the Internet? Here, we are not asking about your knowledge of the programming languages and hardware configurations that make the Internet function. Our colleagues in computer science best explain those technical matters. Rather, we are asking about your understanding of the human uses (and misuses) of that technology in social terms. This first part of the book provides some insights for addressing this question. In the next two chapters, you will read about the social character of the Internet, that is, how people have conceptualized and used the various Internet technologies in accord with or in consideration of one another. The communicative, historical, and linguistic concepts that we introduce in this part of the book form a foundation for the discussions we build on in subsequent chapters. Furthermore, they testify to the growing breadth and depth of the technology's effects on human thought and action.

CHAPTER 1

Using Technology to Communicate in New Ways

The Internet is like a giant jellyfish. You can't step on it. You can't go around it. You've got to get through it.

—John Evans

At the heart of this book rests a basic assumption: Communicating in computer-mediated contexts is somehow different than any other form of communication. Software engineer Ellen Ullman (1996) describes encounters in which these differences have been made apparent to her. She regularly communicates with her fellow computer programmers and her supervisors through her computer. Over the years, she has reportedly acclimated to the shortness and arrogance that many of her colleagues seem to convey in their correspondence. Such behavior is, of course, not restricted to online interaction. However, what has struck Ullman more are the contrasts she has noted between mediated and face-to-face interactions with her coworkers. Two examples illustrate Ullman's keen perceptions.

On one occasion, Ullman (1996) found herself up one night and decided to send a message to a colleague. He happened to be awake as well and, after reading her message, wrote back to inquire why she was up so late. The two exchanged cordial messages that night, yet the next day when they attended a corporate meeting together, Ullman was unsure about how to approach him. They had, after all, been friendly with one another just hours before, yet in the office setting, she questioned, "In what way am I permitted to *know* him? And which set of us is the more real: the sleepless ones online, or these bodies in the daylight?" (p. 6).

On another occasion, Ullman (1996) had struck up a romantic relationship with a fellow programmer. For quite a while, the two communicated exclusively through exchanges of electronic mail (e-mail). He would send her a message, she would reply, and so forth. This continued with increasing frequency, until they were writing to one another almost every waking hour. Eventually, the couple decided to meet for dinner, and when they did, Ullman noticed something unusual about their conversation. "One talks, stops; then the other replies, stops. An hour later, we are still in this rhythm. With a shock, I realize that we have finally gone out to dinner only to *exchange e-mail*" (p. 17).

The questions and patterns that Ullman developed as a practitioner of computer-mediated communication (CMC) did not fully emerge until she saw the assumptions of one form of interaction contrasted with another. What she had learned to accept as norms in the world of computer mediation seemed odd and uncomfortable to her in real life. Some people report a similar feeling of dissonance when working in just the opposite manner, coming from the familiar practices of face-to-face interaction to the subtle distinctions associated with CMC. Either way, people like Ullman, and perhaps you, are aware that some things about the online experience are different.

In this chapter, we examine CMC to understand the experience of online interaction. Naturally, this requires an overview of just what CMC is and how it fits within the field of communication studies and popular culture. Following this discussion, we examine CMC as a blurring between immediate and mediated communication. As shown here, this process of blurring holds important implications for our conceptions of self and society. The question remains, however: How do we communicate differently in this medium than through other traditional modes of interaction? Answering that, we explore popular components of online communication, including e-mail, bulletin board systems (BBSs), internet relay chat (IRC), multiuser domains (MUDs), and the World Wide Web (WWW). The third major section of this chapter introduces the study of cyberspace as a metaphoric means to understanding CMC. To that end, we explore the meaning of the word *cyberspace* and the location of the cyberspace experience before extending our study to the alternative metaphors for our online interactions. We conclude with a reminder that dominant spatial metaphors for CMC may limit our understanding of this environment.

WHAT IS CMC?

In this section, we begin to explore **computer-mediated communication** (CMC) as an integration of computer technology with our everyday lives. The field of CMC studies how human behaviors are maintained or altered by exchange of information through machines. How do we study this process? By pulling on the insights of a variety of researchers and commentators. In communication studies, most scholars avoid setting up disciplinary boundaries so rigid that we miss out on fascinating human phenomena simply because they don't "fit" artificial boundaries. We do not want to neglect the contributions that allied fields like psychology, sociology, and composition studies (to name but a few) have to offer. Even within an area of research as specific as CMC, we must not lose sight of how this mode of human interaction affects so many parts of our lives as to be almost ever present. Nonetheless, it is all too easy for us to blur the distinction between our chosen focus of study and the larger forces of technology shaping our lives. Doing so, we risk making this text an unmanageable mess. For the sake of simplicity, therefore, we propose that our study is limited to the analysis of those technologies that serve more or less directly to mediate intentional human communication.

Here's an example: Although nuclear power plants—each with many computer processors and terminals—remain a significant component of the U.S. energy system, these sites would not play a significant role in the study of CMC. We talk about nuclear power plants—their potentials and their threats—but we seldom talk through them. The presence of computer technology, therefore, does not constitute the only required component for our analysis. We choose, instead, to focus on those technologies that help individuals and groups relate to one another in some fashion, for good or for ill.

As you might guess, the primary focus of our work is the Internet—that network of networks. Although we learn more about the Internet later in this chapter, it is important at this point to know a key distinction we make between the chips and channels that comprise this medium. Although the architecture of computer devices that aid the transmission of digitized information around the world is itself a fascinating topic, such an inquiry is beyond the scope of this book. Rather, we have chosen to focus on the channels of communication made possible by the Internet, on what has been called the "space within [the] lines" where human beings exert individual will, conduct business, and form communities. In this way, the emergence of telephony in the 19th century is quite analogous to our study of contemporary computer technologies. The principle of mediated discourse—whether mainly by way of telephone or through the more sophisticated technologies of today's desktop computers—inspires careful examination because of its potential to alter human interaction without the need for physical presence.

WHY STUDY CMC?

Certainly the student of communication can find plenty of other phenomena to explore, such as small-group interaction, corporate culture building, and health care discourse. However, we focus on CMC because of its impact on all of those contexts. Many student "study teams" find online chat rooms to be more convenient than face-to-face interaction. Many corporate offices streamline internal communication with e-mail. Many patients use the Web to inform themselves about their medical options. In each case, the introduction of online media changes day-to-day life and alters, to some degree, how we relate to each other.

We approach these topics with a desire to understand the blurring of technology with our everyday lives. We study the sophisticated ways in which computer technology—the microchips that process information and execute commands and the software that allows human beings to employ this technology—is integrated into our physical environments, interpersonal relationships, and even senses of personal identity. Although technology has always played a role in social life, the power of computer technology offers a new dimension to this theme. Where computing devices were once rare, expensive, and so complicated as to require expert attention at all times, the computers we use are more subtly embedded in our lives. Our use of telephones, cars, microwave ovens, and even clothing increasingly requires some use of computer technology. Thus, when we study CMC, we don't just explore the use of technology in communication; we study the blurring of technology with our everyday lives.

Thus far, we have identified CMC as the study of how human behaviors are maintained or altered through exchange of information through machines, and we have positioned CMC research within the realm of communication studies. Our next step is to examine a key component of communicating online, the distinction between immediacy and mediation. As we discover, computer-mediated interaction increasingly appears to blur any distinction between these terms.

IMMEDIACY VERSUS MEDIATION

Think back to Ullman's (1996) narratives. She felt tension regarding a colleague with whom she had communicated all night through the Internet. She felt connected, close to her coworker. But when they met the next day, neither had a framework to orient their face-to-face relationship with their online one. One reason to explain this conundrum is the blurring of immediate and mediated communication they experienced. In this section, we explore these terms more closely before discussing their impact on society, self, and reality.

Immediate communication refers to a process where messages are transmitted more or less directly, without the aid of exterior technology. **Mediated communication** separates the communicators through some technology—from the simplest types like paper to the most sophisticated kind of computer devices like a wireless Web unit. When you stop by your professor's office to ask a question and he or she answers you, you both are engaging in immediate communication. When you send your professor an e-mail and he or she responds, even within a few seconds, you both are experiencing mediated communication. After all, regardless of how quickly the interaction takes place, this communication could not occur without the mediation of some technology. The proliferation of mediating technologies raises the question, What kind of academic community emerges if most of your interactions with colleagues and professors are mediated in some way? On a larger level, what kind of culture arises from a mediated society?

Mediated Society

History records many critics who feared that too much mediation, through either bureaucracy or technology (or both), would lead to social collapse. Think back to stories you might have heard of Greek philosophers pleading their cases before tribunals of their peers. One such man, Socrates, stood in a court of law. He was said to be 70 years old, a gadfly who taught the young to disobey their elders and question the social norms of his day. He spoke without notes or script. There was no mechanical device to record his words. Like his student, Plato, Socrates would argue that ideas hewn from truth should be spoken simply and not mediated by devices, whether they are mechanical ones or rhetorical ones (Stone, 1988).

After the death of Socrates, who was forced to commit suicide after being judged guilty in the Athenian court, Plato would go on to argue that even the art of writing should be feared, lest his society lose the power of memory to store culture. Plato argued that words mediated by the technology of writing could be used to deceive masses of people. The democratic nature of ideas fixed onto paper that could be freely interchanged would, he feared, replace the careful and wise debate that he felt was so lacking in the trial of Socrates.

Plato believed that the true self could not be defined by text. Individuals must speak their minds directly to confront the problems of society and maintain their personal ideals. And yet, today, we are surrounded by devices designed to capture, compose, and alter our words and, by extension, ourselves. Some theorists suggest that ours is an age of oversaturation, that our machines and media have begun to overwhelm us with too many choices. Kenneth Gergen (1991) described the resulting impact as **multiphrenia**—the experience in which our identities are defined and shaped by too many choices of self-expression. We turn, therefore, to the role of self in an increasingly mediated society.

Mediated Self

The mediated self constructs a sense of "who I am" through interaction with others by various media. In an oral culture, a person speaks and is judged according to that speech. His or her narrative is communicated without mediation. Community members don't need to sift through layer after layer of image and artifice to get a sense of the speaker. Compare this immediate culture to a mediated one such as that experienced in contemporary America. A speaker, such as a political candidate, is mediated by almost-countless technologies such as edited speeches, camera shots, and Web sites. Every technology communicates a slightly different version of the political candidate so that, after a while, it's hard to discern whether a real person resides underneath the political spin. To illustrate the power of mediated communication in a comical sense, we recall a 1970s *Doonesbury* comic in which a character asked a political figure, "If we turned off the cameras, would you cease to exist?" In the shift from voice to text, from human to machine as mediator of our ideas, we face remarkable new challenges. The most important challenge, in a world in which more and more of our messages are mediated, is to sustain a coherent sense of personal identity.

How did this explosion of mediated selves began? In exploring this question, we delve deeper into the implications of using technological innovation as the sole force that drives and shapes human communities. With the emergence of writing, immediacy became no longer necessary for discourse. In other words, a person's presence was not necessary in order to feel that person's influence. One could inflict a law or tax or faith-justified expectation without the requirement of physical presence. As machine writing supplanted handwriting, when movable type replaced hand-copying of words, it became even easier to manufacture and mass-produce words that simulated ideas, which themselves simulated human interaction. For monks and visionaries, the written word could unite isolated peoples into global faith or political organization.

Consider the example of the *Declaration of Independence*. Here, we see a text used as a distance weapon against a king. You might imagine the power of that document from the stirring speeches delivered before its completion during those sweltering summer days in 1776 Philadelphia. Surely those ideas uttered by visionaries such as Benjamin Franklin, John Adams, and

Ethical Inquiry

In each of the following chapters, we pause to pose a question or present a scenario to help you reflect on the ethical nature of behavior in online communication, whether it be about the behavior of other people or your own. Noted media ethicist Michael Bugeja (1996) argues that the time to think about ethical behavior is before one is put into a position where one's ethics are tested. We believe that as students of the medium (as well as participants and future shapers of it), the readers of this text will be well served by considering these reflections.

As our perspectives on both the outer world and the inner world become increasingly mediated, it is important to remember that despite the distances that may separate people interacting online, the effects of their behavior can be very "real" and immediate to others. Bugeja also reminds us that every choice we make has consequences. We can make our choices, but we cannot control the consequences that follow. As such, it seems that those wanting to exercise communication ethically carefully consider the choices they select.

What kind of choices are you making right now in your own online behavior? Are you making choices about what you say or do in the mediated environment that contrast with your behavior in the immediate world? As you currently practice it, do you hold your mediated communication to a different, perhaps more lax standard? What unforeseen consequences might follow from some of these choices?

Thomas Jefferson propelled a nascent nation to war with a global power, Great Britain. Yet, for the majority of revolutionaries, the message embodied by that declaration was delivered in paper form or read second-hand. Yet across the vast distances of the colonies, from Maine to Georgia, an army was raised and a superior force defeated. Clearly, the technology of writing served to mediate that message in ways that would have been feared by Socrates and Plato. No longer would men and women of intellect debate face-to-face. Aided by technology and its power to mediate human experience, individuals would form nations and overthrow tyrants without ever seeing one another in person. Somewhere beyond those human constructions lies "reality," untouched by human will. But in an increasingly mediated world, even reality becomes subject to manipulation.

Mediated Reality

Beyond our sense of self and society, mediated communication even affects our perception of the world around us. In *Orality and Literacy*, Walter Ong (1982) argues that the technologies of communication influence our thought processes and, by extension, our cultures. In making his case, Ong concentrates on the influence of one of the earliest technologies of communication—writing. He notes that cultures without writing systems privilege the sense of hearing as a tool for interpreting reality. Knowledge within these cultures is community-based and people tend to construct their identities in relation to the community, dependent as they are on contact with each other for information. In contrast, print cultures encourage more individuality and less connectiveness to the community among their participants. Literacy led to people looking for information in the relatively isolated exercise of reading rather than through face-to-face interaction. The dominant sense in literate cultures, as you might imagine, is sight, not hearing. However, the proliferation of electronic media in the 20th century heralded a turn in Ong's estimation. Radio and even television favor the sense of hearing over sight.

Ong calls this turn **secondary orality**—a shift in the way we perceive reality that evokes a more communal culture. The work of another noted scholar, Marshall McLuhan (1964), concurs with Ong's. McLuhan saw the same trend toward what he called a "global village," consisting of people who shared common experiences through mediated messages rather than immediate interaction. We can look to how people turned to electronic media during events such as the assassination of President John F. Kennedy, the explosion of the space shuttle *Challenger*, and the terrorist attacks of September 11, 2001, for examples of how we were able to share events collectively rather than individually. For those of us who witnessed the horrific events of that day unfold before our eyes on national television, this sense of mediated reality was undeniable. Even if we were watching from "safe" distances in Ohio or even California, people across the United States and around the world felt fear, sadness, and anger because of events transpiring hundreds, if not thousands, of miles away. Mediated through this secondary orality, such events evoke a sense of connected culture, even as they shape our perception of each tragedy as somehow connected to our lives. In a mediated world that has the power to appear immediate, "you are there."

So far, we've identified CMC as a means to understand human interaction through mediating technologies, and we have examined the blurring of immediacy and mediation as powerful influences on society, self, and reality. We've approached

HYPERLINK: TECHNOLOGY AND TRAGEDY

The terrorist attacks of September 11, 2001, had a tremendous impact on the world in which we live. In the wake of that tragedy, we have seen changes in U.S. foreign policy (as the "Bush Doctrine" led to conflicts in Afghanistan and Iraq), changes in the law (including the U.S. Patriot Act, which increases the government's ability to watch for terrorism but may erode civil liberties), and, most certainly, changes in the way we travel (long lines and opened bags are now the norm at American airports).

The attacks also had a tremendous effect on the world online as well. According to the Pew Internet & American Life Project, a research organization dedicated to chronicling the Internet's effects, the attacks had substantial effects on both the content of information and the conduct of people communicating online. In a cross sample of some 30,000 Web sites monitored in the weeks after 9/11, the researchers found that 63% of the sites contained some information related to the attacks. The effects were notable on a variety of types of sites, including those sponsored by journalistic, religious, and governmental institutions. For instance, 13 federal agencies actually removed material from their Web sites that might be considered useful to terrorists planning future attacks (Rainie et al., 2002). What was added to and deleted from the content of the Web in the aftermath of 9/11 is telling about our nation's collective fascination with and anxiety over that day's events. (More on the legal aftermath of 9/11 is discussed at the end of chapter 9.)

Yet one of the most interesting statistics to come from the Pew study involves not so much what institutions did or did not post in public forums but what people did privately in response to the tragedy. According to the study's report, "19 million Americans rekindled relationships after 9/11 by sending email to family members, friends, former colleagues and others that they had not contacted in years. Fully 83% of those who renewed contact with others have maintained those relationships . . ." (Rainie et al., 2002, p. 5). Such a personal effect testifies to the depths that those historic events had on individuals as well as society and to the ability of the technology to facilitate human-to-human contact through it all.

these dimensions from an historical overview to argue that today's debates about the implications of e-mail, virtual reality, and the Internet are hardly new: As long as humans have used technology to relate to each other, essential questions of self and truth have emerged.

Tom Standage's (1998) book, *The Victorian Internet,* illustrates that advances in communication—the Internet in the 20th century and the telegraph in the 19th, for example—tend to provoke similar questions among us. Indeed, although the devices are different, the question has largely been the same since the days of Socrates. Will our ideas lose their fidelity—their apparent truth as perceived by others—as communication becomes more and more mediated by technology? Can text and image serve with spoken words toward the goal of identification and human community? Or, perhaps, do these simulations of human interaction deprive us of some key part of ourselves? Consider these questions as we explore corporate, therapeutic, and alternative uses of CMC throughout the book. In chapter 2, we go beyond immediacy and mediation to explore other characteristics of online communication. But we now shift our emphasis to an overview of the various technologies through which we communicate online.

HOW DO WE COMMUNICATE THROUGH CMC?

What constitutes interaction on the Internet today is not the same as it was a decade ago. In fact, people are always finding new ways to use the communication media around them. It was not so long ago that people thought of the telephone as a technology used exclusively for the exchange of oral symbols. You would dial the number of a person or business across the country and expect to talk to a person on the other end of the line. If, however, the topic of your conversation involved discussing anything printed, such as a legal contract, you would have to wait until it arrived through traditional mail-handling services. However, the proliferation of the facsimile machine (fax) throughout the 1970s and 1980s (Walker, Tames, Man, & Freeman, 1996) allowed people to transmit written materials and even images over the same telephone lines they used for speaking (albeit they would not allow you to speak and send a fax at the same time).[1] The fax machine changed our thinking about telephony as a technology for more than just vocal presentation. Now we also know it as a tool for communicating documents—and even electronic signatures—as well.

The Internet has had a similar history. At one time, interaction over it was largely limited to text-based exchanges. E-mail, BBSs, MUDs, and IRCs are forms for the exchange of textual messages. The use of words alone is still a popular means of online communication, but now people can also share images and sounds through their computers. The innovations brought by the introduction of the World Wide Web over the last decade have broadened the sensory data that people can share over the Internet. Scholars have examined communication in each of these five forms of CMC.

Electronic Mail

E-mail is perhaps the most popular and familiar channel for communicating through the Internet. Like its ancestor, the much slower, paper-based "snail-mail" routed through traditional postal means, e-mail involves the exchange of textual messages between two or more parties. Unlike its ancestor, e-mail arrives very quickly and seems to express meaning in a notably variant fashion.

---

[1] The facsimile machine was actually first patented in 1843, some three decades before Alexander Graham Bell patented the telephone itself. Its English inventor, Alexander Bain, conceived an apparatus to connect two pens with a wire. For more than a century, subsequent fax machines were cumbersome and expensive, until Xerox and its Japanese competitors introduced increasingly smaller and less expensive units onto the market in the last quarter of the 20th century. For example, in 1973 there were approximately 30,000 machines in the United States, but by 1983 there were 300,000. By 1989 there were 4 million (Great Idea Finder, 2002).

Judith Yaross Lee (1996) explains that people approach e-mail as a "hybrid medium," uniting rhetorical elements of both spoken and written communication. This results in a form of communication "between the telephone and the letter" (p. 277). The practice of writing e-mail eschews the formality of traditional text. In this regard, e-mail is like the telephone in that there is a quality of orality, of transcribing the message as though one were uttering it from one's lips. Yet e-mail is obviously like the letter because of the dominance of type in its presentation. Consider, for instance, the informal text of the following:

```
Bruce:
How about February 19? That's a Saturday.
Unless you're planning to visit Susan, we could get
together, have lunch, see your apartment, show me the
wilds of Gotham, etc.
MK
```

As you can see, the person who **posted**, or sent, this message wrote in a fashion that was far more conversational than the conventions of formal letter writing would dictate (i.e., a formal salutation like Dear Mr. Esposito). Through their practice, people have made the writing of e-mail a less formal, albeit no less textual, mode of communication.

HYPERLINK: CHAIN MAIL AND THE PROLIFERATION OF INTERNET HOAXES

```
I'm an attorney, and I know the law. This thing is for
real. Rest assured AOL and Intel will follow through
with their promises for fear of facing a multimillion
dollar class action suit similar to the one filed by
PepsiCo against General Electric not too long ago. I'll
be damned if we're all going to help them out with
their e-mail beta test without getting a little
something for our time....
    For every person that you forward this e-mail to,
Microsoft will pay you $203.15, for every person that
you sent it to that forwards it on, Microsoft will pay
you $156.29 and for every third person that receives
it, you will be paid $17.65....
```

Perhaps you have received a solicitation like this yourself from a family member, friend, or colleague. Whether it's getting money from Microsoft or free computers from IBM, e-mail chain letters promise their recipients riches and good fortune just for doing what they might be in the process of doing anyway: sending along more mail. Unfortunately, messages such as these are all too often hoaxes (Emery, 1999), if not outright scams. Another frequently circulated offer, from someone claiming to be a Nigerian national, promises you a share of a fortune locked in a U.S. bank account if you'll only put up a small amount of front money first.

Electronic chain letters are fascinating rhetorical documents whose credibility is largely reliant on the number of "forwards" they have enjoyed rather than the quality of arguments they offer. Some of the claims, such as the one that says Microsoft will give you money just for forwarding an e-mail message, may seem more credible to someone who regularly uses e-mail than they would to an outside observer. It is, after all, difficult to argue with dozens (if not hundreds) of people, some of whom you know, who are willing to take the chance that the claims just might not be false and have already forwarded the message.

Electronic chain letters might also owe their popularity to another aspect of the technology. Unlike their paper-bound predecessors, electronic chain letters are much easier to forward. With a few clicks of your keyboard, dozens of acquaintances can receive the same promising news without the unnecessary hassles of photocopying the message and paying postage to mail it. However easy it might be to forward such messages, it is unlikely that person-to-person e-mail will ever catch on as a valued (and hence financially rewarding) marketing tool. As the wise have often counseled: Any promises that seem too good to be true, probably are.

Bulletin Board Systems

A variant of e-mail called a **bulletin board system** (BBS) is also a form for text-based communication, but distinguished by the size of the audience it attempts to reach and the technological manner in which messages are read. In a BBS, individual contributors send messages to a single computer address. The program then posts these individual messages that visitors can access and read at their discretion. In this manner, a BBS functions like the kiosks or wall-mounted boards you see around your college campus covered with public announcements for fraternal rushes and credit card offers. Unlike these cluttered presentations, however, a BBS organizes incoming materials so that subsequent messages responding to previous messages are ordered one right after another. Such an aggregate is called a **thread** and each can continue to extend for as long as contributors continue to send in submissions. Interestingly, these threads practice a type of hypertext in that contributions layer on and reflect back on one another.

Most BBSs are organized around a topic of special interest, ranging from the practical (e.g., sci.electronics) to the entertaining (e.g., rec.humor). Such special-interest groups are called **newsgroups** (illustrated in Fig. 1.1), and people participating in them have developed a flow for interaction therein. Nancy K. Baym (1997) reports that contributors to rec.arts.tv.soaps are among those BBS groups that keep streams of conversation going by adapting to the technology. In responding to a previously posted message, the custom of cutting and pasting the relevant parts of that message as a point of departure of one's own has arisen. This is not, however, merely a mechanical response. Baym notes that the comments are cut to minimal length, suggesting that people are aware of the expectation that they will cite the ideas of others but that they will do so with brevity.

Another text-based form, the **listserv**, communicates with a wider audience, just as a BBS does. A listserv is a service one registers for in which messages sent to a central e-mail address are forwarded directly to subscribers. Unlike the BBS, then, messages are not stored in a central archive awaiting the individual to access it, but routed by a computer to each individual subscriber's mailbox. A number of organizations use listservs and offer to send periodic newsletters to your e-mail address announcing

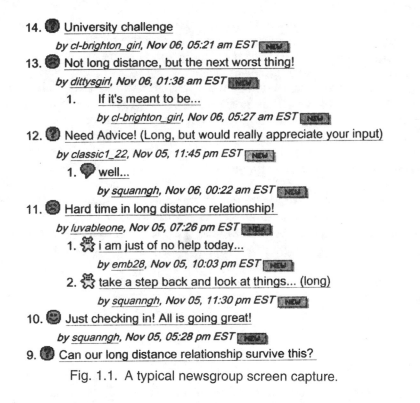

Fig. 1.1. A typical newsgroup screen capture.

their products and services. You may have even had a course in which the instructor used a listserv for messages to be exchanged among all the members of your class. As such examples illustrate, a key distinction between the BBS/listserv and e-mail, then, is that these messages are written as a public rather than a personal address.

Internet Relay Chat

Unlike e-mail, or a newsgroup, **Internet relay chat** (IRC) occurs in real time. Like newsgroups, IRCs are often thematic, addressing the concerns of a particular audience. For instance, iVillage.com, a Web site directed at women, features chat programs for issues such as parenting, beauty, and career, to name but a few. Similar chat rooms exist throughout the Internet.

Although people can "pair off" and conduct a turn-by-turn conversation using chat programs, some of the most popular forums for chatting, including those on iVillage.com, are frequented by groups of people who participate in the conversation at the same time. Because most systems post comments in the order in which they are received, a given discussion might get buried amidst the stream of contributions being offered. Consider the following portion of an IRC log:

```
Goldbricker:  Well, SoSon, what's the solution?
   fieldmaus:  What's "bolderdash" really mean?
     sheri22:  I think JimmEE comment was out of line. How
               would he feel if I said that to him?
       SoSon:  I think we should try to concentrate more on
               education and less on punishment.
```

In typical conversation, one would expect SoSon to have the next turn and be able to reply to Goldbricker's inquiry. However, because the system posts contributions in the order in which they arrive, by the time SoSon begins to write a reply, other contributors have already sent their messages.

Susan Herring (1999) cites that these violations of traditional turn-taking behaviors create a lack of conversation coherence. Yet, despite the seeming confusion that comes with chatting, it continues to be popular. Why? Herring suggests that participants in these forums have found the heightened interactivity and play of language particularly attractive. And in order to cope with the potential incoherence of the numerous exchanges, they have adapted to the situation, developing new communication strategies. For instance, although the conversational overlap in the previous example would be ill suited to effective communication if everyone in the same physical space were attempting to talk at the same time, overlap seems to work in the typewritten environment. Because it takes less time to read than to type, overlap is actually a very efficient strategy. If everyone had to wait on each person to type a response, people would spend a lot more time than is apparently necessary in developing their online conversations. Moreover, despite the influx of multiple messages, people seem to be able to keep track of their particular thread in the conversation because of the textual record that is preserved as contribution after contribution is displayed on the screen.

Multiuser Domains

Another form of synchronous, and primarily text-based, interaction occurs in a **multiuser domain** (MUD). Originally called multiuser dungeons because they were inspired by the fantasy role-playing game "Dungeons and Dragons," MUDs have inspired a plethora of acronyms, each suggesting some specialized quality of its approach to the concept. These include MUDs object-oriented (MOO), multiuser shared hallucination (MUSH), and multiuser character kingdom (MUCK). What is common among all these permutations is that they are text-based virtual realities in which participants interact with an environment, objects, and other participants. Originally constructed of nothing more than the words on the computer screen and the user's imagination, everything about a MUD is invented, although it is all rule-governed by the administering program. Nonetheless, participants enjoy a great deal of freedom in adopting roles, in indicating movement through the virtual environment that they read about on the screen, and in conversing with their fellow participants in a MUD. More recently, graphic components have become salient features to the MUDding experience, and online environments like the SimsOnline and EverQuest feature of blend of text-based interaction with visual depictions.

The classic experience of MUDding could look something like the following. Imagine that you are seated at your computer screen and at the ">" prompt, you type in various commands:

```
>look
Hallway
There are stairs leading upward to the east. There is
an unmarked door to the west.
>east
A large ballroom is at the top of these stairs.
A crystal chandelier hangs from the ceiling and
```

```
Gershwin tunes are playing from an old phonograph
in the corner.
Gumba is here.
>say hello Gumba
You say "hello Gumba"
Gumba says "welcome to my party"
```

Although they certainly might sound like nothing more than a video game guided by typewritten commands rather than a joystick, Pavel Curtis (1997) argues that the virtual realities of MUDs are social phenomena. Accordingly, he identifies three factors that distinguish MUDs from other simulations:

1. MUDs do not have a predetermined end goal. MUDs are ongoing adventures, unlike video games, which have a final level to be achieved.
2. MUDs allow users to add to the richness of the environment by contributing new spaces and objects that become an ongoing part of the administrating program.
3. MUDs typically have more than one user connected at any given time, all of whom are communicating in real time.

These factors contribute to a virtual environment in which people construct identities, relationships, and whole worlds using text. For these reasons, a number of researchers have investigated MUDs. The results of much of that information are presented in chapters in this book dealing with identity, relationships, and community.

The World Wide Web

The **World Wide Web**, often referred to as simply "the Web" or abbreviated WWW, is increasingly becoming a **portal** to the other forms of CMC. That is, people begin their Internet excursions to pick up mail from their e-mail accounts, check out the latest newsgroup messages, or meet some friends in a chat room through the Web. This experience begins when they launch their **browser**, a program that downloads instructions taken from the Internet and displays them on their desktop computer as text, images, animation, and sounds. Mosaic was the first widely available browser, although today Microsoft Explorer, with limited competition from Netscape Navigator, commands a majority of this software market. Perhaps because it is a much more graphical interface, people have lately been turning to this form of CMC as a way into the other, more text-based forms.

Like the other forms discussed thus far, the Web also possesses communicative properties based on its technological abilities and the social practices that have emerged through the use of it. One of the rhetorical effects of the Web has been the ways in which the globally accessible messages posted to it address particular audiences. Ananda Mitra (1997) found that the choice of words and the use of imagery on a Web site indicated whether it was aimed at an ingroup audience of like-minded individuals or an outgroup audience of people unfamiliar with one's culture or ideas. In his review of sites related to the nation of India, Mitra noted that the Web designers were careful to use the multimedia cues available to them in order to distinguish which audience they were attempting to communicate with, an ingroup of Indian nationals or an outgroup of international visitors. For example, a page that prominently features a map of India is directed to an outgroup audience, one that would not be

Hyperlink: Computer Anxiety

If you were fortunate enough to grow up with a computer in your home or in your school, you probably don't give much thought to the intimidation those who are less familiar with the technology might feel. Yet before they can ever experience the Internet, many people must first deal with feelings of apprehension. Communication scholars have studied apprehension, fear of or anxiety about real or anticipated interactions, in many contexts, most notably as it is experienced by public speakers (McCroskey, 1978). However, the same sensations that accompany "stage fright" in the public context can occur to someone anticipating the computer-mediated context as well, resulting in what is commonly known as **computer anxiety**. In fact, as many as 55% of Americans may suffer some degree of computer anxiety (cited in Williams, 1994).

Computer anxiety may manifest itself in a number of ways. According to Larry Rosen, Deborah Sears, and Michelle Weil (1987), a team of researchers who have investigated ways to measure and counter computer anxiety, three manifestations are possible. Those who possess some apprehension about computers "may display anxiety about computers, may have negative attitudes about computers, or may engage in disabling self-critical dialogues when interacting with computers" (p. 177). You may know different people who actively avoid new technologies, criticize them, or express doubts about their own competence when confronted with them: "I just don't understand computers." Everyone from traditional college students to senior citizens may experience some degree of computer anxiety (Cody, Dunn, Hoppin, & Wendt, 1999; Jerabek, Meyer, & Kordinak, 2001).

Craig Scott and Steven Rockwell (1997) found that there was a remedy for those coping with computer anxiety. In a study that examined the relationship among communication apprehension, writing apprehension, and computer anxiety, they found that experience was a strong predicator of future technology use. In other words, the more experience people had with the technology, the less apprehensive they felt about using it. In learning to communicate successfully with others using the Internet, then, it is important for those of us with an interest in CMC to understand that people who are ill at ease with technology require our patience and guidance in coming online. Helping them to acquire the skills necessary to operate technology is a first step in extending the communicative potential of the computer to others.

as familiar with the geographically inspired icon as an Indian would. As Mitra notes, designers use a number of the Web's technological features, including formatting, language, multimedia, and hypertext, to make the distinction to an intended audience.

As can be seen from this brief review, each of the forms of CMC in this section exhibit not only functional differences based on their technological properties, but also communicative differences based on their social applications. Regardless of the distinct forms CMC may take, there are qualities of online interaction that are hauntingly familiar and yet notably different than other contexts. Although we explore these similarities and differences more fully in the coming chapters, we turn now to attempts to make sense of the context through language, for it is in articulating how people talk about the Internet that we may begin to better understand its effects.

In this section, we have outlined five commonly employed tools to mediate our communication: e-mail, bulletin boards systems, Internet relay chat, multiuser domains, and the World Wide Web. We conclude this chapter with an analysis of another kind of mediation—the use of language, specifically, metaphor, to intercede between ourselves and the machines we use.

COMPREHENDING THE INTERNET THROUGH LANGUAGE

According to the Judeo–Christian tradition, the first project God assigns to mortals is to name things:

> And out of the ground the Lord God formed every beast of the field, and every fowl of the air; and brought them unto Adam to see what he would call them: and whatsoever Adam called every living creature, that was the name thereof. (Genesis 2 : 19)

Ever since that divine commission, humankind has been about the business of naming. It is through naming, or more broadly taken, language, that humanity has been able to explain the mundane elements of the world around us (e.g., *cattle, water, underwear*) and to make some sense of the intangible world of constructs that allow us to express our spiritual and social beliefs (i.e., *peace, justice, equity*). Language grants us a certain degree of control over the phenomena of experience, for at the very least language allows us to identify what something is.

When encountering anything for which we do not already have a term, we turn to metaphor in order to draw a comparison between the new phenomenon and a familiar thing. Just consider how children go about explaining experiences in their lives by pulling on the resources of their limited vocabularies when they do not yet have a more defining term. In such cases, a small child might laugh and call for the attention of a "funny face," not yet possessing the vocabulary to label someone a "clown."

In like manner, adults, trying to make sense of the many new technologies of the last century, have often turned to metaphor to make sense of the sometimes fantastic inventions they have encountered. As you've probably seen in period films or cartoons, people at the turn of the 20th century used the phrase "horseless carriage" to describe the automobile. A carriage was a familiar mode of transportation, and referencing it as a means for explaining the automobile helped people describe the function and composition of the machine. More recently, people have used metaphor to describe computer technology as well. Consider how computers were initially integrated into the workplace, and accordingly so many of the terms used to describe computer functions are related to items in the typical office (Jacobs, 1999). For example, we display tools on our *desktops*, we copy text onto our *clipboards*, we place *documents* in *file folders*, and we check our *mailboxes* for messages. Perhaps more important than the visual analogies these choices allowed, however, was the fact that desktops, clip-boards, and the rest were familiar, unthreatening objects in most office employee's experience. As just noted, language allows us to grasp the tangible and the intangible. In attempting to explain the complexities of online interaction, language has again relied on metaphor to make sense of the Internet. A good number of these metaphors have attempted to relate the ethereal qualities of the Internet to more grounded concepts of space. Of the terms bandied about in the last decade or so, none exhibits this quality better than that of *cyberspace*. As discussed in the following sections, coming to an understanding of how to think about electronic forums for interaction and how to express our experiences within them is influenced by our choice of metaphor.

DEFINING CYBERSPACE

You are likely to have heard the term **cyberspace** used in conjunction with the Internet. However, despite its popularity among media reports and marketers, just where this term comes from and what it means is less commonly known. The *cyber* in cyberspace comes from the Greek for "steersman" (*kubernetes*) and carries with it the connotation of control. In desiring to communicate that same sense of control, Norbert Weiner (1954) established the precedent of making cyber a prefix when he first adopted it to christen a field of study he called **cybernetics**—the science of automatic control systems. Cybernetics concerns itself with the quality of controlled feedback in systems like machines (such as when your automobile's dashboard indicates a low fuel tank) and societies (such as when a family must compensate for a member's death). We learn more about the role of cybernetics in the history of communication technology in chapter 2.

The introduction of cyberspace into common usage, though, follows a trail that leads from science fact to science fiction. Authors of science fiction have often predicted technological trends well in advance of their creation in reality. Just take a look at the communicator devices introduced in Gene Roddenberry's 1960s *Star Trek* television series and note the uncanny parallels to the cellular phones introduced in the 1990s. The same is true for cyberspace, as it was first conceptualized in the novella, *True Names*, by science fiction writer and mathematician Vernor Vinge in 1981—many years before the Internet was widely known or available (Frenkel, 2001). Vinge had named his networked space "The Other Plane," and although the name failed to grab the world's imagination, the concept inspired a number of other authors. Among them was William Gibson (1984), who, inspired by Vinge and borrowing from Wiener, coined the more widely embraced designation, cyberspace. In his science fiction novel *Neuromancer*, Gibson defined it in the following manner:

> Cyberspace. A consensual hallucination experienced daily by billions of legitimate operators, in every nation, by children being taught mathematical concepts . . . . A graphic representation of data abstracted from the banks of every computer in the human system. Unthinkable complexity. Lines of light ranged in the nonspace of the mind, clusters and constellations of data. Like city lights, receding. (p. 51)

Interestingly, Gibson was writing a prophetic description of what the Internet might be like almost a decade before the introduction of the technology that would make any truly "graphic representation" of the World Wide Web possible. According to a later interview, Gibson's interpretation of cyberspace came after witnessing children playing with video games. "These kids clearly *believed* in the space games projected," he said, noting that they seemed "to develop a belief that there's some kind of *actual space* behind the screen, someplace you can't see but you know is there" (cited in McCaffery, 1992, p. 272).

Gibson's term seemed to catch on once people began to note the similarities between Gibson's imaginary plane and what can be experienced in various online interactions. Ever since, people have used it to describe "where" online interaction seems to occur. In due course it has contributed a new affix to the English language, allowing its practitioners to indicate computer mediation in everything from *cyberlaw* to *cybersex*.

Finding Cyberspace

Where the term *cyberspace* comes from is far easier to define than what cyberspace is. One possibility is that cyberspace is merely the "consensual hallucination" that Gibson first dubbed it. Indeed, some have compared cyberspace to the nonlinear reality of mind-altering drugs (Bromberg, 1996), whereas others have concluded that cyberspace takes the mind to the next level of human consciousness (Rushkoff, 1994). However, such hallucinatory analogies carry with them the implication of an apparition without substance or effect. Such imagery belies the impact that electronic encounters have on people beyond cyberspace. Shawn Wilbur (1997) deftly argues that although the Web may be the product of ethereal contact, people still find their lives affected by their encounters in cyberspace:

> The deepest roots of virtuality seem to reach back into a religious world view where power and goodness are united in virtue. And the characteristic of the virtual is that it is able to produce effects, or to produce itself as an effect even in the absence of "real effects." The air of the miraculous that clings to virtue helps to obscure the distinction between real effects of power and/or goodness and effects that are as good as real. (pp. 9–10)

To the chat room participant, for instance, the effect of building a relationship online can be every bit as meaningful and rewarding as building one face-to-face (Rheingold, 1993). We must consider, then, that engaging others in the context of virtual reality is more than a substanceless hallucination.

Howard Rheingold (1993) proposes a less psychedelic definition. He contends that cyberspace is "the conceptual space where words, human relationships, data, wealth, and power are manifested by people using CMC technology" (p. 5). Conceiving of cyberspace as a "conceptual space" is among the most useful ways to explain to a geographically oriented culture where the Internet is to be found. With disparate parts of its whole situated in computer systems around the globe, the only "place" where cyberspace could be situated is within conceptual space. And yet what happens "there" is typically consensual, an experience built on interaction. Let us agree to a working definition of cyberspace that defines it as more than a hallucination, and is more likely a "consensual, conceptual space."

HYPERLINK: GET A (REAL) LIFE

Throughout this book, we use the term **real life** to distinguish human behavior that occurs without the aid of computer mediation from that which occurs online. Cybercultural enthusiasts sometimes use the abbreviation IRL for "in real life" to express the same concept. Calling offline interaction "real" might be something of a misnomer because many people who communicate via the Internet consider the effects of online interaction just as impactful as those one might encounter in a face-to-face scenario. The argument goes that if offline interaction is real, than online interaction must be unreal and, thus, meaningless. We do not intend to perpetuate a negative connotation in our selection; however, "real life" has been embraced by the scholarly literature, and so even though it is not without its faults, we use it here for consistency.

Extending the Metaphor

Why is it that the better part of society has embraced the metaphor of space rather than any other? After all, wouldn't something like cyber*library* be a better descriptor of the Internet's information-rich contents? Perhaps if all the Internet did was foster the flow of information, and not facilitate interaction among people, any other metaphor might have dominated, yet it is space that presently influences our interpretation of the Internet. The reasons may be that a sense of space has always been particularly important to people. Space has been instrumental in helping people make sense of the world around them and in enabling their interactions with others.

Once again, we know that the Greeks were among the earliest people who used space to express both tangible and intangible meanings. For example, the Athenian citizens would often gather in a large open plaza called the **Agora**. Here they would exchange ideas, debate politics, and conduct business. Thus the Agora became an important meeting space for Greek culture. Some cyberculturalists have likened the Internet to a modern-day Agora where people go to meet one another (O'Leary & Brasher, 1996). But the Greek contribution to the importance of space also included the use of conceptual space. As discussed earlier, the Greeks expected public speakers to deliver their speeches without the benefit of manuscripts or notes. This led some teachers of rhetoric to develop elaborate systems for memorization.

One popular method had students memorize their speeches by relating parts of their presentation to parts of a visualized house. Within each room of the house students were to place another part of the speech. As one spoke, one was to visualize walking through the structure, opening doors to various rooms along the way. As one opened these metaphorical doors, the messages within them were to stand revealed in one's memory and then to be expressed in one's speech. From early on in Western society, then, the concept of space was of particular importance for both social and intellectual purposes.

Metaphors dealing with space have, of course, continued from the classical period through to the modern period. In medieval times Dante Alighieri's classic trilogy, *The Divine Comedy*, depicted the conceptual realms of hell, purgatory, and heaven as geographic spaces. Each of the three books chronicles Alighieri's journeys through multiple layers of punishment, repentance, and ecstasy. For instance, in *The Inferno*, Alighieri links each of the descending levels of hell to worse and worse crimes, beginning with those who indulged in emotional and physical pleasures on the upper level and ending with the treacherous on the very bottom. Such an arrangement suggests that the intangible world of religious doctrine could be understood through geographic metaphor.

In America, space has been a driving metaphor since the foundation of the colonies. For almost three centuries, the notion of "manifest destiny" dictated that America push back the physical space of the western frontier until the land had been claimed from sea to shining sea. And when America ran out of land to discover, it turned its attention to the "final frontier" of space. More recently, the notion of a frontier has been applied to the metaphoric frontiers of medicine and the inner space of human biology.

Similarly, the Internet has been conceptualized as a frontier. Anthologies with titles like *High Noon on the Electronic Frontier* (Benedikt, 1991) and *Cyberspace: First Steps* (Ludlow, 1996), underscore the role that the spatial metaphor has played in our conception of the Internet, but then so has a lot of more popular usage. To some, claiming domain names on the World Wide Web harkens back to the land rushes of the American West. To others, the lack of rules governing social behavior has been compared to the lawlessness of the Wild West.

Even beyond frontier imagery, other spatial conceptions of the Internet have influenced how we think of it. One of the earliest spatial analogies was that of the "Information Superhighway," a transportation analogy used by the Clinton administration to suggest the manner in which space is transcended by the Internet. Even the way people talk about using the Internet is correlated with space. *Surfing* has emerged as a popular descriptor of the process of interacting with the network. In reality, a surfer is physically located on a wave in the ocean. In like manner then, Internet surfers ride the waves on an ocean of information. However, although surfing is reminiscent of a physical activity, the metaphor is actually borrowed from the practice of flipping through channels of television, whose screen is similar to but whose function is different from the computer's. As Steven Johnson (1997) explains, surfing suggests a rather passive activity, one he would preferably trade in for a more active term. His choice? *Navigating*. Why? Johnson cites that navigating suggests the same sense of the oceanic voyage, but one in which the traveler is making more conscious decisions about direction than a surfer at the mercy of the waves. Interestingly, both surfing and navigating are connected notions of space.

Finally, John Perry Barlow (1995) offers a rationale for this preoccupation with space. He theorizes that a collective loss of our sense of community has set many of us on a quest to find a place to belong. For generations, people lived in small communities where they behaved in relationship to one other. Our increasingly depersonalized urban centers have left many people feeling alone and created in them a longing for the simpler communities of past generations. The Internet, it seems, is the forum, and hence the place, where people have turned to find their sense of community once again.

Critiques of the Spatial Metaphor

Because it helps us to comprehend, to some degree, the daunting complexity of the phenomenon, you might not think that the spatial metaphor for framing the online environment would raise objections. Yet David J. Gunkel and Ann Hetzel Gunkel (1997) warn that "the activity of naming is never a matter of 'mere words.' It is one of the primary mechanisms of appropriation and control" (p. 132). In particular, Gunkel and Gunkel are concerned with the rhetoric of cyberspace as a "new world" awaiting conquest, promising wealth, and offering utopia. They remind us that previous "discoveries" of new worlds, such as the voyages of Christopher Columbus to North America, served to perpetuate existing frames of reference more than introduce new ones. As in that historic case, the discovery of America brought more changes to the native people and geography than it did to Europe, most notably by instigating the virtual genocide of the native peoples.

Gunkel and Gunkel (1997) want for us to consider how our conception of a metaphor could limit our perceptions of and responses to the network of networks. "Naming is always an exercise of power and must therefore be taken seriously" (p. 133), they note. Getting too accustomed to the notion of cyberspace as a new world has the potential to limit our thinking about what this new context for interaction could be and should not be. The new worlds of Columbus' voyage, of the later push toward America's western frontier, and of the more recent mission to outer space have carried with them some sense of moving over terrain, of tapping into riches, and of finding a better place.

In the case of cyberspace, Gunkel and Gunkel indicate that these three dimensions could foreclose some of the potential within the online experience. For instance, grounding ourselves in a three-dimensional analogy like the geographically situated "new world" could foreclose the possibility of perceiving the Internet in more fluid, nonphysical terms. Also, if the benefits of the new world are conceptualized as economic boons (a la Columbus' quest for gold and spices), alternative conceptions of social and cultural configurations could be lost. Cyberspace might be a space for socializing and not just pillaging. Finally, perceiving it as an unpolluted utopia, where all society's ills can be solved, ignores the lessons of the past, when other new lands and new media were promised to solve humanity's problems.

Alfred Chueh-Cin Yen (2002) agrees that cyberspace may have become too dominant a metaphor, noting, "Insight gets lost when one metaphor assumes enough prominence to crowd other ones out, especially if the prominent metaphor has misleading qualities" (p. 1209). He is particularly concerned with the use of the western frontier analogy and its use to defend limited, if any, regulation of the online environment. The western frontier might have offered abundant land and escape from the social and legal restrictions of the East in 19th-century America, but it also brought fostered violence, racism, and greed. These darker qualities seem to be largely glossed over in popular culture, but they do point to the flip side of an overly romanticized vision of what the West was like or what the Internet might be like.

Indeed, in recent years we have seen the Internet boom turn to bust. Countless Internet startup companies, lured by the promised riches of cyberspace, have gone bankrupt, causing ripples in the economy that caused the late 1990s economic highs to crash into economic woes at the beginning of the 21st century. Still, the lure to think in terms of space persists, as corporate giants tout the metaphor in imagery and slogan.

Netscape displays its ocean-going clipper ship and Microsoft asks, "Where do you want to go today?" Both corporations still cling to symbols of space.

Other critics have challenged society's collective fascination with the spatial metaphor, yet for differing reasons. Among them, Jonathan Koppell (2000) has questioned the uniqueness of what transpires online compared to other interactive media. "Ham radio operators have a global network of friends and acquaintances who came together solely through their use of that instrument. Do they exist in 'hamspace'? And why is the manner in which people make first contact so significant? Do pen pals exist in 'penpalspace'?" Koppell surmises that Internet enthusiasts have offered claims of a "there" being there to promote the online experience and to avoid less flattering comparison to other media, most especially the often-reviled television set. Still, he contends, this does not constitute a noteworthy step forward in human communication.

CHAPTER SUMMARY

As this section demonstrates, the language we use to understand the Internet is both helpful and contested. Clearly, the final word on what online interaction is and is not has yet to be uttered, but as students of the emerging cyberculture, we must be sensitive to how the choices we make influence how we experience it. Throughout this chapter, we have provided you tools for gaining a deeper sensitivity toward online communication. Exploring the emerging field of CMC, we have identified the continuum of mediation and immediacy as a primary axis to understanding society, self, and reality in the contemporary world. We have also toured some of the tools through which our relationships are increasingly mediated. Finally, we have surveyed the role of cyberspace in making sense of online communication. At this point, we are ready to examine on a historical and functional level the next question that animates this section: Just how do these tools work?

ONLINE COMMUNICATION AND THE LAW

This feature appears at the conclusion of each chapter in this book. We include these sorts of discussions because legal definitions of and challenges to various forms of CMC, in corporate and personal contexts, affect more than legislators or courtroom participants. Legal decisions about online communication have already begun to affect us all.

Case in point, you may recall the legal controversy surrounding the online music swapping service Napster several years ago. Not only did the Napster case establish boundaries for regulation in an online medium, but also it serves as an interesting example of this chapter's focus on metaphor. At the time, artists whose songs were being traded through Napster accused the service of **piracy**. You are probably familiar with pirates of old from sources in popular culture, such as Disney's *Pirates of the Carribbean* amusement park ride and the 2003 film it inspired. Although those pirates took over ships at sea and sailed away with their goods, the metaphor suggests that modern media pirates commit an equally criminal act when they reproduce artistic works and profit from them without ever compensating the artists. According to the plantiffs in the case, Napster was guilty of such piracy. The term piracy was not originated to describe online thefts (unscrupuolous vendors have profited from imitations of film, video, and recordings for decades), but it does seem apt to apply this metaphor once again within the online context.

The legal principle being tested here is **copyright**. Copyright is a property right that protects persons who created original intellectual and artistic works (including songs, films, and books). It legally guarantees that they should retain control over those materials for a set period of time and, thus, enjoy the profits of their creative labor. Although Napster itself was not copying the materials per se, the courts found that it operated for the purpose of violating copyright, since it did not arrange for its visitors to pay fees to the songs' copyright holders, and thus shut it down.

However, the proverbial genie was out of the bottle, and Napster imitators with names like Kazaa, Morpheus, and Grokster sprung up quickly to fill the gap left by closure of the trendsetting service. To meet the demand for online music, numerous Internet and music companies launched their own paid subscription services. However, those legitimate offerings did little to stem the tide of people who wanted to trade music for free. Hence, the Recording Industry Association of America (RIAA) starting going after the "little fish" and began subpoenaing the account names of persons who have been heavily trading on the Napster clones. Legal action in many of these cases is pending, but news of the RIAA crackdown has had a cooling effect on Kazaa's traffic, which was down by more than a million visitors in the 2 weeks after the announced lawsuits (Graham, 2003).

We take a closer look at some of the RIAA's tactics in chapter 7, but for now whatever turn the online music controversy takes next, you can be sure that it will continue to challenge our established legal system to adapt to the uncertain new terrain of cyberspace.

Glossary

Agora: An open meeting space within the Greek city of Athens, commonly used for transacting all kinds of social exchanges.

Browser: A software program that interprets information from the Internet and displays it as text, images, animation, and sounds (e.g., Mosaic, Netscape Navigator, Microsoft Explorer).

Bulletin board system (BBS): A publicly accessible collection of organized messages posted by various contributors.

Computer-mediated communication (CMC): The ways in which human behaviors are maintained or altered by exchange of information through machines.

Computer anxiety: Fear of using or considering using computer technology.

Copyright: A property right over intangible materials such as books, musical compositions, and films.

Cybernetics: The science of automatic control systems.

Cyberspace: The consensual, conceptual space where online interaction occurs.

Immediate communication: "Live," face-to-face human interaction.

Internet relay chat (IRC): Synchronous exchanges of primarily text-based messages through an online channel.

Listservs: A type of e-mail in which one posts messages to and receives messages from others through a program that delivers to all those who subscribe to it.

Mediated communication: Human interaction that is aided by some exterior technology such as print, radio, or the Internet.

MUD: A multiuser domain in cyberspace where participants exchange messages with one another and image themselves to interact with their computer-generated enviornment.

Multiphrenia: Conception of human identity as being splintered because of overlapping technological and cultural forces.

Newsgroup: Any one of the BBS groups devoted to a particular topic (e.g., alt.culture).

Piracy: The illegal act of reproducing artistic works and profiting from them without compensating the owner of the copyright.

Portal: A starting point for one's Internet excursion.

Post: The act of putting a message onto the Internet.

Real life: Human behavior occurring in contexts other than those involving computer mediation.

Secondary orality: The perceptual return to privileging spoken rather than written discourse as the dominant sense for interpreting the social world.

Thread: A series of e-mail messages posted to a BBS that follows a particular line of conversation.

World Wide Web: Network of documents, pictures, sounds, and other "texts" organized in a point-and-click method that mirrors most desktop computers.

Topics for Discussion

1. Keep a journal over a 24-hour period of how much time you spend involved in Internet communication. Rank-order your activities. They might include the following: chatting with friends, conducting research, paying bills, and just "surfing" for entertainment. What are your primary reasons for going online?

2. Have you, like Ellen Ullman, noticed distinctions in the way you interact with people online versus in real life? Identify an important message you have communicated to a friend or loved one. Write a brief explanation of how the context you chose, face-to-face or mediated, affected the message. As part of your response, consider how the message might have been affected if you switched contexts (i.e., sent the news via e-mail rather than giving it face-to-face).

3. Make a list of 10 people who are most important to you. Would you describe the majority of your interactions with them as immediate or mediated? Do you think that a majority of mediated relationships might adversely affect your emotional well-being?

4. In this chapter, we have reviewed several metaphors used to make sense out of technology, such as the computer as an office, the Internet as a highway, and the Internet as an ocean. What other metaphors for the Internet have you heard or could you substitute for those involving space? Either identify another metaphor you are familiar with or create you own and write a paragraph in which you relate it to certain Internet phenomena. Consider both what your metaphor reveals particularly well and what it might obscure about online interaction.

REFERENCES

Barlow, J. P. (1995, March–April). Is there a there in cyberspace? *Utne Reader*, pp. 52–56.

Baym, N. K. (1997). Interpreting soap operas and creating community: Inside an electronic fan culture. In S. Kiesler (Ed.), *Culture of the Internet* (pp. 103–120). Mahwah, NJ: Lawrence Erlbaum Associates.

Benedikt, M. (Ed.). (1991). *Cyberspace: First steps.* Cambridge, MA: MIT Press.

Bromberg, H. (1996). Are MUDs communities? Identity, belonging, and consciousness in virtual worlds. In R. Shields (Ed.), *Cultures of Internet: Virtual spaces, real histories, living bodies* (pp. 143–152). Thousand Oaks, CA: Sage.

Bugeja, M. J. (1996). *Living ethics: Developing values in mass communication.* Boston: Allyn & Bacon.

Cody, M. J., Dunn, D., Hoppin, S., & Wendt, P. (1999). Silver surfers: Training and evaluating Internet use among old adult learners. *Communication Education, 48,* 269–286.

Curtis, P. (1997). MUDding: Social phenomena in text-based virtual realities. In S. Kiesler (Ed.), *Culture of the Internet* (pp. 121–142). Mahwah, NJ: Lawrence Erlbaum Associates.

Emery, D. (1999). *Current Internet hoaxes.* Retrieved July 13, 1999, from http://urbanlegends.about.com/library/bl

Frenkel, J. (Ed.). (2001). *True names and the opening of the cyberspace frontier.* New York: Tom Doherty Associates.

Gergen, K. (1991). *The saturated self: Dilemmas of identity in contemporary life.* New York: Basic Books.

Gibson, W. (1984). *Neuromancer.* New York: Ace Books.

Graham, J. (2003, July 22). Swap songs? You may be on record industry's hit list. *USA Today,* p. 1D.

Great Idea Finder. (2002, September 23). *Fax machine.* Retrieved July 16, 2003, from http://www.ideafinder.com/history/inventions/story051.htm

Gunkel, D. J., & Gunkel, A. H. (1997). Virtual geographies: The new worlds of cyberspace. *Critical Studies in Mass Communication, 14,* 123–137.

Herring, S. (1999). Interactional coherence in CMC. *Journal of Computer-Mediated Communication, 4.* Retrieved February 29, 2000, from http://www.ascusc.org/jcmc/vol4/issue4/herring.html

Jacobs, J. Q. (1999). *Cyberspace is a parallel world: A metaphor analysis.* Retrieved July 17, 2003, from http://jqjacobs.net/anthro/metaphor.html

Jerabek, J. A., Meyer, L. S., & Kordinak, S. T. (2001). "Library anxiety" and "computer anxiety": Measure, validity, and research implications. *Library & Information Science Research, 23,* 277–289.

Johnson, S. (1997). *Interface culture: How new technology transforms the way we create and communicate.* San Francisco: HarperCollins.

Koppell, J. G. S. (2000, August). No "there" there: Why cyberspace isn't anyplace. *The Atlantic Online.* Retrieved July 17, 2003, from http://www.theatlantic.com/issues/2000/08/koppell.htm

Lee, J. Y. (1996). Charting the codes of cyberspace: A rhetoric of electronic mail. In L. Strate, R. Jacobson, & S. B. Gibson (Eds.), *Communication and cyberspace: Social interaction in an electronic environment* (pp. 275–296). Cresskill, NJ: Hampton Press.

Ludlow, P. (Ed.). (1996). *High noon on the electronic frontier: Conceptual issues in cyberspace.* Cambridge, MA: MIT Press.

McCaffery, L. (1992). *Storming the reality studio: A casebook of cyberpunk and postmodern fiction.* Durham, NC: Duke University Press.

McCroskey, J. C. (1978). Validity of the PRCA as an index of oral communication apprehension. *Communication Monographs, 45,* 194–203.

McLuhan, M. (1964). *Understanding media: The extension of man.* New York: Routledge.

Mitra, A. (1997). Diasporic Web sites: In group and outgroup discourse. *Critical Studies in Mass Communication, 14,* 158–181.

O'Leary, S. D., & Brasher, B. E. (1996). The unknown god of the Internet: Religious communication from the ancient agora to the virtual forum. In C. Ess (Ed.), *Philosophical perspectives on computer-mediated communication* (pp. 233–269). Albany: State University of New York Press.

Ong, W. J. (1982). *Orality and literacy: The technologizing of the word.* New York: Routledge.

Rainie, L., Fox, S., Madden, M., Schneider, S., Foot, K., Halavais, A., Massanari, A., Larsen, E., Siegl, E., & Dougherty, M. (2002). *One year later: September 11 and the Internet* [Online]. Pew Internet & American Life Project. Available: http://www.pewinternet.org/

Rheingold, H. (1993). *The virtual community: Homesteading on the electronic frontier.* Reading, MA: Addison–Wesley.

Rosen, L. D., Sears, D. C., & Weil, M. M. (1987). Computerphobia. *Behavior Research Methods, Instruments, & Computers, 19,* 167–179.

Rushkoff, D. (1994). *Cyberia: Life in the trenches of hyperspace.* San Francisco: Harper-Collins.

Scott, C. R., & Rockwell, S. C. (1997). The effect of communication, writing, and technology apprehension on likelihood to use new communication technologies. *Communication Education, 46,* 29–43.

Standage, T. (1998). *The victorian internet.* New York: Berkley Books.

Stone, I. F. (1988). *The trial of Socrates.* Boston: Little, Brown.

Ullman, E. (1996). Come in, CQ: The body on the wire. In L. Cherny & E. R. Wise (Eds.), *Wired women: Gender and new realities in cyberspace* (pp. 3–23). Seattle, WA: Seal Press.

Vinge, V. (1981). *True names.* New York: Dell.

Walker, R., Tames, R., Man, J., & Freeman, C. (1996). *Inventions that changed the world.* New York: Reader's Digest.

Weiner, N. (1954). *The human use of human beings: Cybernetics and society.* Boston: Houghton Mifflin.

Wilbur, S. P. (1997). An archaeology of cyberspace: Virtuality, community, identity. In D. Poster (Ed.), *Internet culture* (pp. 5–22). New York: Routledge.

Williams, S. (1994, June 12). Technophobes: Victims of electronic progress. *Mobile Register,* p. 9E.

Yen, A. C. (2002). Western frontier or feudal society?: Metaphors and perceptions in cyberspace. *Berkley Technology Law Journal, 17,* 1207–1263. Retrieved July 17, 2003, from http://ssrn.com/abstract=322522

CHAPTER 2

UNDERSTANDING HOW NEW COMMUNICATION TECHNOLOGIES WORK

Websites are like shifting sands. The average life of a Web page is 100 days. After that either it's changed or it disappears. So our intellectual society is built on sand.
—Brewster Kahle (cited in Marks, 2002)

The history of the World Wide Web is written in scientific papers, hastily scrawled designs, and the shifting sands of digital papyrus. It's no wonder that one site seeking to archive every web page created since 1996 resides in the new Library of Alexandria, the location of an ancient collection lost to the ages. With its sister sites located in California, the Internet Archive Wayback Machine allows you the chance to sift through 10 billion web pages, including a growing number from the "ancient" Internet, before the dot-bomb implosion, when folks first began to craft simple web pages with an easy-to-learn language called Hypertext Markup Language. Visit the Wayback machine, typing in the address for MSNBC, and you might peruse the news when Bill Clinton was president. Visit Yahoo from 1996 and a far simpler World Wide Web than you'll find today. Why would you want to? For the same reason that you might investigate the history of the printed word or television. Innovations offered by these media profoundly altered the ways in which we communicate our perceptions about our selves, our relationships, and our world. Fortunately, it's easier to learn about the history and basic functions of online communication than it is to thumb through a Gutenberg Bible.

This chapter offers a bookend of sorts to the previous chapter's introduction to the role of computer technology in human communication. Having introduced the tools of CMC, both functional and metaphoric, it is appropriate that we examine more closely how these tools work. In this chapter, we place computer technology in an historical context, surveying the emergence of online communication from the perspective of cybernetics. We then step beyond chapter 1's exploration of mediated and immediate communication to overview five qualities that distinguish Internet technology from other forms of communication: packet-switching, multimedia, interactivity, synchronicity, and hypertextuality. These functions help explain how CMC works to blur the distinction between mediation and immediacy.

Throughout this chapter, we approach computer technology as important—critical, even—to understanding the whirlwind of changes affecting the ways we communicate with friends across the street and strangers around the globe. But before we go further, it is important to remember that human communication cannot be explained by computer technology alone. As we hasten to explore technology as a force that shapes identity and culture, we must not fall into the trap of **technological determinism**. Technological determinism assumes that our growing ability to alter or replace nature provides a central reason for most personal and social trends. A technologically determinist perspective on an historical event, say World War I, would focus primarily on the innovations in killing machines like the machine gun and the use of mustard gas to explain what some critics viewed as the dehumanization of the 20th century. Certainly, technology plays a key role in social innovation—and crisis. However, in this text, we approach technology as merely one key component to understanding identity and culture, preferring to view human experience as an intersection of all three. Indeed, as we begin our brief history of cybernetic technology, we find that personality and cultural assumptions played significant roles in the evolution of what would become the Internet.

A BRIEF HISTORY OF CYBERNETIC TECHNOLOGY

Charting the development of mediating technologies in human history is a subject deserving of several volumes, so substantial has been their influence on societies. Yet it is beyond the scope of this book to delve too deeply, too specifically into much more than a review of the most significant highlights of the story in establishing the forerunners to today's mediating technologies. Thus, although the history of computers encompasses everything from the mechanical adding machines of yesteryear to tomorrow's visions of computers that abandon silicon for more subtle architectures that mimic human DNA, it will suffice to say that the history of computers is a narrative of human beings seeking to employ technology to alter their worlds. To understand this history within our limited space, then, we explore a brief narrative beginning with conceptions of thinking machines, continuing through to cybernetic devices, and arriving at today's Internet as a contemporary cybernetic organism.

Thinking Machines in the 19th Century

Some of the earliest mechanical calculating machines mirrored the processes of ancient clock makers and loom designers. Yet Charles Babbage (1791–1871), perhaps more than anyone, introduced these machines to nonscientists (Fig. 2.1). Here, it is important to remember that during the height of Britain's Age of Empire, scientists and planners could easily be compared to modern rock stars. During the 19th century, their clever mechanical devices and globe-girdling plans employing science as a civilizing force earned them popular acclaim. But it was Babbage who generally receives credit for striving to develop a device that remarkably resembles the modern computer—**the analytical engine**. As Shurkin (1984) explains in his book, *Engines of the Mind*, Babbage was a dabbler whose interests ranged from the scientific study of whether some beggars were really poor (or just faking it) to inquiries into which types of paper and ink made for the most comfortable reading experience.

Babbage's lifelong obsession, however, was his dream to create a steam-driven machine that would compute tables and formulas. Like today's computers, his analytical engine would consist of "memory" (columns of wheels with engraved numbers) and a form of "central processing unit" that manipulated the numbers with the aid of punch cards. As it turned out, Babbage's engine was too sophisticated to be produced; his

Fig. 2.1. Charles Babbage (1791–1871), developer of the analytical engine.

mechanics required tools that had not been invented yet. But his engine is at the heart of today's thinking machines.

You can imagine how these calculating machines might have worked by picturing a mechanical loom such as the **Jacquard loom** (Fig. 2.2). This device offered a means for a weaver to mass-produce patterns of cloth by punching holes in cards. The hooks guided the thread only where there were holes in the cards, leaving the empty sections alone: The data—the description of the pattern—were coded in terms of a binary alphabet represented by the holes and "nonholes" in the cards; thus the communication between weaver and weaving machine used a language, as all communication does, and the cards formed the channel of communication for this language (Moreau, 1984). Whether these devices were mechanical or electrical, in the case of the room-filling vacuum tube computers of the early to mid-20th century, the principle was the same. Computers could manipulate data—manifested in the form of cards or electrons—according to the desires of their users.

Cybernetic Devices in the Early 20th Century

Throughout the 19th- and early 20th-century evolution of computers, critics feared their potential to rid human beings of their capacity to act with purpose within some ethical framework. Here again, technological determinism is at work. For many, the mechanized warfare of World War I confirmed their worst fears, that centuries of the industrial revolution had wrought nothing less than the end of civilization. It is, therefore, fascinating to observe how the introduction of cybernetic devices in the next

Jacquard Loom.

B, breast-beam; *c*, cloth; *d*, driving-crank; *h*, harness;
j, Jacquard apparatus; *jl*, Jacquard lever; *l*, lay;
pc, pattern-cards; *p, p*, picker-sticks; *sb*, swivel-batten;
sh, shipper-handle; *t*, take-up wheel.

Fig. 2.2. The Jacquard loom.

global conflict would occur simultaneously with a renewed attention to the process through which individual and cultural narratives affect technological innovation.

You may recall our definition of CMC as the study of how human behaviors are maintained or altered by the exchange of information through machines. From this perspective, cybernetics helps us understand the process through which that exchange takes place. As discussed in chapter 1, cybernetics is the science of automatic control systems. The study of cybernetics can range from the most complicated phenomena, like the process of atmosphere renewal, to the most apparently simple devices, like the thermostat you probably have in your home or office. As you know, a thermostat receives input in the form of a preset temperature, generally "programmed" by turning a dial or setting a switch. If the temperature in your room slips below that preset number of degrees, the thermostat sends a message to the central heating system in your home or building to increase the energy used to heat your space. If the degree of heat in your room rises above a certain level, however, the thermostat instructs the heater to shut down. This all might sound most mechanical—and, to be sure, machines are essential to the process—but the heart of cybernetics is the manner through which physical devices and natural forces are controlled and altered by human agency.

Norbert Weiner is a scientist and writer who popularized the study of cybernetics with his book, *The Human Use of Human Beings* (1954). Weiner's work with cybernetics began with the efforts of antiaircraft gunners who wanted to build machines that would help them plot and anticipate the movements of enemy aircraft. Weiner helped develop devices that would provide feedback to the weapons so that when a gun missed its target, it could compensate. After missing the plane with its first round, the gun would adjust for distance, wind velocity, the acceleration of its target, and various other factors before firing another round. This time, after firing twice, the machine would have a more accurate "fix" on its target—teaching itself how to respond to changing environmental and human factors. Unfortunately for the pilot of the enemy aircraft, the machine would learn quickly and eventually (within seconds) hit its target.

Recalling the example of the thermostat, you can see a similar principle: Machines can alter their behavior according to the programs of their operators. Of course, if you have ever been in a room where the thermostat didn't work properly (or if you can imagine yourself in the unhappy position of being a pilot in the sights of a computer-mediated weapon), you recognize that human computer interaction goes both ways. In a cybernetic environment, computers and humans share information to alter each other's behavior. Perhaps one of the most significant impacts of Weiner's work is a more sophisticated concept of information. From the perspective of cybernetics, **information** is an exchange of data necessary for one system to influence the behavior of another system.

As a student of communication, you might find this definition of information to be somewhat strange. After all, from a more common perspective, information is simply a container for our messages. One of the authors of this book used to think it quite clever to play on the implied breakdown of the word to describe communication as the process of putting facts *in formation*. Weiner's approach, however, emphasizes the challenge of communication scholars to identify their topics. Do we study the process through which data—facts, sounds, gestures—are transmitted as an engineer would study the efficient movement of words through telephone lines? Or, instead, do we study the human choices and social consequences that shape our communicative acts? The cybernetics-oriented definition of information allows a middle ground central to the foundation of this book. We approach CMC as a study defined not only by its range of interests, but also by its perspective on human discourse where individuals and technology shape each other in surprising ways.

> ### Ethical Inquiry
> One of the most significant attributes of cybernetic systems is their ability to adjust independently to external stimulus without the aid of human intervention. As we've discussed, Norbert Weiner warned about the possibilities of a machine intelligence supplanting that of humankind. More recently, the *Terminator* and *Matrix* series of films depict a grim fate for humanity that allows its tools to enslave us all. Prior to these pop culture dystopias, however, remains the choice between innovation and intervention. Should we ensure a machine ethic such as that created by science fiction author Isaac Asimov, who created various "laws of robotics" dictating that machines should not harm human beings? Or, as a corollary, should we imagine a form of ethics that would make it wrong to destroy a machine whose consciousness begins to mimic that of a human being? In other words, as our machines more and more resemble human beings in power and intellectual capability, should they begin to enjoy "machine rights" similar to human rights?

In *The Human Use of Human Beings*, Weiner (1954) warned that human beings cannot allow their will and consciences to be controlled by machines. His call to cultivate "fertility of thought" was a reaction to what he viewed as an increasing "massification" of media. In a world in which ideas can be considered interchangeable, where original thoughts are rare, the value of individual opinions becomes random. Human lives, Weiner warned, would become just as random as the "dry foam of data" described by Gibson and Sterling (see next page). Do you think that Weiner was simply afraid of the machines he created or, perhaps, was he correct?

HYPERLINK: WHAT'S "THE DIFFERENCE ENGINE"?

Before Charles Babbage's experiments with the analytical engine, he imagined a simpler mechanical device that would solve certain equations. His "difference engine" provides a central character of sorts for a book of the same name, written by Gibson and Sterling (1991). In the book, Victorian scientists develop a difference engine that can be used to predict and potentially control the movements of ordinary people. The authors provide a nightmarish vision of the power of this steam-driven thinking machine:

> Paper-thin faces billow like sails, twisting, yawning, tumbling through the empty streets, human faces that are borrowed masks and lenses for a Peering Eye. And when a given face has served its purpose, it crumbles, frail as ash, bursting into a dry foam of data.

The "Peering Eye" is the machine that surveys all human conduct through its acquisition of information. The threat, predicted by *The Difference Engine*, is that a machine provided too much information may no longer find human beings to be useful.

THE INTERNET AS CYBERNETIC ORGANISM

Our understanding of self-regulating machines is essential to understanding the Internet, for, in many ways, we are talking about a cybernetic organism. To understand this idea, start with the military goal of **command and control**. This term refers to the notion that information, properly channeled, can ensure that individuals will act as a unit within a framework larger than themselves. To fight fascism in the early 20th century or protect a nation from a nuclear-powered foe throughout the Cold War, command and control were essential to the well-being and continued existence of the United States.

The irony is that a military system of command and control—so useful in World War II, when gunners needed the help of machines to keep up with increasingly rapid aircraft—facilitated the evolution of a system that simply could not be controlled: the Internet. The Internet emerged during a period of tremendous fear on the part of the U.S. government. In 1957, the Soviet Union had launched its Sputnik satellite, marking a major victory in the Space Race. Immediately, U.S. policymakers geared up their efforts to "catch up" with the Soviets. The fact that a satellite crafted by the Soviets had virtually free reign over U.S. airspace led some to believe that floating missiles and space-based weapons were not far behind.

Scientists, military planners, and educators needed to pool their efforts. After the Sputnik launch, the United States formed the Advanced Research Projects Agency (ARPA). Among their projects, ARPA scientists envisioned a "galactic network" of computers that would not relay on a central system to function. Rather, they would form a network with a common protocol that could respond to changes, even the

HYPERLINK: VANNEVAR BUSH AND HIS AMAZING MEMEX

Long before there was an Internet, and the countless megabytes of data it now contains, a research scientist named Vannevar Bush (1945) envisioned a prototypical hypertextual system for cataloging information. Writing at the end of World War II, Bush foresaw the need for a better means of keeping track of all the research publications being produced in the wake of the many scientific discoveries during his times. What Bush suggested was a device he called the **memex**. Although the technology to realize such an invention did not yet exist in 1945, Bush theorized that a memex could help people cope with the vast amounts of information that existed on any given topic. In design, it would be housed in a desklike structure, with screens for displaying data and internal mechanisms for retrieving and archiving it. Information within the memex would be stored on numerous sheets of microform. Most importantly, the reader would have the ability to establish links among various sources of information stored within the memex for future retrieval. Bush indicated that customary systems for cataloging information were based on arbitrary systems, like alphabetizing. The memex, he contended, operated more like the human mind, which works through associations. For example, a woman might associate ice cream with kissing, not because "I" and "K" are near one another in the alphabet, but because she received her first kiss at the Dairy Queen. Bush's memex would allow users to make such idiosyncratic connections among topics.

Although Bush's vision for the memex, per se, was never realized, his ideas were highly influential in the development of hypertext systems and, ultimately, the World Wide Web. Accordingly, the same woman, writing a web page today, could create a hyperlink from a mention of her first kiss to the Dairy Queen site. The ability to associate ideas within a rich pool of possible references was prophesied in the 1940s and realized in the 1990s, but the effects of Bush's uninvented invention will impact us throughout the new century.

elimination of individual computers from the network. Although it is inaccurate to say that ARPA scientists sought to create a nuclear war-proof computer network, the Defense Department funding their efforts began to imagine that their project could result in one anyway.

One of the leading figures of that era, J. C. R. Licklider, wrote some of the essential proposals for the information transmission systems we use today. In papers like "Man–Computer Symbiosis" and "The Computer as a Communication Device," Licklider envisioned "the invention of the 'mouse,' 'windows,' and 'hypertext'" (Bennahum, 2003). Most importantly, he wove a deep concern for the implications of their devices into the deliberations of the women and men developing the programs and equipment that would spawn the digital age:

> For the society, the impact will be good or bad, depending mainly on the question: Will "to be on line" be a privilege or a right? If only a favored segment of

the population gets a chance to enjoy the advantage of "intelligence amplifica-
tion" the network may exaggerate the discontinuity in the spectrum of intellectual
opportunity. (Licklider, cited in Taylor, 1990)

Leading efforts within the ARPA, Licklider funded projects that led to the Internet as
we know it.

A milestone toward that goal occurred in 1969 when universities launched
ARPANET, a network of computers that would draw from each other's resources
in a time-share relationship and provide the foundation for the unbreakable computer network. This innovation was revolutionary because of its ability to facilitate
the transmission of overlapping messages with different destinations through the
same network. Of course, the technology being used to move information between
computers was so exotic that few civilians could understand it. Zakon (2003) recalls
that the company that won the contract to manufacture Interface Message Processors
for this network received a congratulatory telegram from Senator Ted Kennedy for
their plans to build the *Interfaith* Message Processor, thanking them for their efforts
to stimulate religious communication among people with different views of God. Although politicians were slow to grasp the significance of this evolution in computer
science, many universities caught on quickly.

The first universities to sign on to the project were UCLA, Stanford, University
of California, Santa Barbara, and the University of Utah. But dozens, and eventually
hundreds, more followed. Throughout the 1970s, their research efforts were being
used to test e-mail, newsgroups, and other experimental ways for scientists to interact with one another. During the 1980s, as network researchers experimented on
various protocols for moving "packets" of information, ARPANET split into military
and civilian components. Before long, people referred to the computer system where
computers transfer information simply as the "Internet."

WHAT IS THE INTERNET?

The history and evolution of this network of networks are fascinating. But we cannot
proceed without a specific definition of the **Internet**. Here, we borrow from the former Federal Networking Council's (1995) definition, which includes three primary
elements:

- The Internet is linked together through a global address system.
- The Internet uses a common form of transmission protocol.
- The Internet allows public and private communication.

Let's consider these requirements for an Internet in turn.

First, a global address system ensures that a message can actually reach its destination. Imagine that your address (say, 1600 Pennsylvania Avenue, Washington, DC)
was shared by other people; instead of there being one site to indicate the placement
of your house, there would be several. Mail delivery would get pretty complicated!
The Internet works because *each address in the network refers to only one location*.

Second, the Internet requires a common form of transmission. In other words,
computers must be able to route their messages through according to consistent
rules—just like drivers from California must know that stop signs mean the same

thing, even when they visit other states. The Internet works because every computer knows the rules of the road.

Finally, the Internet must allow for the layering of communication, both public and private. In other words, the Internet does not have simply one function, but many simultaneous uses. Thus, it is possible for the same Internet connections to facilitate overlapping, but separate, transmissions of information. The same principle is found in the Eisenhower highway system, which was planned to serve both the needs of civilian travel and military preparedness. The same stretch of highway that allows the movement of trucks and private cars was also designed, in many places, to serve as a landing strip for aircraft in case of war.

Thus, the Internet is a network of computers that allows for the transmission of data for multiple purposes through a common set of protocols according to a global address system. Notice that among these three qualities, "ease of use" cannot be found. For most people during the period of Internet evolution, from 1969 through the 1980s, access to this network of networks required patience with a communication system designed by engineers for engineers. Only with the emergence of the World Wide Web did the Internet become more than a technical marvel.

Up until the 1990s, manipulating information in what had become the Internet required users to comprehend arcane commands. If you wanted to access a file online, you needed to submit a specialized code. There was no such thing as "point and click." Tim Berners-Lee, looking to simplify information exchange among high-energy physicists, took the Internet to an entirely new level by proposing the World Wide Web.

As discussed in chapter 1, the World Wide Web is exciting because of its transformation of how people interact with computers and each other. With the invention of Web browsers such as Mosaic, Netscape, and Explorer, the same ease of use that non-scientists came to expect from their desktop computers became available beyond the desktop through the use of a point-and-click interface. The World Wide Web mirrored the Internet in its impact on computer networking. What was, at first, a clever way for scientists to share research soon became—for many users—the primary manifestation of the Internet, just as the Internet outgrew its military ARPANET predecessor.

The Browser Wars

This manifestation of the Internet reflected more than technological innovation, though. It represented a struggle between powerful companies to shape the future of online communication. After popularizing their "Navigator" software, Netscape sat atop the browser heap and appeared to be unbeatable. Every day, people downloaded their software and discovered the World Wide Web as a user-friendly point-and-click library, shopping mall, and community. On the sidelines, Microsoft began to implement its plans to dominate another market by creating their "Explorer" browser and loading it with every personal computer shipping with the Windows operating system. Most importantly, Netscape and Microsoft began to design browsers that called for slightly different rules for how web pages were displayed. Most folks never considered the difference, having gotten used to accessing computer contents without knowing any programming languages or network protocols, but browsers are generally picky about the codes they translate. Pretty soon, a triumph realized by the Web, the ability to communicate pictures, sounds, and words to any computer anywhere in the world, was thwarted. One might read today's dominance of Microsoft Explorer over its erstwhile rival, Netscape, as a story of corporate conflict, but one might also read this history as a tale of cybernetic systems response as Internet users gravitated to a common browser to reduce the uncertainty and Babel-like confusion wrought by the browser wars.

HYPERLINK: A POST-BEIGE REVOLUTION

With its "1984" advertisement mocking the plodding predictability of personal computers—their no-nonsense green or black screens, their neutral beige coloring, their orientation toward business and other "practical" concerns, their stupefying complexity—Apple Computer launched a revolution in hardware and software design, "a defining moment, not only of the heralded computer revolution but also of what has become our media landscape" (Stein, 2002, p. 169). Whereas IBM developed machines-as-tools, Apple offered computers-as-toys: a bright screen that displayed a friendly "hello," icons that represented data in the form of folders, papers, and even a trash can, and a mouse that inspired users to feel like they were physically manipulating their textual environments with a point and click.

These innovations, borrowed from previous experiments in people-friendly graphical user interfaces, were first ridiculed, then studied, and ultimately copied by any computer company that planned to last beyond the 1980s. But imitation spelled doom for Apple, a company that fell prey to a host of internal and external faults. By the mid-1990s, an Apple computer was seen as a device for a particularly small brand of holdouts, those idealists who had not "given in" to the Wintel empire of Microsoft Windows and Intel processors. Even the development of a very fast Power PC chip could not turn the company's fortunes. Apple's flamboyant and notoriously thin-skinned cofounder, Steve Jobs, had long since left the company, shoved aside through a combination of corporate politics and his own hubris. Market share had slipped from more than 10% to less than 6%, making Apple Computer an also-ran in an industry of giants.

In desperation, Apple begged Jobs to return as interim chief executive officer, to turn around the company that was launched with a "hello." Within months, Apple introduced the iMac—a computer designed with a faster processor, an easier Internet configuration, and (most importantly) a radically new look compared to any other machine on the market. The first iMacs featured a somewhat turquoise shell and see-through covering; the mouse looked like a flying saucer. Combined with an ambitious advertising campaign ("Think Different") and a revitalized sales strategy, the iMac helped energize the company, allowing it to continue its challenge to Wintel. In an interview with Jobs, *Time Digital's* Chris Taylor struggled to make sense of the popularity of this machine, finally asking, "Would you call it postmodern?" Jobs simply responded, "I call it post-beige."

At the same time, folks have begun to challenge the notion that one needs a computer to go online. Increasingly we access Internet content through Personal Data Assistants, mobile phones, and wearable hardware that blurs the distinction between computation and fashion. New protocols for the transmission of text, pictures, and other media allow content that formerly could only be viewed on a browser to be accessed through a growing range of devices that free us from the need to go to a particular *place* in order to go online. With the growth of the "wireless web," liberated from the miles of cable and wires that formed much of the network infrastructure of the last century, one discerns an emerging world in which information resides everywhere one might imagine. Suddenly, we enter a period defined by Howard Rheingold (2002) as the age of **Smart Mobs**: networks employing sophisticated media to interact and respond with their environment in ways that surpass individual decision making, along with other forms of organization.

Smart Mobs reflect a contemporary look at the changing ways in which individuals interact through the aid of (frequently) wireless technology. As Rheingold (2002) explains, Smart Mobs represent a colloquialism for "mobile ad hoc social network." Mobility refers to the potential for groups to move from place to place, for individuals within them to shift from group to group. If you've ever spent time in an airport, watching a traveler march along a concourse with a cell phone in one hand and a laptop computer in the other, you are witnessing the impact of mobility on an increasing component of the workforce. For many "road warriors," the 24-hour copy shop, with its bank of high-speed Internet-connected computers, is all the office needed. "Ad hoc" refers to another component of fluidity in which decisions and modifications need not be deliberated over time; individuals and groups act now, responding to the needs of the moment. Thus, one harried traveler shows up at her assigned gate, only to discover that the flight has been canceled. Accessing a discount ticket agent through her laptop, she confirms another flight. A quick mobile call to her colleagues waiting in a distant city ensures that they can meet each other on time. Rheingold (2002) adds that the "social network" concept imagines persons as nodes connected by links to one another. Less tightly bound to one another than families or tribes or hierarchical organizations, more and more Smart Mob members are composed of freelancers, part-timers, and corporate mercenaries.

As we discuss in more detail later in the book, Smart Mobs reflect an important evolution in our understanding of the use of machines to shape human behavior. Smart Mobs reflect the potential for individuals and groups to form superorganisms capable of responding to changes in their environments, able to draw from individual strengths in creative ways, and utterly more difficult to control than traditional aggregates. How, for example, would a police force bent on blocking a demonstration respond to individuals who text message one another, reporting a safe place to congregate? Once the group gathers, the police might disperse them—but a few text messages later and the group could re-form blocks later. The key distinction is best viewed above. Unlike a "dumb mob" of people marching from place to place, capable of being blocked by a relatively lean force, the Smart Mob remains composed of individuals who follow idiosyncratic paths, connected by invisible lines of wireless communication, gathering, dispersing, and re-forming according to shared information and hundreds of informants. From a "bird's-eye view," an observer would witness strangers moving in order, but without apparent guidance—like birds in a flock that shift according to the winds and the seemingly random decisions of individual members. Leaderless, boundaryless, the Smart Mob reflects an extension of Internet Age thinking that offers stunning implications for public life. The way these groups communicate, therefore, demands closer attention.

WHAT ARE SOME CHARACTERISTICS OF ONLINE COMMUNICATION?

Thus far, we have surveyed a brief history of computer technology from the perspective of cybernetics, exploring the evolution of the Internet as a feedback mechanism that grows so rapidly and in so many intriguing ways that it is hard not to imagine it as a living organism. Consuming resources, responding to change, and generating offspring, the Internet may not be alive in a literal sense, but it displays characteristics that are certainly vibrant. In this section, we explore the question of whether the Internet might be seen as a new kind of mass medium—or maybe an entirely new form of communication. We then outline five characteristics of the Internet that help explain the ways in which CMC assists and alters contemporary communication. Here, we concentrate on the traditional Web, mediated by computers and accessed through browers.

Morris and Ogan (1996) suggest that the Internet represents a new form of mass medium. They note that traditional mass media like newspapers and television have promoted an affiliation between the producers of messages and the audience for those messages characterized as a one-to-many relationship. As an example, a network anchor speaks to millions of Americans every night on the evening news. The Internet may be seen as a mass medium that adds one-to-one (as in e-mail), many-to-many (as in listservs), and many-to-one (as in corporate Web sites) to the mix. Viewing the Internet as a mass medium does help explain some aspects of what happens online. For instance, a traditional mass media theory like uses and gratification can help to explain why people visit particular sites on the World Wide Web (Kaye & Medoff, 1999). However, limiting one's view of the Internet to that of only a mass medium, and relying only on the preestablished theories of mass media, would fall short of addressing the interpersonal aspects that are present online.

In contrast to the Internet-as-mass medium approach, J. Michael Metz (1994) suggests that CMC "is a field of theoretical study in its own right, not merely a channel to study within other theoretical contexts" (p. 33). Metz's point is well taken. In recent years, those in the field of communication studies have grown increasingly aware that *context* factors into the ways that messages are produced and interpreted. Such emerging contexts exhibit qualities that help distinguish them from more traditional areas of study like interpersonal, organizational, and mass communication. Thus, scholars have begun offering specialized courses in health, family, and, of course, CMC. As shown in this and the following chapters, elements of CMC could be taught in an interpersonal, organizational, or mass communication classroom. Yet the qualities that distinguish computer-mediated from other contexts for communication might not be fully addressed in any one of those courses.

Many scholars would agree that there are some telling distinctions between other forms of human communication and that conducted on the Internet. One of them is Sheizaf Rafaeli, who identifies five qualities that distinguish the Internet from other forms of communication (Newhagen & Rafaeli, 1996). These distinctions are packet-switching, multimedia, interactivity, synchronicity, and hypertextuality. Let us explore what Rafaeli says about each of these in turn.

Packet-Switching

Rafaeli counts this technical aspect of the medium as one of its distinguishing features. As discussed earlier, the Internet was developed as a means for sending messages over multiple pathways rather than a single line like a telephone does. At one end of the transmission, a computer breaks down a message into packets of information. Each packet is then routed toward its destination, where it is reassembled by another computer. Other media use packet-switching to some degree. For example, your telephone network may break your voice into packets. However, the telephone network creates a "pathway" of sorts to ensure that each packet arrives at its destination quickly—an important quality in voice communication. Packet-switching on a computer network works differently, by assigning each packet its own source and destination address as if it is an individual letter sent through the postal system.

Here's another example: Let us say that your younger sibling wants to view the Disney site on the World Wide Web. At your request, the collection of codes that tell your home computer how to display the Disney site are broken down into smaller units, or packets, and sent through a number of different paths along the computer network. The codes are then reassembled on arrival so that your sibling can view what is up on the Disney site. You may be somewhat confused by the fact that most households rely on a telephone connection to link to the network. Although it is true that the telephone connection between your home computer and your Internet service provider (ISP) does not operate on packet-switching itself, the ISP, in all likelihood, is connected to the network of networks that forms the Internet and thus receives information via packet-switching before passing it along to you.

Multimedia

For now, this characteristic operates in only one form of Internet communication that is explored in more depth here, the World Wide Web. If you have explored the Web in some breadth, you are already aware that it facilitates messages in the forms of text, images, animation, and sound. In other words, the Web can communicate through multiple channels. Compare this to *USA Today*, which has the properties to convey text and images but not sound, or the latest Madonna compact disk, which has the properties to convey sound but not text or images (excluding, of course, the colorful packaging it comes in). A quick peek at the Disney site, however, provides a multimedia experience. Here one can view trailers for Disney's upcoming theatrical releases or play recordings from its latest Broadway musical.

Interactivity

It should be fairly self-evident that the Internet allows for interaction among its communicators. However, it is important to note that as far as different media go, interactivity occurs at various levels. Consider broadcast television, for instance. The meteorologist at the local TV station provides you a forecast for the next day's weather. Whether you are pleased that it will be sunny or disappointed that it will snow, you cannot express your reaction to the forecaster through the television. In fact, if you want to communicate with that person, you would probably have to choose another medium, perhaps the telephone, to communicate the message. The quality of interactivity is discussed in greater depth in chapter 3. For now, suffice it to say that people communicating over the Internet have some degree of interactivity. If you have exchanged e-mail messages with anyone, then you are already aware that two-way communication is possible, if somewhat delayed by the nature of the technology involved.

Synchronicity

Messages exchanged over the Internet transverse not only space but also time (Strate, 1996). CMC allows for two types of time to elapse in online communication. **Synchronous communication** occurs when two or more participants are interacting in real time. You have experienced synchronous communication if you've ever played with a set of walkie-talkies in real life or experimented with IRC. These messages tend to be more conversational in nature, as they are composed off-the-cuff. In contrast, Internet messages can also be exchanged with lag time between them. **Asynchronous communication** occurs when participants interact with significant spans of time between their exchanges. You have experienced asynchronous communication if you have ever traded traditional letters with a pen pal or jokes with a friend over e-mail. Given that the authors have time to think them through, asynchronous messages tend to be better planned than synchronous ones.

Interestingly, the time between when a message is sent and when it is responded to contributes to indications of relational cues. Although many nonverbal channels are filtered out of most CMC (i.e., gesture, facial expression, intonation), the management of **chronemics** can still present shared meaning between communication partners. We all know that in face-to-face conversations, a silent pause can "say" a lot about a person's reaction. The length of the pause in asynchronous exchange seems to hold meaning as well. Walther and Tidwell (1995) found that people based their perceptions of liking by the amount of lag time between asynchronously exchanged messages. When the messages exchanged between two people were task-oriented (i.e., "Do we have a system in place to keep track of this?"), the more prompt the reply was, the more intimate (and, by inference, respectful) the relationship between the conversants was perceived. On the other hand, when the messages were social in nature (i.e., "What is your schedule when you are here—any openings? We should make plans."), the slower (and presumably more thoughtful) replies were perceived as the more intimate expressions. Thus, the management of time is a consideration for the manner in which our messages are expressed on the Internet.

Hypertextuality

Rafaeli's fifth distinguishing characteristic for Internet communication is hypertextuality. **Hypertext** is a type of nonsequential writing that challenges traditionally held notions about the way meaning is created through the experience of reading. As noted in chapter 1, Ong (1982) argues that writing was a technology that shaped how people think and ultimately how people interact with one another. Think of the ways in which the conventions of reading have shaped some of your perceptions. If you pick up a new book, you have been trained to start on the first page and read each page in turn rather than starting in the middle and jumping around the text. Likewise, you assume that words will flow in a left-to-right order across the page:

.arbitrarily reversed was order word the if frustrating be would It

Although such practices as page and word order seem normalized today, they are actually social conventions that evolved with the invention of writing and, later, print. Capitalization and punctuation are additional inventions used to make reading an easier task. That these conventions are invented rather than inherent characteristics of reading can be demonstrated by looking to other writing systems. For instance, the Chinese use not only a different alphabet but also a different word order, reading in a fashion that is mirrorlike to American language practices, with words flowing right to left across the page.

Writing in the days before a widely accessible source of hypertext was made manifest in the World Wide Web, Landow (1992) theorized that hypertext challenged several notions of our traditional reading of a text. He had been working with students of literature who were experimenting with the ways in which the relationships among the reader, writing, and text seemed altered in electronically linked (rather than printed) documents. In particular, he noted that the transition to hypertext represented a move from linearity to multilinearity, from centrality to a system of links, and from hierarchy to cooperation.

FROM LINEARITY TO MULTILINEARITY. As the examples of word order just cited indicate, the traditional practice of reading suggests that the reader proceed in linear, or sequential, manner. In this sense, readers are at the mercy of the author, who determines what topics will be addressed in what order. In contrast, some of that authorial control is yielded to the reader in a hypertext document. This control is facilitated by hyperlinks. **Hyperlinks** are selected words or images related to other sections of the same document or other documents. When one selects a hyperlink, typically by positioning one's cursor over it and clicking one's mouse, the computer program displays that other section or document for the reader. For example, as a reader of an electronic document on the history of writing, one might choose to select a hyperlink to Theodore Nelson and see an image of the man who first proposed hypertext.

In Landow's conception, every symbol in a hypertext document has the potential to be a hyperlink to another set of symbols, yet in practice, a limited number of hyperlinks are available to readers, meaning that authorial control is still a determining factor in the presentation of hypertext in practice. Nonetheless, readers have more choices about which hyperlinks to pursue or ignore in their own reading of the text, and that in itself is a noteworthy transfer of power (see Table 2.1).

Table 2.1
Different Types of Hyperlinks

Target link	Connects one point in a given document to another point in the same document.
Relative link	Connects one page at a given site to a different page within that site.
External link	Connects one site to a distinct site.

Source: Adapted from Shipley and Fish (1996).

Hyperlink: The Dark Side of the Rainbow

Over the last few years, various fans of the rock group Pink Floyd have turned to the Web to share their vision of what Roger Waters, Dave Gilmour, and bandmates *really* meant when they recorded their groundbreaking 1973 album, *Dark Side of the Moon*. Many careful students of this album claim that the band intended their album to follow the plotline of the film, *The Wizard of Oz*! One researcher of the odd coincidences between these works, Charles Savage (1995), points out:

- The Pink Floyd song "The Great Gig in the Sky" is closely matched to the film's tornado scene, rising and falling as the tornado spins across the screen.

- The album ends with the sounds of heartbeats—just as Dorothy listens to the Tin Woodsman's chest.

- " 'Black ... and blue' from 'Us and Them' is sung as the Wicked Witch of the West appears dressed in black. That is shortly followed by 'and who knows which is which' (witch is witch) as she and Glenda confront each other."

Did Pink Floyd intend for listeners of *Dark Side of the Moon* to start the album just as the MGM lion roared? No one is sure. But it's fun to imagine that they did. Ironically, *The Wizard of Oz* itself has invited a host of rereadings. Henry M. Littlefield found that the original book could be interpreted as a response to the free silver movement of the 1890s. From this perspective, characters in this child's fantasy could be reconfigured to stand in for characters and symbols of the political struggle of that age: the yellow brick road representing the gold standard, the Scarecrow representing the farmers, and the Cowardly Lion representing political leader William Jennings Bryan.

Hypertext challenges us to think past the question of whether Pink Floyd *meant* to relate their music to *The Wizard of Oz* or whether Lyman Frank Baum *meant* to write a subtle allegory of his time. Most fans of these works doubt whether either artist intended to create this strange set of connections. But that's not quite the point of our analysis. Hypertext allows us to imagine and interpret **synchronicities**—immediate but not necessarily intended connections and cross-references between people and ideas that unify public life and ground human experience.

From Centrality to Links. Landow (1992) also argues that traditional texts create a fiction that they exist independent of the world of texts around them. Novels, in particular, seem to create self-contained universes, seemingly oblivious to the worlds of literature they inhabit or the influences that contributed to their creation. In this way, they seek to establish their own centrality to the experience of reading. A hypertext document, on the other hand, dispels this fiction and accepts a decentered position as one of many texts that contribute to a reading experience. In this way, a given hyperlink situated in a passage from the novel *Being There* might lead to a biographical essay on its author, Jerzy Kosinski. Documents thus exist in relationship to rather than independently of one another. Landow calls each of these fragments a **lexia**, and it is the relationship of one lexia to another that moves the experience of reading away from centrality in hypertext. In the present practice of hypertext on the World Wide Web, a single page at any given Web site would function as a lexia.

FROM HIERARCHY TO COOPERATION. Finally, Landow sees hypertext as marking a significant shift from a hierarchical to a networked relationship between author and reader. In the traditional conception, the author has long been valorized as the creator of meaning. Certainly, literary scholars have long hallowed authors like Nathanial Hawthorne and Maya Angelou, to name but two canonized artists, for their creative gifts. Yet the hierarchy that places the creative genius of the author above the common intelligence of the reader is flattened in hypertext. Here author and reader must work together to make meaning out of the available symbols. Thus, the experience that comes from reading a given set of lexias flows from both the creative production of the author and the choices made by the reader. Such increased participation in constructing the reading experience is reminiscent of our earlier discussion of how online communication is facilitating a return to community. As experimentation with hypertext continues in forums like the World Wide Web, it will be interesting to see how the conventions of reading change for a new generation of meaning makers.

The changing relationship between author and reader in a hypertextual environment understandably raises significant questions. Doesn't it *matter* whether the author intended that a particular text would communicate a specific meaning? Shouldn't we respect the author's wishes in reading a text in a certain way? The problem with this line of questioning is that we rarely can peer so clearly into the author's psyche that we can hardly presume to know for sure what he or she *really* meant. The worst part? Some authors aren't too sure either.

Hypertextual analysis provides the reader the power to shape the meaning of a text by providing the means to establish meaning between and across texts. The World Wide Web provides an arena where various narrative interpretations are tested against common sense. Those that endure become part of our social fabric. Others remain as pages that people seldom visit. Either way, the texture of our communities becomes a lot more interesting.

CHAPTER SUMMARY

In this chapter, we have explored the technology of CMC from historical and functional perspectives. We offered an abbreviated history of computer technology, with particular emphasis on the role of cybernetics in the evolution of the Internet. Following this overview, we delved into five characteristics of online communication: packet-switching, multimedia, interactivity, synchronicity, and hypertextuality. At this point, we switch gears and head into the second major section of this text—a survey of issues related to online identity.

ONLINE COMMUNICATION AND THE LAW

Who owns hyperlinks? This may seem like a meaningless question. Hyperlinks may be placed on any web page, linking to any other web page, but they cannot be "owned" by anyone. However, British Telecommunications PLC (BT) claimed otherwise in 2000, arguing that they possessed a patent granting them exclusive use of the hyperlink. They didn't mind other folks using the technology, but they figured they should earn a small fee for each click. Some observers called this the "rock star" of the patent world, particularly when BT ceased their efforts to license the technology and launched a lawsuit against the ISP Prodigy: the first of many, they promised. Responding to the suit, a range of groups began to search out examples of hypertext use that preceded BT's patent. They knew that a solid example of hypertext use prior to BT's 1989 patent would annihilate their claim of creating the technology that enables the World Wide Web. Although plenty of examples of hyperlink use do, indeed, precede BT's claims of usage dating back to the 1970s—including films of hypertext taken during the 1960s— the 2002 judgment against BT hinged on a more subtle argument. Ruling against BT, the U.S. District Court for the Southern District of New York found that the firm based their patent on a "hub and spoke" notion of transmission, but the Internet functions more like a "network of networks," without the need for a hub computer (Donner and Juran, 2002). Since that ruling, BT has backed away from their plans to profit from hyperlink technology, and Internet users may breathe a bit easier.

Glossary

Analytical engine: A 19th-century concept that serves as the predecessor to the modern computer.

ARPANET: Early computer network designed for the U.S. Defense Department.

Asynchronous communication: The exchange of messages with significant lag time between them.

Chronemics: The use of time as a nonverbal channel for communicating qualities such as liking or dominance.

Command and control: The channeling of information to ensure that individuals act efficiently as a unit.

Hyperlink: Selected words or images that connect to other sections of a document or other documents in a hypertext environment like the World Wide Web.

Hypertext: A form of nonsequential writing that composes a text out of smaller bits of material that exist in relation to one another in a multilinear, decentralized network.

Information: An exchange of data necessary for one system to influence the behavior of another system.

Internet: A network of computers that allows for the transmission of data for multiple purposes through a common set of protocols according to a global address system.

Jacquard loom: A device that allows a weaver to mass produce patterns of cloth by following the patterns of punch cards.

Lexia: A chunk of material in hypertext.

Memex: A theoretical machine for the storage and retrieval of information linked together by hypertext.

Smart Mob: A network that employs sophisticated media such as mobile phone technology to interact with and respond to its environment in ways that surpass individual decision making skills.

Synchronicities: Immediate but not necessarily intended connections and cross-references between people and ideas that unify public life and ground human experience.

Synchronous communication: The exchange of messages in real time.

Technological determinism: The perspective that our growing ability to alter or replace nature provides a central reason for most personal and social trends.

Topics for Discussion

1. Select any one of the forms of CMC discussed in chapter 1 (e-mail, BBS, MUD, IRC, or the Web) and explain how Rafaeli's five qualities are or are not apparent. As part of your response, consider how communication practiced in that form is different from communication in the other forms.

2. Spend some time exploring a site on the World Wide Web. When you are finished, consider how hypertext influenced your interpretation of the reading experience. Then write a brief explanation for each of the following qualities: How did you proceed in a nonsequential rather than a linear fashion? How did the site decenter itself in relation to other sites through hyperlinks? In what way did you collaborate with the web master in making meaning out of this site?

3. Conduct a Yahoo search for resources about the Internet. Select five Web sites that appear to offer timely and credible information about one or several of these topics: search engines, Web portals, e-mail, the role of the Internet in education, the impact of CMC on business. Bookmark these online resources for your upcoming research efforts.

REFERENCES

Bennahum, D. S. (2003). J. C. R. Licklider (1915–1990). Retrieved from http://memex.org/licklider.html

Bush, V. (1945, July). As we may think. *Atlantic Monthly, 176,* 101–108.

Donner, I., & Juran, B. (2002, September 5). *Who invented hyperlinks?* Retrieved from http://www.haledorr.com/publications/pubsdetail.asp?ID=1299952002

Federal Networking Council. (1995, October 30). *FNC resolution: Definition of "Internet."* Retrieved from http://www.itrd.gov/fnc/Internet-res.html

Gibson, W., & Sterling, B. (1991). *The difference engine.* New York: Bantam Books.

Kaye, B. K., & Medoff, N. J. (1999). *The World Wide Web: A mass communication perspective*. Mountain View, CA: Mayfield.

Landow, G. P. (1992). *Hypertext: The convergence of contemporary critical theory and technology*. Baltimore, MD: Johns Hopkins University Press.

Marks, P. (2002, November 23). Way back when. *New Scientist*. Retrieved from http://www.newscientist.com/opinion/opinterview.jsp?id=ns23701

Metz, J. M. (1994, April). Computer-mediated communication: Literature review of a new context. *Interpersonal Computing and Technology: An Electronic Journal for the 21st Century, 2*(2), 31–49.

Moreau, R. (1984). *The computer comes of age: The people, the hardware, and the software* (J. Howlett, Trans.) Cambridge, MA: MIT Press.

Morris, M., & Ogan, C. (1996). The Internet as mass medium. *Journal of Communication, 46*(1), 39–50.

Newhagen, J. E., & Rafaeli, S. (1996, March). Why communication researchers should study the Internet: A dialogue. *Journal of Computer-Mediated Communication, 1*(4). Retrieved from http://www.ascusc.org/jcmc/vol1/issue4/rafaeli.html

Ong, W. J. (1982). *Orality and literacy: The technologizing of the word*. New York: Routledge.

Rheingold, H. (2002). Smart mobs: *The next social revolution*. Cambridge, MA: Perseus.

Savage, C. (1995). *The dark side of the rainbow*. Retrieved from http://members.aol.com/rbsavage/floydwizard.html

Shipley, C., & Fish, M. (1996). *How the World Wide Web works*. Emeryville, CA: Ziff–Davis.

Shurkin, J. (1984). *Engines of the mind: A history of the computer*. New York: Norton.

Stein, S. R. (2002). The '1984' Macintosh ad: Cinematic icons and constitutive rhetoric in the launch of a new machine. *Quarterly Journal of Speech, 88*(2), 169–192.

Strate, L. (1996). Cybertime. In L. Strate, R. Jacobson, & S. B. Gibson (Eds.), *Communication and cyberspace: Social interaction in an electronic environment* (pp. 351–377). Cresskill, NJ: Hampton Press.

Taylor, R. W. (1990, August 7). *In memoriam: J. C. R. Licklider: 1915–1990*. Retrieved from http://memex.org/licklider.pdf

Walther, J. B., & Tidwell, L. C. (1995). Nonverbal cues in computer-mediated communication, and the effect of chronemics on relational communication. *Journal of Organizational Computing, 5*, 355–378.

Weiner, N. (1954). *The human use of human beings: Cybernetics and society*. Boston: Houghton Mifflin.

Zakon, R. H. (2003). *Hobbes' Internet timeline 6.0*. Retrieved from http://www.zakon.org/robert/internet/timeline/

PART II

THE SELF AMONG OTHERS

A generation ago, a communication technology grabbed the nation's interest, and its enthusiasts eagerly incorporated the latest equipment for their systems, adopted quirky aliases for themselves, and spent hour after hour doing nothing more than talking to other enthusiasts. If this behavior seems a lot like the way people behaved when the Internet caught on in the 1990s, it is because there are some intriguing parallels between the previous popularity of Citizen's Band (CB) radio and the recent popularity of the Internet. Although amateur radio broadcasts had been evolving since the late 1940s, its popularity peaked in 1977, when an estimated 11 million Americans were taking to the airwaves broadcasting messages to one another (Drew, 1997). In fact, the film *Frequency* (Hoblit, 2000) nostalgically recalled the joys of this form of mediated communication. Although there are far fewer CB hobbyists today, people's interest in communicating with others who are not physically present has not diminished. Arguably, the introduction of e-mail into people's professional and personal lives has made such mediated communication an even more frequent occurrence.

Thus, today we can find people adding webcams to their computer systems, rechristening themselves with fanciful pseudonyms, and spending countless hours chatting with people they have never seen nor are likely to see. Yet despite the Internet's popularity, some people question the quality and effects of this latest form of mediated communication in our lives. This part of the book addresses both people's behavior in and the concerns about CMC. We consider behaviors like the creation of identities, the formation of relationships, and the maintenance of virtual communities. But we also address concerns like misrepresentation, hostile messages, and Internet addiction. In short, we discuss a host of issues that involve how individuals affect and are affected by the others they engage through communication.

REFERENCES

Drew, K. (1997, March 20). Breaker, breaker: CB radio is back. *Christian Science Monitor*, p. 3.

Hoblit, G. (Producer/Director). (2000). *Frequency* [Motion picture]. New York: New Line Cinema.

CHAPTER 3

FORMING ONLINE IDENTITIES

Looking at the proliferation of personal Web pages on the Net, it looks like very soon everyone on Earth will have 15 megabytes of fame.

—M. G. Siriam

For 3 years, women who participated in a CompuServe discussion group grew closer and closer to a woman they knew as Julie Graham. During that time, Julie posted messages that disclosed increasingly intimate details of her life, including the fact that she was a mute, paraplegic victim of a car crash who had wrestled with suicidal depression. Her plight so moved her fellow participants that after a number of months of interacting with her online, one well-intentioned woman set out to find Julie and offer her face-to-face comfort and support. Much to this woman's surprise, "Julie Graham" turned out to be a fiction, and the facts behind the person creating her were quite contrary to what the woman and others had read. First of all, Julie wasn't a mute paraplegic. Second, she wasn't housebound, but a full-time professional psychologist. Third, she wasn't a she, but a man who had created the online persona of Julie to delve deeper into the female psyche by impersonating one. When the sleuthing woman reported her discovery to the rest of the bulletin board's participants, outraged contributors condemned the experiment, remarking that in impersonating one of them, the psychologist had violated their privacy (Stone, 1991).

Why were the women upset with "Julie's" deception? After all, how could these women feel betrayed by someone with whom they had never met face-to-face? Despite the intuitive conclusion of those outside the context that these were "just words," the self that this psychologist presented and the one that his conversation partners perceived seemed quite authentic. CMC contexts, like no other person-to-person media before them, offer communicators the ability to manipulate their personal identities in ways that call into question assumptions about what is possible and what is appropriate in the presentation of self.

Professor Sherry Turkle has been particulary helpful in illuminating just how computing technologies have challenged us to reevaluate how we think about ourselves. Turkle has thus labeled the computer an evocative object, that is, an object to think with (Rheingold, n.d.). As we review shortly, computers have been helpful in showing us just how multifaceted our lives are. Whereas popular conceptions of psychological health have considered an unfragmented, unitary self the ideal, Turkle suggests that the ability to move from one aspect, or self, to another and to do so with an understanding of the process is a more healthy conception of who we are. Computers, with their ability to multitask various jobs simultaneously, serve as a metaphor for our own lives in which we are called on to fill more than one role, oftentimes simultaneously. The computer's communication applications, those in which we practice CMC, are just some that allow us to practice, to explore, and ultimately to reflect on the nature of who we are in terms of not just one self, but our many selves.

Thus, this chapter explores several key issues dedicated to questions of identity in communicating through mediating technologies. An **identity** is a complex personal and social construct, consisting in part of who we think ourselves to be, how we wish others to perceive us, and how they actually perceive us. In particular, CMC research has looked at the second of these fragments: how we wish others to perceive us. The process of setting forth an image we want others to perceive is known as **self-presentation**.

In considering how people go about constructing their self-presentations online, we review research that considers several different channels for CMC. In particular, this research has focused on human interaction in MUDs, IRC, and BBSs, although much of what has been suggested about the nature of these text-only media can be applied to e-mail and even the more graphically rich environment of Web sites. (A review of the tools just described can be found in chapter 1.) Social convention has dictated that most MUDs, many IRC channels, and several BBSs serve a more playful than professional function. Thus, because their objectives tend to be social rather than task-oriented, they present especially rich opportunities for experimentation with self-presentation. As shown here, these text-only media have introduced new forums for communicating one's identity. The lessons learned from people's use of them underscores how we construct our identities and points to ways we can more competently communicate about ourselves in the mediated environment.

In the following sections, this chapter introduces several concepts in understanding the communication of online identity. To begin, we consider the process of

Hyperlink: 15 Megabytes of Fame

Andy Warhol, the 20th-century artist who enjoyed a noteworthy reputation in art and popular culture circles, once said, "In the future everyone will be world-famous for fifteen minutes." Warhol was, of course, offering a sarcastic commentary on how society has become obsessed with celebrity status. Today, more than ever, it seems that there are figures who are famous simply for being famous, and people seem more likely to know the names of the entertainers who star in their favorite television shows than the names of their state's elected officials who legislate the laws that govern their lives. Some critics have noted that the Internet has only added to this dilemma, allowing more people than ever to engage in the pursuit of celebrity by allowing them to create mass-distributed images for themselves.

A watershed example of this quest occurred when DotComGuy established his Internet presence, a unique domain name, and an irresistible public relations gimmick. The former Mitch Maddox (he legally changed his name to

DotComGuy) decided to live a year of his life online using products and services purchased exclusively through the Internet (Sheff, 2000). Beginning on January 1, 2000, DotComGuy moved into a house whose furnishings were limited to little more than a computer and the dozens of webcams used to broadcast his homebound activities day and night. In keeping with the promotional agreement that he made with his sponsors, DotComGuy never left his home and so bought everything from toilet paper to movie videos online. In making his exploits available to a worldwide audience, DotComGuy garnered the attention of numerous media outlets in addition to the fans who regularly chatted with him on his Web site, www.dotcomguy.com.

More recently and more popularly, people have taken to recording their thoughts, and consequently increasing their notoriety, through Weblogs, or **blogs**. From the mundane to the idiosyncratic, blogs are journal-like Web sites, where authors may, for instance, record their day-to-day experiences, publish new poetry, or post links to sites of interest that they have found online. For example, while news organizations were boasting of "embedded" reporters during the Iraqi war, a number of bona fide military were blogging the events from an even more immediate first-hand account of the events (Hastings, 2003). Estimates put the total number of blogs at nearly a half-million, with some garnering the attention of several thousand devoted readers and others only a handful of interested visitors (Levy, 2002). At either extreme, the bloggers put their talent, wit, or off-the-wall perspectives on display, trying to achieve the attention that they, and so many others, crave. (We'll take another look at bloggers' activities as voices outside of the mainstream in chapter 9.)

Of course, these examples are just the tip of the celebrity-seeking iceberg. From personal Web sites that function as electronic wedding albums to pay-per-view sites where amateur exhibitionists engage in all manner of revealing activities on live webcams, the Internet has seemingly put celebrity within everyone's grasp. Now instead of 15 minutes of fame, perhaps Warhol's prophecy could be revised to guarantee everyone 15 megabytes of fame as M. G. Siriam suggests in the opening quotation. Of course, in the rush to package, publish, and market themselves, those in pursuit of star status must compete with everyone else seeking the public's notice. What is an unknown to do in this competitive climate?

Perhaps another sarcasm taken from popular culture offers some perspective. A popular soft drink campaign mocked its competitor's use of celebrity endorsements to sell their products. "Image is nothing" quipped each ad in the series, attempting to remind us that the famous are not omniscient experts: Just because someone plays basketball well does not mean that he or she knows your tastes better than you do. As we encounter would-be Internet icons (or even consider becoming such icons ourselves), we should take the soft drink maker's advice under consideration. Is our own admiration of these stars based on legitimate contributions they have made to our lives or merely based on their own pursuit of fame?

perceiving an audience through telepresence. Next, we review the construction of identity through a performance metaphor, examining how people construct online personas. After that, we examine the distinctions among nameless anonymity, inventive pseudonymity, and one's real-life identity. Finally, we conclude with some suggestions for protecting real-life identity in an era of enhanced technological access to potentially damaging personal information.

THE PRINCIPLE OF TELEPRESENCE: IS ANYONE OUT THERE?

One of the foundational issues in establishing a sense of online identity has to do with the degree to which people feel they are able to experience a connection to others through technology. Some people are able to look at a computer screen and declare, "Those are just words," whereas others report that they are able to perceive personal characteristics and relational content through text-only messages. As in many such cases where the same phenomenon can render different interpretations by different audiences, human perception functions to make the experience richer or poorer.

Whenever we interact in face-to-face contexts, we take our surroundings, and the multiple senses that are stimulated, for granted. When you take a walk in the park, you probably are aware, but don't deeply contemplate, all the sensations that make the experience real to you: the sight of oak trees, the sound of singing robins, the smell of spring blossoms, and the feel of the dirt path beneath your feet. These stimuli create a feeling of presence for you. In mediated contexts, such as reading a description of a walk through the virtual park of a MUD, requires that you perceive the same sensations as creating (or re-creating) the experience for you. This is **telepresence**, "the extent to which one feels present in the mediated environment, rather than in the immediate physical environment" (Steuer, 1992, p. 76). Even slight distinctions among mediating technologies can vary the experience of telepresence. Consider, for example, the difference between an audio recording cut in the studio and one made at a concert. A concert recording can seem more realistic because of the addition of background noises that recreate the experience of being a part of an audience for a listener.

According to Steuer (1992), the sense of "being there" that many report experiencing while engaged in the virtual realities communicated through cyberspace can be explained in terms of telepresence. His model (as depicted in Fig. 3.1) suggests that varying degrees of vividness and interactivity on the part of the medium indicate how realistic a person will perceive the limited stimuli offered to be.

The quality of **vividness** refers to the amount of sensory information the medium makes available to a person. According to Steuer, a sense of vividness is created by both the breadth of senses engaged and the depths to which any one of those senses is stimulated. If you compare media rated as "high" in vividness with those rated as "low," you will see a difference in both the breadth and the depth of sensory information available. For instance, compare 3-D films, which rate relatively high on vividness, to books, which rate relatively low. A 3-D film, such as the Universal Pictures classic *The Creature from the Black Lagoon*, is a more vivid depiction of an alternate reality than that available in the latest Tom Clancy novel. The film displays more breadth than the book because it makes use of our senses of both sight and hearing. The book would only engage our sight. The film also represents greater

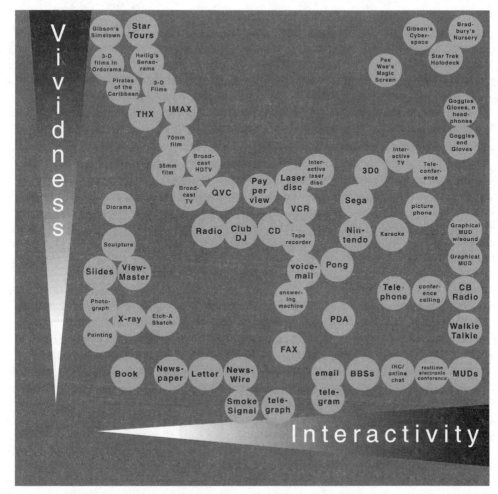

Fig. 3.1. Various media technologies classified by vividness and interactivity. (Courtesy of Jennifer Cool, 2001. Reprinted from Steuer, J. (1992). Defining virtual reality: Dimensions determining telepresence. *Journal of Communication, 42*(4), 73–93 by permission of Oxford University Press)

depth of vividness. Three-dimensional cinema uses technology to create an illusion of multiple layers to enhance our visual perceptions more than traditional filming or photography. Books lack such sensory depth, relying instead on our imaginations to add dimensions of meaning to the words we read in them.

The sense of realism that comes with telepresence is also enhanced by the degree of interactivity the medium presents to people. A measure of **interactivity** deals with the degree to which a person can manipulate the environment of a medium. A sense of interactivity is suggested by three factors. The first of these is *speed*, or how quickly a user can manipulate the environment. The second is *range*, or how much a user manipulates the environment, and the third deals with *mapping*, or how the actions of a user are related to reactions in the virtual environment. Let's return to the earlier example of books and compare them to another text-based communication medium, MUDs. With a few exceptions, books offer limited interactivity to readers. Readers can do little to change the content of books in any sort of timely fashion. Even if a typographical error is found in a textbook and it is reported to the publisher, a correction is unlikely to appear until a subsequent edition of the book is printed in 2 to 4 years. Thus, only limited control can be exerted over the speed or range of manipulation over this medium. One genre of book does allow some sense of mapping, the third quality of interactivity, and that is the "choose-your-own-adventure" books, popularized in the 1980s. These books allowed readers to determine the sequence of a story by choosing among limited choices of what page or chapter to read next. However, the vast majority of books are low in interactivity.

In contrast, MUDs are forums for greater participation. A MUD allows one to make contributions to the ongoing conversation and action in real time. Not only is one's contribution quickly transcribed onto the screen, but it can alter the course of events or conversation, indicating a much more significant degree of content manipulation than was possible with books. Finally, one's decision to move around objects or one's own position within the MUD is reacted to by the program governing its operations. Hence, when one directs one's character, <bud>, to "leave library," the program accommodates the directive and displays "bud leaves library," providing a sense of mapping as one's actions appear to cause a reaction in the virtual world.

One of Steuer's (1992) more interesting selections for his comparison of various media includes one technology that only exists as fiction, the holodeck that originated on the television series, *Star Trek: The Next Generation* (1987–1994). The holodeck was a room aboard the starship *Enterprise* that created recreational environments for the ship's crew during their long sojourns in space. Using holograms and force fields, the holodeck simulated everything from New Orleans' jazz clubs to alien landscapes in convincing detail. The holodeck not only provided a practical plot device to get the series' characters out of outer space from time to time, but also served as an idealized conception of the heights to which mediating technologies could aspire. The holodeck provided a forecast for an as-yet-unrealized medium that is exceptionally high in vividness and interactivity. Likewise, Steuer's dimensions determining telepresence help us appreciate just how complex a thing it is for the mind to interpret different mediated messages as realistic.

Ultimately, the qualities for any given medium for CMC are fixed, that is, each medium is programmed to grant us so much vivid detail or allow a certain amount of interactivity. Beyond this, the perceptions of the individual users also play a signficant role in determining just how much telepresence is interpreted (Tu, 2001). Even the relatively "lean" messages of text-based CMC systems may be perceived to be quite rich by someone tuned into the cues that are available. Likewise, even the most graphically rich and interactive Web site might seem flat to someone else. In the end, the quality of telepresence is subjectively experienced, and it is that subjectivity that makes some feel that interacting online is real and others that it's not a real deal.

PERFORMING IDENTITY ON THE INTERNET

People's perceptions of the amount of telepresence in a given medium suggest that they are likely to consider how the messages they fashion through media are reflections on them. Perhaps you have acquaintances who do not leave messages on telephone answering machines, declaring, "I don't like those machines." Such individuals are probably a bit self-conscious about what they say or how they sound on tape. This kind of self-awareness is but another manifestation of humanity's long struggle with identity. Again, an important aspect of identity is how we present ourselves to others. To some degree, we can control what others know of us by making some choices in life, yet certain qualities of our identities are predetermined for us. In face-to-face interactions, people infer qualities of our identities based on our gender, race, clothing, and other nonverbal characteristics. Because many of these cues are invisible online, Internet technologies offer us the possibility of controlling more aspects of our identity for public consideration than has been possible before. As the following examples demonstrate, fashioning identity has been a perennial concern of human civilization.

Manipulating one's identity is nothing new to Western culture, and, indeed, neither are many of the insecurities associated with such a practice. Consider, for example, the ancient Greek myth of Oedipus, preserved for us in the works of Sophocles. According to the playwright's account, a prophet had declared that the king's newborn son was destined to kill his father. Hoping to avoid this fate, the king sent the infant off to be killed itself, but the soldier charged with the task instead left the baby to be raised by shepherds. Years later, the grown Oedipus, oblivious of his ancestry, unknowingly traveled back to the kingdom. Along his journey he got into an argument with a stranger, which culminated in the stranger's death. Unknown to Oedipus, he had just fulfilled the prophecy by slaying his own father, who was actually the king in disguise. Oedipus traveled on to the city of Thebes, where, after solving the riddle of the monstrous Sphinx, he was proclaimed king and given the queen as his bride. That queen, as you might have guessed, turned out to be his own mother. Before the play is over, Oedipus discovers his true identity and, in anger for not recognizing the situation sooner, gouges out his own eyes with the pin of a broach. With such grisly repercussions, even for those ignorant of their circumstances, is it any wonder that societies such as the Greek's, and the Western cultures that followed them, have placed such a heavy emphasis on consistency in individual identity?

In addition to Greek tragedies, the problematic nature of personal identity has also been a theme for comedies. In fact, a source of humor in a number of William Shakespeare's timeless comedies is the misrepresented identity, specifically the switching of identities that involves gender-swapping. Modern audiences were reminded of how complex and fun such manipulations of identity could be in the 1998 Academy Award winner for best picture, *Shakespeare in Love*. In the film, noblewoman Viola de Lesseps (portrayed by Gwyneth Paltrow) wants to be an actor, but both her elevated social class and her gender forbid her from mingling with common performers. Only when she disguises herself as a boy is she able to win a role on stage working with Shakespeare at his Globe Theatre. She traded her skirt for a pair of pants, tucked her long hair under a hat, and deepened her voice to perpetuate her disguise. According to the fictional movie, these events allegedly inspired Shakespeare to use gender-swapping as a plot device in his comedies, including *As You Like It* and *All's Well That Ends Well*.

Although comparatively few of us elect to take on the characteristics typically associated with the opposite gender, most of us are adopting specific ornaments for our appearance and attitudes to suit the roles we find ourselves fulfilling during daily life. Consider the process you undergo in the morning when deciding what clothes to wear. Do you purposefully choose a professional outfit because you have to go to work or make a presentation for a class? Or do you throw on the first thing you trip over on your floor? If you know you have to work or make a presentation, would it be inappropriate to show up in baggy sweat pants and a T-shirt? Certainly, just as it would be inappropriate to show up for a touch football game in a blazer. Most of us are aware that costuming is an important aspect of the parts we play and the self we choose to present at one time or another.

Casting Call: Performing Multiple Roles

Communication scholars have long pulled on the works of noted sociologist Erving Goffman, who wrote extensively on how people work to present themselves in everyday life. Goffman would have agreed with Shakespeare, who wrote:

> All the world's a stage,
> And all the men and women merely players.
> They have their exits and their entrances;
> And one man in his time plays many parts. (*As You Like It*, Act II, Scene 7)

It was Goffman's (1959) contention that everyday life was a performance of sorts, and that our behaviors and attitudes could be explained in terms of a theatrical metaphor. Accordingly, Goffman wrote of how people adopted particular roles when they were in public view by putting on a face. The effort people invest in "staying in character," as it were, Goffman calls **face-work**, noting that people are persistently attending to the requirements of a particular face lest they break the image of their role. Over the years, Goffman's work has been instrumental in advancing the understanding of how elements of performance contribute to what and how people communicate. More recent researchers have echoed Goffman's fascination with the theatrical metaphor and have invoked similar language in attempting to explain how people construct identities online.

Pulling on another theatrical term, Amy Bruckman (1992) dubs text-based forums like MUDs "identity workshops." A workshop in theatrical training presents an opportunity for actors to experiment with various roles. An actor in training might take on the role of a vocal football coach one moment and then change over to a portrayal of a sidewalk mime the next, all to exercise the range of his or her acting ability. In like manner, then, an identity workshop presents people with a chance to display different manifestations of themselves. One could very well maintain an identity as a rough-and-tough sailor in one MUD but portray a sensitive artist in another chat room.

Turkle (1995) confirms the notion that the computer enables users to explore multiple roles. Turkle says, "In . . . computer-mediated worlds, the self is multiple, fluid and constituted in interaction with machine connections; it is made and transformed by language" (p. 15). This view of the self as multiple and fluid—subject to multiphrenia described in chapter 1—rather than singular and static is further explored in Turkle's writings by drawing a comparison to the multiple tasks one can accomplish in a windows-based environment. Current software allows users to change from using a word-processing program to author a research paper, to sending e-mail to one's boss, to participating in a MUD, all by merely clicking from window to window. Thus, one can quite readily switch roles from student, to employee, to fantasy figure. Certainly, this is a manifestation of the concept of multiphrenia. However, Turkle clearly suggested that people control the multiple roles rather than suffer from the burden of having to negotiate among them.

Why do people engage in such role-playing then? Turkle (1995) suggests that one reason is that people can experience an identity they could not successfully portray in real life. A benefit of such role-playing is that individuals can gain a new perspective on their world and their place in it. Borrowing from anthropology, Turkle uses the term **dépaysement** to describe the experience of seeing the familiar through unfamiliar eyes. In interviews with people who adopted identities distinctly different from their own for their online personas, most notably those who changed their genders, Turkle found that the experience of living a life unlike their own opened them up to the struggles and pleasures that come along with living with another gender, race, class, or other distinction.

A good example of how role-playing might promote better understanding comes from the simulations conducted by Andrew Vincent of Macquarie University in Syndney, Australia (Vincent & Shepherd, 1998). Coming to the simulations, Vincent's students tend to have limited comprehension of the political problems facing the Middle East, which is unsurprising given the distance that the conflict is from most of his students' experiences and the complexity of the issues involved. Following a format similar to that of a model United Nations program, Vincent assigns both students in his course and those at a cooperating institution to roles of various contemporary figures in the conflict (e.g., the leader of the Palestinians, the prime minister of Israel). Through several weeks of Internet-based exchanges, the role-players try to come to some agreements. By the end of the simulation, students begin to understand more about the Middle East situation, for, as one of Vincent's students explained it:

> Putting yourself in someone else's shoes—you may get the role of particular character but you don't necessarily agree with them but you have to try to develop their mindset. It's interesting. Right in there at the moment we've got a girl with leanings towards the Palistinians playing Benjamin Netanyahu [then Israeli prime minister], so it's a complete turn-around for her. It's imperative to be able to see other points of view and realise that they're just as valuable as yours. (Vincent & Shepherd, 1998)

That kind of insight is educational, indeed.

Another reason for role-playing might reside in the increased control people experience over their online identities. In real life, one can adopt a limited number of roles, given that one's gender, race, age, accent, and other nonverbal determinants influence people's perceptions of how well one functions in a given role. For instance, a middle-aged, Euro-American man might decide he wants to experiment with a female identity. With the appropriate costuming and mannerisms, he might be successful in appearing to be a female to someone he has not previously met, but if he wants to know what it is like to be an African American, he is less likely to be able to pull off such a charade. However, in an online forum, he can more readily adopt and enact a change in his gender, race, or any other characteristic he chooses.

In whatever identity he selects, he can exert greater control over his identity in the online environment than in face-to-face interaction. In face-to-face interactions, we communicate not only through our words but also through our appearance. For example, in real life, someone might decide to discount your opinion because of your age, because he or she perceives that you are either too young or too old to know much about a topic. But in online forums, what people know about others is based on the disclosure of information that one wishes others to know (Cutler, 1996). If one's age is not relevant to the persona one wishes to have others perceive, then one needs merely not to reveal this information to prevent skewing others' perceptions one way or another.

In fact, research from John Bargh, Katelyn McKenna, and Grainne Fitzsimons (2002) shows that people are better able to express and have others perceive their "true self" online than off. In their experiment, participants were asked to disclose components of their inner, nonpublic selves before logging into a chat room. Their conversation partners were then asked to rate qualities about these people after their chat. Compared to a similar group of face-to-face conversants, those online were more accurately perceived. That is, their faceless conversation partners were better able to match their descriptors of the participants with the descriptors that the participants themselves had offered. Bargh et al. theorize that the qualities of the medium itself help to ease one's tensions about disclosing details that might be otherwise socially taboo. As we see shortly, the ability to be heard, but not seen, can be quite liberating. Let us consider first the role that language plays in text-only media such as chat rooms.

Learning One's Lines: Performing Through Language

In the presentation of self in text-only media, one is not recognized by one's physical appearance, but through one's verbal behaviors. Obviously, one might offer a description of one's persona or disclose personal characteristics that contribute to others' impression formations. Yet according to Mark Giese (1998), there is another way that people come to identify an individual as participants interact with one another. "In a sense I am 'recognized' by a host of personal markers that include my writing style, my .sig [signature attachment], the way I conduct myself with various members of the groups and my contribution to the cooperative narrative." In short, both what people say about themselves and how they behave with others contribute to a perception of personal identity online. The use of language is consequently of immense importance in cyberspace, for it is through the use of language that people construct their identities.

Language is thus the primary vehicle for establishing one's own and perceiving another's online persona. A term for such figures originated among fantasy game-players and embraced among CMC practitioners is **avatar**. An avatar is a representation of oneself in a virtual environment, in other words, one's alter ego or persona. If you've ever used Instant Messenger icons on America Online or created a signature file to attach to your outgoing e-mail messages, then you are already somewhat familiar with the process of employing an avatar online.

The selection of a rather unusual term to express the relationships between identity and cyberspace is perhaps justified by the unusual nature of the medium itself. As with all mediated environments, one does not have a body in the nonspace of cyberspace, only a representation of oneself, wholly constructed by individual choices. Even in the case of a handwritten letter, which is seemingly devoid of many nonverbal cues, readers (like handwriting experts) infer qualities about the person on the other end based on something (loops in letters, dotting of letters) other than the content of what is written. Only in cyberspace is the proverbial playing field leveled of such biasing cues, suggesting that a new type of representation is occurring in this context.

Of course, the practice of representing oneself through language and controlled cues (as in Web pages that offer photographs or sound bites) is not above suspicion. People tend to mistrust what they cannot verify through other sources. We all know that lies are constructs of language. Even telling someone to "put it in writing" does not preclude deception. Socrates, whose philosophical treatises formed the foundations for Western thought, never committed a word to paper. (What we know of the insights attributed to him were set down by his pupil, Plato.) Socrates was suspicious of writing, fearing that someone could just as easily misquote him as quote him. The persistent fear that language does not provide an accurate depiction of reality is revisited in the construction of avatars. How are we to know that what we read is what we get? Contributing to a lack of ease in dealing with people only though their online presentations is the much-touted practice of gender-swapping.

Gender-Swapping: Performing in Virtual Drag

The opening vignette of this chapter illustrates one well-known case in which gender-swapping was not favorably received. **Gender-swapping** occurs when an individual of one gender self-presents as a member of another gender. As you probably know, gender is a social construct that provides guidelines for how we expect people of a certain biological sex to behave. For example, men are expected to be masculine and thus strong and women to be feminine and thus compassionate. Such expectations are reinforced throughout our lives, so when we encounter someone who seemingly violates these stereotypes, we can be frustrated by the inconsistency. Several years ago, *Saturday Night Live* featured a character called Pat, and the confusion over whether Pat's name and behaviors were indicative of a man or a woman revealed how obsessed we are with gender (Bruckman, 1996).

Research has indicated that when people gender-swap (and more typically than not it is men portraying women), they tend to adopt the same rigid gender roles that their culture has come to expect (Bornstein, 1994). As such, masculine avatars devote a great deal of attention to, and will eagerly come to the aid of, female avatars (Bruckman, 1996). The perpetuation of stereotypical responses to gender such as this may explain why when someone is exposed for gender-swapping, others can respond with disbelief, confusion, or anger.

Reports of gender-swapping, and the anxieties that accompany it and other forms of misrepresentation, may yet prove to be overly exaggerated. According to research reported by Diane Schiano (1999), most people in online forums act as idealized versions of themselves (rather than markedly distinct individuals), and the majority of MUD participants maintain only one character. In fact, she found that participants experienced "an awareness of social pressure to maintain the authenticity and accountability afforded by a single primary identity." Such a finding corroborates survey results among people making presentations of self through personal Web sites. Approximately 67% of those responding to the survey reported that they do not feel it is appropriate for anyone to misrepresent themselves online (Buten, 1996). Interestingly, 91% agreed that they accurately represented themselves on their own home pages. Such research clearly suggests that although experimentation with identity is possible, it is neither encouraged nor the norm for the presentation of self.

HYPERLINK: THE DOGGONED LOG-ON

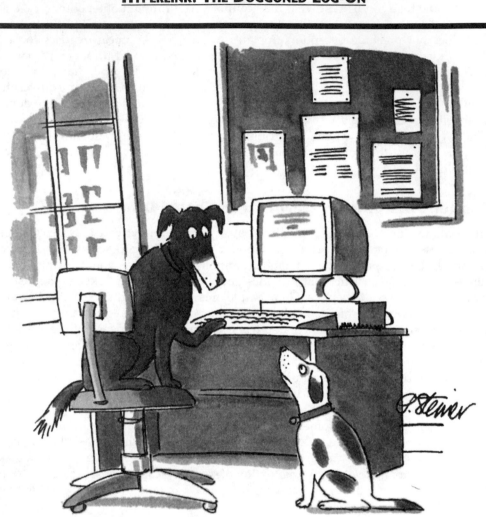

"On the Internet, nobody knows you're a dog."

A perennial feature of *The New Yorker* magazine has been its whimsical cartoons. Over the years, they have provided witty commentary on social practices, including the one that appeared in the July 5, 1993, issue, featuring two dogs reflecting on the nature of personal identity on the Internet. As one dog sits poised in front of a computer screen, he turns to his companion and says, "On the Internet, nobody knows you're a dog." The cartoon, drawn by Peter Steiner, represents in stark brevity the point of much academic contemplation on the nature of self in online contexts (the contents of this chapter included). On the surface, the cartoon makes light of how easily online identity is manipulated, so much so that even an animal could successfully disguise itself. On a deeper level, it, like many other examples of humor, picks at the scabs of our collective insecurities. The dogs the cartoon depicts are almost conspiratorial in their misrepresentation of identity. Moreover, the label *dog* is not only applied to a beloved household pet, but also used to describe an undesirable person (e.g., "That dog left me at the altar"). Perhaps without ever intending to, the cartoon "On the Internet, nobody knows you're a dog" illustrates twin concerns associated with online identities: the playfulness they promote and the suspicions that surround them.

ANONYMITY, PSEUDONYMITY, AND IDENTITY

When people enter chat rooms, contribute to bulletin boards, or participate in MUDs, they can exercise control over elements of their self-presentation. In choosing names, signature files, or personal descriptions, they make conscious decisions about how they wish to be perceived by others. The range of possible selves one might elect to present could be considered along a continuum (see Fig. 3.2) of identification (Marx, 1999). At one end of this continuum would be the nearly emptied state of anonymity. Along the continuum would be differing levels of an invented self-representing pseudonymity. At the opposite end, then, would be the identity presented in real life (or as close as one could get to it through the limited stimuli of mediating technologies). In the section that follows, we look at the manipulation of identity along this continuum.

Anonymity

Although most Americans would consider being "up-front" with people to be a common value, the fact is that in many instances we value privacy even more than frankness. There are certain legitimate circumstances in which our safety is protected by issuing our messages anonymously. In mediated contexts, **anonymity** is a state of communicating where the identity of the communicator is not readily apparent. People use anonymity to solicit dates in newspaper and magazine advertisements, to

Anonymity   Pseudonymity   Real-Life Identity

Fig. 3.2. A continuum of identity manipulation.

report knowledge of criminal activities on police tip lines, to engage in whistle blowing activities that draw media or legal attention to corporate misdoing, and to seek shelter when involved in abusive relationships (Wayner, 1999). In such circumstances, not being obliged to disclose one's true identity, and thus risk one's personal security, may well encourage important messages that might not otherwise be communicated.

The ability to communicate anonymously has been a particularly thorny issue in CMC. Although anonymity can function to protect people from reprisals it can also distance them from accountability, that is, taking responsibility for what they say. As we explain in the final section of this chapter, some people misuse the anonymity that online communication technologies afford to commit crimes. According to Gia Lee (1996), the debates over online anonymity have centered on three key issues. The first issue has to do with the informative aspect of identity. Knowing the reputation of the person issuing a statement is a double-edged sword. On one hand, knowing who has said something suggests the credibility that person has to speak on that topic. For example, having information about a source's expertise on a given topic influences how much one will trust the source's position. On the other hand, knowing characteristics like the sender's gender, race, and social standing could lead to an unfair hearing based on a receiver's personal biases and stereotypes. The second issue concerning anonymity deals with group pressures. One side of this argument suggests that people who must be associated with their ideas will only express things they truly believe. Knowing that others will judge them by what they say serves to minimize blind attacks. The other side of this argument suggests that anonymity allows others to express unpopular opinions or question conventional wisdom. Such statements can function as agents of change when those who issue them are not suffocated by group pressures to remain silent. The third issue involves the enforcement of existing legal restrictions on speech. Without knowing who has issued them, it is impossible for law enforcement agents to prosecute those who commit libel, obscenity, or copyright infringement.

Although there are no quick fixes to these debates, scholars and legal experts have suggested that a compromise would be to enact "a principle of truth in the nature of naming" (Marx, 1999). As such, either the people issuing anonymous messages or the ISP facilitating them would indicate that their statements were anonymous. Such "visible anonymity" (Lee, 1996) would still protect the interests of the source while signaling to the receiver that the source has, for whatever reason, chosen not to associate with the message.

Pseudonymity

If anonymity lies at one end of the identity continuum and one's real-life identity lies at the other, then pseudonymity covers a good deal of the area in between. **Pseudonym** comes from the Latin words for "false" and "name," and it provides an audience with the ability to attribute statements and actions to a common source. Like an anonym, a pseudonym provides its owner with some degree of protection. But unlike an anonym, a pseudonym allows one to contribute to the fashioning of one's own image. Authors and performers have long recognized such a virtue. In the 19th century, Samuel L. Clemens recognized that the river pilot's call, "Mark twain!" reflected his desire to be an author associated with life on the Mississippi River. A century later, would-be actor Bernard Schwartz realized that Tony Curtis was a much more glamorous name for earning recognition in Hollywood.

Although celebrities have popularized adopting pseudonyms, the practice of renaming oneself in different communication contexts is by no means inaccessible to common people. In fact, pseudonyms were quite popular among people who communicated on a medium that could be considered the predecessor to the Internet, CB radio. As we noted earlier, CB enthusiasts adopted **handles** to identify themselves when broadcasting messages over the airwaves. Because these messages were in the public arena, many people chose to participate in public discussions without giving out their real names (and some security) by using their handles instead. They also chose handles that allowed them to fashion some perception of their unique identities. As CB radio grew increasingly popular throughout the 1970s, participants adopted identities like "Stargazer" and "Midnight Delight," each of which conjures up distinct images of what the person behind them might be like. One researcher found that women users in particular tended to adopt handles that suggested either the temptress imagery of an Eve figure or the loyalty and purity of a Mary figure, depending on what type of image they wanted to project (Kalcik, 1985). The precedent established by CB users to choose a pseudonym that reflects some aspect of their personal disposition was paralleled by Internet communicators in the decades that followed.

Haya Bechar-Israeli (1995) investigated the function and personal importance of pseudonyms among IRC participants. Not surprisingly, Bechar-Israeli concluded that pseudonyms, or **nicks**, as these nicknames are known among IRCers, served as attempts to present the self in a single line of text. Although he was able to categorize the nicks he discovered in a range of categories (as shown in Table 3.1), the most frequently selected pseudonyms were referential of some quality of one's identity. Nearly one-half of these participants chose to disclose something about their character <shydude>, profession <medoctor>, state <sleepless>, or appearance <handsom> through their nick. Though very few people chose to use their actual names in this setting, a clear majority tended to share qualities about their identities that they wanted others to perceive through their choice of pseudonym.

The ownership of one's pseudonym is something fiercely guarded in these contexts. As Bechar-Israeli observed, when a participant discovers his or her nick in use by another, the original owner reacts with hostility toward the perceived identity thief. Hence, even though play with identity is possible in such environments, consistency of presentation is practiced, even valued, among participants.

Table 3.1
Six Types of Nicks

Category	Examples	Percentage
Self-related names	<shydude>, <handsom>	45
Names related to medium, technology, and their nature	<pentium>, <aixy>	16.9
Names of flora, fauna, objects	<tulip>, <froggy>, <cheese>	15.6
Plays on words and sounds	<whatthehell>, <myTboy>, <uh-uh>	11.3
People using their real names	<Cortne>, <SusanLee>	7.8
Names related to figures in literature, films, fairytales and famous people	<madhatter>, <rainman>, <elvis>	6.1
Names related to sex and provocation	<sexsee>, <sexpot>, <hitler>	3.9
Total		106.6

Note: The total adds up to more than 100% because of the multiple coding method used.
Source: Adapted from Bechar-Israeli (1995).

This same sense of perpetuated and consistent identity is found among personal Web sites. Unlike text-only channels like MUDs and chat rooms, Web sites allow the transmission of text, pictures, animation, and sounds to convey an online identity. However, the inclusion of any of these additional sources of information is still under the control of the author, allowing the individual to determine what identity will be presented. Daniel Chandler (1997) pointed out that the ubiquitous "under construction" sign found on so many personal Web sites is indicative of a process of creating identity (Fig. 3.3). People are building a representation of themselves for the consideration and approval of others.

Certainly, electing pseudonymity can produce an advantageous effect for those behind the false names, especially in opening channels to those who might be reticent to interact if their true names were known. In particular, research has indicated that working with pseudonyms can be a liberating experience for students. Andrea Chester and Gillian Gwynne (1998) conducted a class in which they and their students interacted exclusively online. Fully two thirds of their students later reported that they participated more in the online environment, where "there was no pressure to adhere to the scripts normally governing classroom behavior." The use

> **Ethical Inquiry**
>
> As discussed previously, when individuals operate in anonymity, they can function both for and against the best interest of others in a community. Can you think of specific situations where people function better if they can operate in anonymity or pseudonymity?
>
> One example that you might consider is the Xenia, Ohio, police officers who operate under pseudonyms to patrol chat rooms for child sexual predators. Using a screen name like "Lessa," a 36-year-old officer goes in and out of chat rooms, not soliciting conversation but responding to the inquiries of predators looking for underage sexual partners. The officers are careful not to entrap the predators, allowing them to initiate and perpetuate the conversations and agreeing to meet with them for a presumed sexual encounter in the small Midwestern town. Like many other law enforcement agencies around the country, the Xenia Police Division has managed to arrest dozens of pedaphiles in the last handful of years thanks to their ability to "go undercover" online.
>
> Such undercover work is certainly a form of deception, but one most people would say is necessary in order to protect society. Do other instances of identity manipulation receive similar allowances? Or does any form of identity manipulation cross an ethical boundary that you are uncomfortable transgressing?

of a pseudonym, one of the prerequisites for the course, allowed the participants to choose when and how they would disclose things like their gender, race, and other social demographics.

The veneer of the Internet allows us to determine how much of an identity we wish to front in online presentations. These images can range from a vague silhouette

Fig. 3.3. The "under construction" sign seen on many web pages.

to a detailed snapshot. Whatever the degree of identity presented, however, it appears that control and empowerment are benefits for users of these communication technologies.

HYPERLINK: A RAPE IN CYBERSPACE

Few online characters are more infamous than Mr. Bungles, "a fat, oleaginous, Bisquick-faced clown dressed in cum-stained harlequin garb and girdled with a mistletoe-and-hemlock belt whose buckle bore the quaint inscription 'KISS ME UNDER THIS BITCH!'" (Dibbell, 1993, p. 37). The Mr. Bungles character is reviled not so much for his distasteful self-presentation as for his repulsive actions in LambdaMOO. In MOOs, those present not only exchange lines of dialogue, but can also offer descriptions of their actions.

On one fateful evening, Mr. Bungles joined one of the dialogues in LambdaMOO and proceeded to disrupt the normal conversational atmosphere with vulgar statements and vile actions performed by a **voodoo doll**. A voodoo doll is a program that allows its user to ascribe actions to another character and have them appear on the screen as though the owner of that character had issued them. Using his voodoo doll, Mr. Bungles directed a number of characters to perform sexual and sadomasochistic acts. As he proceeded to seize control of character after character, he ignored their protests and the objections of others present throughout his escapade. Eventually, a participant with a superior program was able to block Mr. Bungles' voodoo spell, silencing his mocking laughter and confining his tasteless activities.

In an ethnographic essay of the LambdaMOO experience, Julian Dibbell (1993) recounts not only these events, but also the conversations among the participants that followed the Mr. Bungles episode. Despite the fact that Mr. Bungles' assault had taken place on an entirely symbolic rather than a physical level, LambdaMOOers talked of the act as a rape because of the violation they felt as victims or perceived as witnesses. Although some participants found "rape" too strong a word to describe what had happened, those who had been victimized by Mr. Bungles insisted that the experience of having their virtual selves violated had the same impact on them as if they had been physically assaulted. In the months that followed, LambdaMOOers debated the actions and the fate of Mr. Bungles with great passion, demonstrating just how impacting words on a screen can be. Ultimately, Mr. Bungles was executed in the virtual world for his actions. In the real world, of course, this meant that his character name was retired, forbidden ever to log onto LambdaMOO again. However, the effects of his actions were far-reaching, leading LambdaMOOers to struggle with the difficult process of becoming a society. (This process is discussed further in a chapter 6 Hyperlink.) It is interesting, however, how our perceptions can lead to the interpretation of lines of text as a crime.

PROTECTING IDENTITIES IN THE INFORMATION AGE

"A good reputation is more valuable than money." So said the Roman statesman Publius Syrus in 42 BC, noting the importance that a good name carried in his time. Today, people are discovering just how costly it can be to have a good name tarnished. Although criminals have found ways to uncover people's personal information in the past (most provocatively by routing through trash, looking for carelessly discarded personal documents) and malcontents have attacked people's reputations in many public forums, the introduction of information technologies has raised the profiles, and the stakes, involved in protecting one's identity online and off. In this section, we look at two identity-related threats of growing concern in the Information Age: identity fraud and shadow identities.

Identity Fraud

Most of us spend a good deal of time, consciously or unconsciously, building a good reputation. We strive to make our credit card and automobile loan payments on time, we work hard to earn passing marks in our college courses, and we obey the laws to avoid marring our records. With all the hard work that we invest in building and maintaining our reputations, it seems almost inconceivable that someone could come along and wipe that out with as little information as our credit card or Social Security number. However, your reputation can be grievously injured if a criminal targets you for identity fraud.

Identity fraud occurs when an individual acquires personal information that allows him or her to impersonate you online or in real life and make purchases or commit crimes in your name. According to the Federal Trade Commission (2003), more than 27 million Americans were victims of identity fraud between 1998 and 2003. Armed with as little information as your name and nine-digit Social Security number, criminals can steal your identity and misrepresent you in online forums and in real life. It happened to Kenneth Morse of New York. After Morse disclosed his name and Social Security number in an online forum, someone began purchasing sport utility vehicles in New Jersey in his name (Sandberg, 1999). Although the culprit was stopped as he attempted to make his third vehicle purchase, Morse had months of letter writing and phone calls ahead of him as he worked to convince creditors that he was not the "Kenneth Morse" who made the inappropriate purchases.

Although your Social Security number is a particularly potent piece of personal information that criminals can use to impersonate you, it is by no means the only piece of information that they can use to their benefit and your detriment. Depending on what information on you they might already have, the additional disclosure of your credit card number, its expiration date, your date of birth, or your mother's maiden name may be all they need to misrepresent you. One of the more troubling instances of identity fraud occurred when a handful of computer help-desk employees supplied a whole ring of identity counterfeiters with people's personal information. After data collecting from more than 30,000 actual clients, the technicians sold the senstive personal information to a number of con artists, who in turn opened bogus accounts with other creditors and ran up fantastic charges (Hawkins, 2002). Passwords are also especially vulnerable pieces of information in online settings. A criminal equipped with your password could use your Internet account to send messages that you would never consider issuing.

A particularly chilling case of identity fraud occurred when a northern California woman who had never even logged on discovered that she was the target of a stalker who was setting her up for disaster. Her alleged stalker, a man to whom she had been introduced by friends and had then rebuffed when he became too intense about developing a relationship, had sent out alarming messages in her name. The stalker, masquerading as the woman, issued a number of statements suggesting that she was interested in having a rape fantasy fulfilled. More than this, the impersonator provided contact information and a schedule of the woman's daily activities to help. After one of the recipients of this e-mail contacted her by telephone, the woman turned to the police and they began to investigate the source of her alter ego. Ultimately, her former acquaintance was arrested, but the fear that this stalker caused through his intimidation complicated her life immeasurably (Foote & Van Boven, 1999).

If you suspect that you or someone you know is the victim of identity fraud, the Federal Trade Commission (FTC, 1998) recommends quick action. First, contact one of the three major credit bureaus (listed in Table 3.2) and direct them to flag your file so that no one can open a new account in your name. Second, notify creditors of any accounts that have been tampered with (e.g., Visa or J. C. Penney) by phone and then follow up by writing to them. Third, file a police report. The FTC offers more helpful hints at their Web site, www.ftc.gov. As more aspects of our lives become entwined with information technologies, we will find that we must be increasingly vigilant of how our personal information is distributed. As the above case indicates, not all instances of identity fraud are preventable, but Table 3.2 suggests steps that savvy consumers can take to safeguard their identities from such assaults.

Table 3.2
Steps for Protecting One's Digital Identity

- Consumers should guard their personal identifying information. Before divulging it, they should find out how it will be used and whether it will be transferred to third parties. They should find out whether they have the choice of "opting out" of having the information shared with third parties (such as direct mail services).
- Consumers should ensure that items containing personal information—such as charge receipts, insurance forms, and bank statements—are disposed of safely (preferably shredded).
- Consumers should disclose their Social Security numbers only when absolutely necessary. They should ask to use alternate numbers as identifiers whenever possible, including on driver's licenses.
- Consumers should carry with them only the credit cards and identification they actually need. Consumers who lose credit cards should notify their creditors by phone and request that a "fraud alert" be placed in their file.
- Consumers should pay attention to billing cycles. Bills that do not arrive on time may have been misdirected by identity thieves.
- Consumers should periodically check their credit report by contacting one of the three major credit bureaus: Equifax (www.equifax.com), Experian (www.experian.com), or Trans Union (www.tuc.com).

Source: Adapted from Federal Trade Commission (1999).

Shadow Identities

Another identity that is being further compromised by Internet technologies is the public identity of people, organizations, and their creations. Entities like manufacturers, film studios, and retailers go to considerable lengths to protect their images from misrepresentation (see the Online Communication and the Law section for another example of how corporations fight to safeguard their identities). Certainly, many of these entities have established a presence on the World Wide Web to promote their preferred image. For example, organizations ranging from the American Red Cross to Xerox sponsor sites that provide a positive perspective on their mission, growth, and services. In an increasing number of cases, some corporations may even conduct business *entirely* online (e.g., Amazon.com). Suffice it to say, such organizations would prefer not to have their reputations tarnished by anyone, certainly not by an easily accessed competing Web site.

Robert Wright (1996) explained that "shadow identities" can be created for virtually any site on the Web thanks to the way search engines work. When search engines are directed to look for a word or phrase on the Internet, they do not necessarily discriminate among the sites containing the indicated word or phrase. They merely report back the matches they have found online. Some of the matches they find might indeed be the **shadow pages** that Wright described, pages that can incriminate a reputation. Thus, in searching for information on a popular retail chain like K-Mart, the search results might also include a "K-Mart Sucks" page. Prior to the advent of the Internet, a disgruntled employee or dissatisfied customer had limited range and could only "bad-mouth" an organization to personal acquaintances. Now that angry person can reach a global audience, casting doubt on the prestige and potency of an international reputation.

Likewise, individuals may have damage done by their own reputations because of the shadowy influence of these sites. In the case of Dr. Gloria Brame, an Atlanta-based therapist, she discovered that a company was posting pornographic materials to the domain name www.gloriabrame.com. Naturally, Brame feared that this lewd representation, which she of course had no role in creating, could still damage her reputation. She was fortunate that when she sued, the ISP hosting the site shut it down; not all shadow pages go away so easily (O'Brien, 2003).

Take, for instance, the example of McSpotlight (www.mcspotlight.org), which emphasizes its shadowlike nature by using a form of McDonald's famous "golden arches" in its logo (see Fig. 3.4). McSpotlight provides a library of resources confronting the

Fig. 3.4. The McSpotlight home page: "Will they sue us?"

Hyperlink: Judging Information on the Web

Of course, credibility on the Web is a perennial concern, particularly given that information found there may be inaccurate, biased, or outdated. Because Web sites often look like professionally published documents, they can create a perception of accuracy by virtue of being online. However, before you quote information from any online source in your research paper, you may want to ask yourself a few questions about the site that you have found.

Who Is the Author?

The first way to judge the credibility of a Web site is to consider its author. For instance, an "unsigned" site begs the question, How do we know whether the author is justified in making these claims? Also, you may want to check to make sure that a person's credentials meet the subject matter of the page. A degree after the name doesn't assure that the author is qualified to discuss this particular topic.

What Possible Biases Might Motivate the Author?

Discover the author's affiliation—especially given the fact that some groups that post Web sites possess enough bias to call their claims of "facts" into question. Remember, though, that a biased claim is not always bad. Indeed, when you're discussing a polarizing issue, it's a good idea to cite someone who is direct about his or her idea—as long as you justify your choice of this evidence and identify the bias to your reader.

When Was the Page Developed?

Watch out for Internet ghosts. Many pages online were posted months or years ago and are no longer supported. In many cases, the information found on these sites may be perfectly useful. But an old page that is no longer actively maintained by the author (indicated, perhaps, by a "last updated" line that states a very old date) may soon "disappear." Your citation is more likely to be credible if it exists when your audience, such as your instructor, looks it up!

There is no single set of standards available to judge the credibility of the millions of web pages out there. Indeed, the very concept of some universal standard is troubling to some people, who believe that standards are set by some folks to keep others from speaking their minds. Although this is a persuasive argument, you must nonetheless be prepared to defend your choice of online evidence because—like it or not—the Web is simply not granted the same kind of authority as a published text in most academic settings.

worldwide influence of McDonald's restaurant franchise, as a number of people object to its food, employment practices, and advertising techniques. In the words of one of the site's founders, "McDonald's spend a fortune each year on advertising. And everybody knows their point of view. But the people campaigning on the other side had, up to this point, been limited in how far they could get their arguments heard. This was partly financial, partly practical and partly geographical. The Internet solved all those problems in one" (quoted in Meikle, 2002, p. 77). McSpotlight grew out of a very long trial in Great Britain in which a couple of activists were tried for libeling the corporation through material that they originally distributed in printed pamphlets in the early 1990s. The trial ended with the judge finding the defendants guilty of libel, yet the materials that they originally published and distributed to a few thousand people in the United Kingdom are now available online to millions around the world. Still, McDonald's has not pursued shutting down the site. Why? The most likely reason is that the added attention to the site and the bad publicity that could result from such a campaign would be far more costly to McDonald's worldwide than to just leave the site alone to function in comparative obscurity.

Although shadow pages may express legitimate concerns and issue relevant chal-lenges to existing entities, they do present some interesting hurdles for establishment and interpretation of identity. You may find your own name or that of the organiza-tion you are employed by in the crosshairs of one of these character assassins and, so, find yourself in the position of having to cope with or offer rebuttal to the statements made on a shadow page. Yet, even if you do not find yourself or those you work for the target(s) of shadow pages, as an information consumer you are likely to have to consider what shadow pages have to say. For instance, if you go online to shop for a new car and find among your search results a shadow page labeled, "WARNING: Do not buy this model!" you might choose to ignore it entirely or, on reading it, choose to forgo purchasing the vehicle.

Clearly, shadow pages serve to remind us that we should not accept any message without some critical thought as to the motives of the producer. Many people and organizations active on the Web have something to sell you; likewise, many of those who author shadow pages have axes to grind. As information consumers, we have to consider critically what any information producer has to offer, be it a representative of the original entity or its shadowy opposition.

CHAPTER SUMMARY

As this chapter illustrates, establishing our own identities as well as determining the identities of others is surrounded by a host of issues, ranging from the metaphysical to the mundane. Although technology has introduced them into a new context, many of the questions about identity that we confront are as old as humanity's search for knowledge: Who am I? How can I get others to understand me? Can I accept that these people are who and what they claim to be? Certainly, we have not answered these enduring questions in this chapter, but we have reviewed concepts that have cast these queries into new light. As Turkle has suggested, we are made to think about the nature of identity through these technologies. By examining points about telepresence, performance, and pseudonymity, we have indicated directions that peo-ple are following in pursuit of answers to these questions in this electronic era. We have also noted identity vulnerabilities that technology exposes. Both identity fraud and shadow identities are problems that everyone, not just Internet users, must be prepared to confront.

ONLINE COMMUNICATION AND THE LAW

The law has long acknowledged the value of name recognition. That is why companies with distinctive names like Pepsi, CNN, and Michelin have sought the legal protection of trademark laws in order to exert control over the use of their names in public forums. And it was because name recognition is so popular in the world of marketing that corporations and entrepreneurs rushed to secure the **domain names** of well-known products and producers. Domain name is, of course, another term for the Uniform Resource Locator (URL), the address of a site on the World Wide Web.

In the mid-1990s, a number of enterprising **cybersquatters** laid claim to recognizable domain names, paying nominal fees to the Internet Corporation for Assigned Names and Numbers (the official entity responsible for assigning domain names) and then turning around and leasing the names to the corporations who originally copyrighted them. Think of a domain name as the cyberspace equivalent to a vanity plate on your automobile: It not only identifies you, but does so with distinction. In some cases, rather than agreeing to capitulate to a perceived extortion racket, some corporations took the cybersquatters to court . . . and won. In fact, legislation has subsequntly been enacted to protect the owners of copyright in the form of the Anticybersquatting Consumer Protection Act. This law allows a copyright holder like CNN to reclaim a domain name, even those that are close enough to cause confusion in the public's mind, such as www.cnnews.com (4th Cir., 2003).

Yet the legal right to a domain name just because someone owns a trademark blurred in the case of *Hasbro v. Clue Computing, Inc.* Hasbro is the toy manufacturer that owns the copyright to the popular board game "Clue." In 1996, Hasbro discovered that Clue Computing, Inc., a small Colorado-based consulting firm, already held the domain name "clue.com." Lawyers for Hasbro argued that by claiming the domain name first, the consultants were engaged in dilution of the trademark; in other words, it weakened the recognition of the trademark ("clue") with the product (the board game).

The Massachusetts judge hearing the case, however, did not agree. He ruled that although extorting money from a trademark holder was illegal, a company that used a domain name for its own legitimate purposes did not dilute trademark. Furthermore, *clue* itself is such a common word that Hasbro was unable to establish that every use of the word suggested the product (Kaplan, 1999).

The legalities of domain names are far from solved, however. The addition of new domains like ".biz" and ".info" opens new avenues for competing presences on the Internet. "Whitehouse.net," for instance, is a well-known parody site mirroring "Whitehouse.gov," but what happens when the next "dot.domain" opens up? How much effort will copyright owners have to exercise in order to protect their good name?

Glossary

Anonymity: Communication without one's identity being apparent.

Avatar: An incarnation of oneself in a virtual environment.

Blog: A journal-like Web site where authors regularly post new contributions of prose, poetry, hypertext links, and other materials for readers.

Cybersquatter: An entrepreneur who registers for a domain name and then sells the rights to use that domain name to another person or corporate entity for a profit.

Dépaysement: Process of seeing the familiar through different eyes.

Domain name: A recognizable URL, or address on the World Wide Web, typically used by corporations and individuals to distinguish themselves through a popular term or trademark (e.g., www.mcdonalds.com).

Face-work: Effort invested in maintaining a role.

Gender-swapping: The adoption of a gender other than one's own in presenting oneself in mediated contexts.

Handle: A pseudonym on CB radio.

Identity: A construct formed by the interaction of the self with the social environment.

Identity fraud: A criminal's misuse of another individual's personal information (e.g., credit card number) to make unauthorized purchases or commit crimes using the victim's name.

Interactivity: The quality of telepresence that measures a person's ability to manipulate the content of the medium.

Nicks: Pseudonyms in an IRC.

Pseudonym: An alias, or "false name," a person adopts to identify him or herself.

Self-presentation: The process of creating a perception of oneself for others.

Shadow page: A page on the Web established to attack the reputation of a person, a corporation, or another site.

Telepresence: Experiencing an environment through a communication medium.

Vividness: The quality of telepresence that measures the breadth and depth of sensory stimulation a medium presents.

Voodoo doll: A computer program used in synchronous conversation forums like MOOs that allows its user to enter lines of text describing another's dialogue or activity.

Topics for Discussion

1. Review Steuer's classification of various media technologies in Fig. 3.1, then select one medium and think of an example for it (e.g., *The Little Mermaid* as an example of a videocassette recording). Write a brief essay in which you explain the amount of telepresence the medium possesses by comparing how high or low it is in terms of vividness and in terms of interactivity.

2. Consider how unified your own self is by listing five different roles you fulfill in your daily life. Along with each role, note what steps you take to be perceived as competent in that role. What implications does your own experience with role-playing have for online behavior?

3. Log on to a chat room or MUD as a participant-observer for a few hours. As you observe the contributions of various participants, see if you can identify any "stars." Summarize a significant exchange you witnessed during your tenure and provide a brief explanation of the participants' behavior in terms of the theatrical metaphor.

4. Create an avatar of your own. In addition to dubbing your persona with a nick, provide a description of the qualities you would want to communicate to others. Once you have done so, consider how closely or distinctly your avatar compares to your presentation of identity in real life. What elements have you added to or omitted from the description?

5. Draw a reproduction of the continuum of identity manipulation presented in Fig. 3.2. and indicate where your pseudonym would rest (more anonymous or closer to your real life). Write an explanation for why you situated your pseudonym where you did. What factors contribute to your perception that you are more or less "true" to real life through this presentation?

REFERENCES

Bargh, J. A., McKenna, K. Y. A., & Fitzsimons, G. M. (2002). Can you see the real me? Activation and expression of the "true self" on the internet. *Journal of Social Issues, 58,* 33–48.

Bechar-Israeli, H. (1995). From <Bonehead> to <cLoNehEAd>: Nicknames, play, and identity on Internet relay chat. *Journal of Computer-Mediated Communication, 1.* Retrieved January 22, 1998, from http:www.ascusc.org/jcmc/vol1/issue2/bechar.html

Bornstein, K. (1994). *Gender outlaw: On men, women, and the rest of us.* New York: Vintage Books.

Bruckman, A. (1992). *Identity workshop: Emergent social and psychological phenomena in text-based virtual reality.* Retrieved January 22, 1998, from ftp://ftp.lambda.moo.mud.org/pub/MOO/papers

Bruckman, A. S. (1996). Gender-swapping on the Internet. In P. Ludlow (Ed.), *High noon on the electronic frontier: Conceptual issues in cyberspace* (pp. 317–325). Cambridge, MA: MIT Press.

Buten, J. (1996). *The personal home page institute.* Retrieved, January 22, 1998, from http://www.asc.upenn.edu/usr/sbuten/survey.htm#top

Chandler, D. (1997). *Writing oneself in cyberspace.* Retrieved January 22, 1998, from http://www.aber.ac.uk/~dgc/hompgid.html

Chester, A., & Gwynne, G. (1998). Online teaching: Encouraging collaboration through anonymity. *Journal of Computer-Mediated Communication, 4.* Retrieved January 10, 2000, from http://www.ascusc.org/jcmc/vol4/issue2/chester.html

Cutler, R. H. (1996). Technologies, relations, and selves. In L. Strate, R. Jacobson, & S. B. Gibson (Eds.), *Communication and cyberspace: Social interaction in an electronic environment* (pp. 317–333). Cresskill, NJ: Hampton Press.

Dibbell, J. (1993, December 21). A rape in cyberspace: Or, how an evil clown, a Haitian trickster spirit, two wizards, and a cast of dozens turned a database into a society. *Village Voice,* pp. 36–42.

Federal Trade Commission. (1998, May 20). *Legislation could help protect consumers from credit identity fraud.* Retrieved January 10, 2000, from http://www.ftc.gov/opa/1998/9805/identity.htm

Federal Trade Commission. (1999, April). *Identity crisis: What to do if your identity is stolen.* Retrieved January 10, 2000, from http://www.ftc.gov/bcp/conline/pubs/alerts/idenalrt.htm

Federal Trade Commission. (2003, September 3). *FTC releases survey of identity theft in U.S.* Retrieved September 7, 2003, from http://www.ftc.gov/opa/2003/idtheft.htm

Foote, D., & Van Boven, S. (1999, February 8). You could get raped. *Newsweek,* pp. 64–65.

4th Cir. affirms transfer of Cnnew.com to CNN in cybersquatting case (2003, February 18). *Intellectual Property Litigation Reporter,* p. 13.

Giese, M. (1998). Self without body: Textual self-presentation in an electronic community. *First Monday, 3.* Retrieved January 10, 2000, from http://www.firstmonday.dk/issues/issue3_4/giese/index.html

Gigliotti, D., Weinstein, H., Zwick, E., Norman, M., & Parfitt, D. (Producers), Madden, J., & Greatrex, R. (Directors). (1998). *Shakespeare in love* [Motion picture]. United States: Miramax Films.

Goffman, E. (1959). *The presentation of self in everyday life.* Garden City, NY: Anchor.

Hastings, M. (2003, April 7). Bloggers over Baghdad. *Newsweek,* p. 70.

Hawkins, D. (2002, December 9). A big-time identity crisis. *U.S. News & World Report, 133,* 34.

Kalcik, S. J. (1985). Women's handles and the performance of identity in the CB community. In R. A. Jordan & S. J. Kalcik (Eds.), *Women's folklore, women's culture* (pp. 99–108). Philadelphia: University of Pennsylvania Press.

Kaplan, C. S. (1999, September 17). Judges pick David over Goliath in domain name suits. *Cyber Law Journal.* Retrieved January 10, 2000, from http://www.nytimes.com/library/tech/99/09/cyber/cyberlaw/17law.html

Lee, G. B. (1996). Addressing anonymous messages in cyberspace. *Journal of Computer-Mediated Communication, 2.* Retrieved January 10, 2000, from http://www.ascusc.org/jcmc/vol2/issue1/anon.html

Levy, S. (2002, August 26). Living in the Blog-osphere. *Newsweek,* p. 42.

Marx, G. T. (1999). What's in a name? Some reflections on the sociology of anonymity. *Information Society, 15,* 99–112.

Meikle, G. (2002). *Future active: Media activism and the internet.* New York: Routledge.

O'Brien, P. (2003, May 6). Registrars, abuse, and the internet: The question of responsibility. *Computer & Online Industry Litigation Reporter,* p. 12.

Rheingold, H. (n.d.). *Mind to mind with Sherry Turkle. Brainstorms.* Retrieved July 2, 2003, from http://www.well.com/user/hlr/texts/mindtomind/turkle.html

Sandberg, J. (1999, September 20). Losing your good name online. *Newsweek,* pp. 56–57.

Schiano, D. J. (1999). Lessons from LambdaMOO: A social, text-based virtual environment. *Presence: Teleoperators & Virtual Environments, 8*(2), 127–140.

Sheff, D. (2000). Net nut in a shell. *Yahoo! Internet Life, 6*(6), 100, 102–104.

Steuer, J. (1992). Defining virtual reality: Dimensions determining telepresence. *Journal of Communication, 42*(4), 73–93.

Stone, A. R. (1991). Will the real body please stand up? Boundary stories about virtual cultures. In M. Benedikt (Ed.), *Cyberspace: First steps* (pp. 81–118). Cambridge, MA: MIT Press.

Steiner, P. (1993, July 5). On the Internet, nobody knows you're a dog. *The New Yorker,*
    p. 61.

Tu, C. (2001). How Chinese perceive social presence: An examination of interaction
    in online learning environment. *Education Media International, 38,* 45–60.

Turkle, S. (1995). *Life on the screen: Identity in the age of the Internet.* New York: Simon &
    Schuster.

Vincent, A., & Shepherd, J. (1998). Experiences in teaching Middle East politics
    via internet-based role-play simulations. *Journal of Interactive Media in Education.*
    Retrieved July 1, 2003, from http://www-jime.open.ac.uk/98/11/vincent-98-11-
    01.html

Wayner, P. (1999). Technology for anonymity: Names by other nyms. *The Information
    Society, 15,* 91–97.

Wright, R. (1996, July 8). The cybersmear. *Time,* p. 46.

RELATING ONLINE

Those strangers, who had no arms to put around my shoulders, no eyes to weep with mine, nevertheless saw me through. As neighbors do.

—John Perry Barlow

One night, while checking my email, an advertisement bar for Match.com caught my attention. I went to the site and signed up for a free trial membership. I never expected to meet the person I'd spend the rest of my life with. Maurice was busy restoring his recently purchased home and, as a result, had no time to meet quality singles using more "traditional" methods. The bar/club scene was not his style. There was something about Maurice's profile that caught my attention. Something about him seemed familiar. We exchanged a few emails then had a telephone conversation to set a date to meet. Our first date was phenomenal. After eating at a Thai restaurant, we walked around the little town where I lived and then down to the beach. We sat on the beach and talked for hours. We casually dated for five months until one fateful trip to New Orleans to celebrate Halloween, my favorite holiday. It was during this trip we realized how compatible we really were. We have been inseparable ever since. Maurice proposed one evening in December 2001 on the Marin Headlands, overlooking the San Francisco city lights and the illuminated Golden Gate Bridge with the stars twinkling above. It couldn't have been more perfect or more romantic. (Match.com, 2003)

As in this testimonial posted on Match.com, one of the Internet's leading dating services, some of you might also know the story of someone who has initiated a personal relationship over the Internet. Others may well have struck up a friendship or experimented with some romantic relating of your own with someone you have never physically encountered. The distance-transcending technologies of the electronic age have enabled people like the author and Maurice to initiate, escalate, and maintain interpersonal relationships to degrees that were once considered possible only when two parties shared common physical space.

Whether or not CMC can be an effective context for building relationships has been an issue of contention among scholars since the formal study of networked interaction began. Early research concluded that computer usage focused people on more task-oriented messages and precluded the development of social relationships among users. However, a growing body of literature argues not only that people use networked technologies for social purposes but also that, in some cases, people prefer the medium for interpersonal relating. Albert Bressand, a respected French economist, has even said that systems we presently refer to as information technologies are more aptly named relationship technologies: "The new machines of today are between man

Table 4.1
Three Perspectives on Relating Online

Perspective	Claim	Relationships
Impersonal	The lack of cues limits the quality of interaction.	Relationships are unlikely to emerge in CMC.
Interpersonal	Learned behaviors can help compensate for the lack of cues.	Relationships can emerge in CMC.
Hyperpersonal	The lack of nonverbal discriminators actually helps some find their voice.	For some the ability to relate is more substantial in CMC.

and man, rather than between man and nature. And relations rather than material products are what is processed in these machines" (Schwartz, 1996).

This chapter reviews the arguments against and for the growth of interpersonal relationships through CMC. In tracing the development of these arguments, we borrow a pattern from Joseph Walther (1996), who suggested that CMC has been characterized as impersonal by some, interpersonal by others, and potentially "hyperpersonal" in his view (Table 4.1). After reviewing the theories relevant to each of these levels of interactivity, we consider some of the implications of conflict and attachment that persons relating online should consider. By the end of this chapter, we hope that you have a firmer understanding of why the prospect of relating online might mean less than they imagine to some and more than they hope to others.

IMPERSONAL COMMUNICATION: DEFINING LIMITS TO CMC

Can you recall the last time you flirted with someone you were interested in? What behaviors did you engage in? Chances are you found yourself smiling a lot, leaning in that person's direction, and looking directly into that person's eyes. Certainly, you might have carried on a conversation with the person, but your interest was probably signaled more by what you did than by what you said. You were likely to use a lot of **nonverbal cues** to indicate your interest. Facial expressions, posture and movement, and eye contact are all channels through which we can share meaning without using language. As you probably already know, nonverbal communication constitutes a major portion of our face-to-face messages, with specialists estimating that anywhere from 65% to 93% of the social meaning in communication comes through these channels (Birdwhistle, 1970; Mehrabian, 1972).

Until recently, the character of most forms of CMC has meant that limited amounts of nonverbal information could be exchanged between people over computer networks. From its inception and continuing through contemporary practice, the Internet primarily has been a vehicle for sharing verbal messages. Of course, the advent of technologies like webcams, photographic devices that upload television-like images to Web sites, certainly presents a challenge to this common conception, but in many network channels, including e-mail, messages are still comprised mainly of textual information. Early research into communication using computers, then, was dealing with media characterized by displays of words and symbols without the apparent benefit of other cues. Accordingly, this led to a reference for computer-mediated being a **cues-filtered-out approach** to communication (Culnan & Markus, 1987). Because there is less information exchanged between people, then, it is not surprising that some would find this medium more impersonal compared to the richness of face-to-face interaction.

Social Presence Theory

Initial research into interaction using computer networks seemed to confirm that this cues-filtered-out quality led to an impersonal perception of CMC. Much of this work was laid on the foundation established by **social presence theory** (Short, Williams, & Christie, 1976). Social presence is the degree to which we as individuals perceive another as a real person and any interaction between the two of us as a relationship. Social presence theory suggests that different media convey different degrees of perceived substance to an interaction. The degree of the connection is based on the amount of nonverbal information available to the receiver through any particular channel.

Thus, you might feel a certain degree of social presence while listening to your favorite morning radio personality. The nonverbal qualities of his voice might suggest to you that this person is fun, sharp-witted, and engaging. You might even faithfully tune into his show, and only his show, because you want to maintain loyalty to him. Even though the two of you have never met, and he is certainly not physically present, you still have a sense, listening to him, that he is "there" with you. Consider how much more nonverbal information is available about your favorite television personality. Is it any wonder people begin to feel that they know the actors they watch on a weekly basis? In contrast, think of how much social presence you feel when reading your local newspaper. Few of us identify with our local journalists as strongly as we do with radio and television personalities, and according to social presence theory, that is because we lack sufficient cues to prompt us to perceive the reporters as "real" as we do the broadcasters.

In comparison to other media for interpersonal interaction, then, computer-mediated channels would provide less presence than other channels. In different situations this could be more or less desirable. This is what Ronald Rice (1987) discovered in one of the early examinations of how people in organizations were using CMC systems. Rice found that people perceived that the appropriateness of using a channel such as e-mail corresponded to the amount of social presence required for successful completion of the task. Hence, users rated tasks like exchanging information and asking questions as a highly appropriate use of the computer network. Such tasks require less social presence than some others. On the other hand, users rated tasks like resolving disagreements and persuading others as inappropriate to communicate online. Because the participants apparently believed that these tasks require more of a perception of social presence in order to be effective, they would be more likely to choose another medium for exchanging these messages.

Further research corroborated the assertion that the quality of social presence factors into people's choices among communication media. In a survey of college students, Lisa Flaherty, Kevin Pearce, and Rebecca Rubin (1998) conclude that people do not necessarily use computer-mediated channels for the same purposes as they do the face-to-face channel. Hence, they assert that the Internet and face-to-face communication are not **functional alternatives**. In the process of constructing their survey, they identified six commonly accepted motivations for human interaction: inclusion, affection, control, pleasure, relaxation, and escape. What they found was that there were statistically significant differences for people's motivations when it came to choosing channels. Only the motivation of pleasure was rated as comparably high between the

Internet and face-to-face communication, meaning that people turned to both of them for the enjoyment they derived from interacting with other people.

For the remaining motives, however, people chose one channel over another to fulfill specific needs, and generally people preferred face-to-face interaction to meet their other needs. For example, their research implied that a lonely worker is more likely to join his or her coworkers in the lunch room than to log onto a chat room in order to fulfill his or her need for inclusion. The results of this study suggest that the Internet and face-to-face communication are **specialized channels**, meaning, quite simply, that people choose them to fulfill particular needs. Consequently, a person might turn to the Internet if he or she wants to enjoy some conversation, but the same individual would seek out a physical presence for affection.

Social presence theory offers one possible explanation for why some people may find online communication impersonal. Because many computer-mediated channels provide fewer nonverbal cues to interpret the meaning of messages, the relatively "lean" messages they deliver can be perceived as less personal. People who prefer the nods, smiles, and touches that can accompany a face-to-face interaction would probably find little warmth in the phosphorescent glow of the computer screen. However, social presence is not the only theory that sides with an impersonal perspective on CMC.

Social Context Cues Theory

Whether or not we are consciously aware of it, we all tailor our communication behaviors to the settings around us. Both what we say and to whom we say it are influenced by our social environment. Consider how you adapt your own messages to the settings around you. As a competent communicator, you are unlikely to shout in a library or in a place of worship. Yet there are places, like at a football stadium or rock concert, where shouting is acceptable, if not necessary. How is it that you know where it is and is not appropriate to shout?

According to Lee Sproull and Sara Kiesler (1986), **social context cues** serve as indicators of appropriate behavior. They govern both contact, telling us with whom we should and should not communicate, and content, regulating what kinds of information we should and should not disclose. Some social context cues include geographic, organizational, and situational variables. Thus, in the example just given, the geographic location suggested the appropriate level of volume. Of course, a combination of these variables could work together to suggest the appropriate social context. Let us say that you and your coworkers stop by the local diner for a bite to eat after work. Away from the office at last and surrounded by your peers, you feel comfortable enough to express some discontent with your mutual supervisor. Suddenly, your boss walks into the restaurant and sits down within earshot of your table, and you change the subject. The arrival of the supervisor suggests a new situation in which you discontinue talking about her in order to comply with the social norm of not talking about persons who can hear you without including them in the conversation. In response to strong cues, then, we focus on others, make subtle differentiations among stimuli, and exert greater control over ourselves in order to meet social expectations.

As you might have surmised, many social context cues are conveyed through nonverbal channels, and, as previously established, computer-mediated channels lack as many nonverbal cues as we are familiar with in face-to-face contexts. Accordingly, Sproull and Kiesler (1986) found that the short supply of social context cues has an effect on the nature of human behavior in mediated contexts. In a survey of e-mails exchanged among employees of a Fortune 500 company, they found that communicators were more likely to exhibit self-absorbed behavior, to display little differentiation among people of different status, and to act more uninhibited. In fact, evidence from their survey suggests that this last quality was particularly pronounced in the newer context. Scores indicated that people within this organization encountered an uninhibited message an average of 4 times a month in face-to-face conversations but 33 times a month over e-mail. One example message from the research demonstrates the degree of this uninhibited behavior. As you read the following message, imagine saying this to 100 of your coworkers:

> It's great to worry about fine points, but I think we should concentrate on getting rid of those aspects of [product] which are TRULY MONSTROUS to the native users (such as yours truly). I had to ask about three people to figure out how to get the @#$%*ing insertion point beyond a graphics frame. The answer, it appears, is some incredibly arcane nonsense about show structure, select after anchor, and repaginate. WHY CAN'T I JUST POINT THE BLOODY MOUSE BELOW A GRAPHICS FRAME AND GET AN INSERTION POINT? (p. 1506)

Such inhibitions seem to flourish under conditions with weak social context cues. The e-mails that the respondents in this survey exchanged tended to lack information about a sender's location, department, position, job, age, or gender, qualities that serve as social context cues. Sara Kiesler, Jane Siegel, and Timothy McGuire (1984) argue that the lack of social context cues leads to feelings of anonymity, reduced self-regulation, and reduced self-awareness. From one perspective, this state can foster greater personal independence, getting one out from under the thumb of social control. On the other hand, it can foster the flouting of social standards, leading one to utter things that are later regretted. In short, the short supply of social context cues can create perceptions of impersonal replies and impersonal interpretations of messages.

The Impersonal Perspective Reconsidered

As the initial work from both the social presence and the social context cues theories exemplifies, many of the early studies in CMC were conducted in organizations. According to J. Michel Metz (1994), this resulted in a bias of conceiving of computer networking as a task-oriented rather than a socially oriented medium. Moreover, Metz points out that these efforts may have overlooked the presence of nonverbals within text-based messages. In citing one of the earliest ethnographies of MUDding (Reid, 1991), Metz points out that people interacting in those environments have innovated methods for implying emotional content as part of their messages through **emoticons**. These emotional icons take on four different forms as outlined in Table 4.2. Although these emoticons arguably are but echoes of traditional nonverbal cues, they do serve the same function as their face-to-face counterparts in that they provide more communicative information to the receiver. The innovation of emoticons suggests that new norms for communicating social presence and social context are likely to emerge over time, not because they have to, but because people want them to.

Despite such compensations for the character of the medium, relating in cyberspace may yet be handicapped by one crucial factor: time. According to Walther (1992), social

Hyperlink: Emoticons—Frequency and Force

Emoticons have a long history within CMC, and in a number of instances, scholars have examined the role they play in affecting meaning in online communication. "Smiley" emoticons, in particular, are basic ASCII (American Standard Code for Information Interchange) art. This means that they are pictures made up of the typographical symbols found on a keyboard. The basic smiley consists of a colon, a dash, and a parenthesis, typographical characters that are unlikely to appear in sequence with one another in normal syntax but, when looked at sideways and using a little imagination, resemble a happy face: :-). (Recent Microsoft products will convert this sequence into a more familiar, uprighted, happy face ☺.)

Alecia Wolf (2000), for instance, found in a review of online newsgroups that gender played a role in emoticon use. In those groups that were predominantly female, emoticons were used frequently to express humor; when the groups were predominantly male, they were used to indicate sarcasm. Interestingly, when males and females shared groups, the rate of emoticon use increased, with males using them much more in the presence of mixed-gender groups. Wolf found encouragement in the adoption of a stereotypical female practice, expressing emotion, in a medium whose communicative practices are stereotypically defined by men.

Subsequently, Joseph Walther and Kyle D'Addario (2001) asked, beyond who was using emoticons, what effect they have on the meaning of messages. In their study, they found that a high rate of people recognized the intention of the emoticons (with 98% of their respondents recognizing that a :-) indicates happiness) but that they had little effect on the impression that the meaning of a particular message made. That is, the verbal message seemed to be more relevant to meaning than the emoticon that accompanied it, which, at best, could complement the statement. The researchers tested this by exposing volunteers to the same verbal message, allegedly from an actual e-mail, but showing different participants different smileys, or none at all, with the message. Thus, a message like, "That econ class you asked me about, it's hell. I wish I never have another class like it," tended to be perceived in a negative light, no matter whether there was a :-), a ;-), a :-(, or nothing at all punctuating it. Walther and D'Addario suggest that emoticons may lack force because they are too easy to type, and thus not perceived as being as thoughtful as the words one chooses, or because after more than 20 years of use they have lost the emotional effect that they once produced. In fact, they may be more generative than communicative, helping the writer, not the reader, "by helping to express, to check, and if need be to edit, that which may be unclear during the initial message production" (p. 343).

Table 4.2
Forms of Emoticons

Form	Description	Example(s)
Verbalization	Textual representations of vocal rather than verbal utterances	<snort> ha ha ha
Descriptions of physical actions	A narration of the speaker's activities, usually set off by asterisks or brackets	*I raised my glass.* <smugly turning to go>
Stress	Emphasis of key words or phrases by using all capital letters	Please bring the car by on the NEXT day.
Smileys	Arrangements of keyboard characters read side-on and used to suggest a message's emotional intent	:-) Grinning happily ;-) Winking reassurance :-P Sticking out one's tongue in jest

Source: Adapted from Reid (1991).

relationships in cyberspace simply take longer to develop than those in face-to-face interaction. People who meet in person have multiple channels in order to process information about a potential partner. People who meet in cyberspace may have only one, the text that they exchange. Given the more limited source of input, it takes longer for a bond to emerge between people. This **social information-processing** perspective would also explain the lack of relational development in early studies of CMC. Groups that met briefly and for an experiment would not have had sufficient interaction time to develop a relationship.

Although we now turn to an examination of how CMC can be interpersonal, we cannot simply dismiss those who find the experience impersonal. Interacting in any given context is a subjective experience. As Walther and others argue, it is not inherent characteristics of the media that make the experience impersonal or not, it is our own perception that helps make it so.

INTERPERSONAL COMMUNICATION: OPENING CHANNELS THROUGH CMC

The research just discussed establishes support for why individuals perceive net-worked interaction unfavorably. Yet despite its evidence, this body of research seems to fall short of an explanation for why some people feel that they have found satisfy-ing relationships with persons they have never met. Remember the couple from the beginning of this chapter? How can we explain the connections people like them find in their mediated conversations?

Martin Lea and Russell Spears (1998), two researchers who have investigated online interaction, submit that we still have a great deal to learn about the complex nature of human relationships in mediated contexts. Specifically, they say that research to this point has been guided by several assumptions and biases that have proven to be unfair to online relationships. Lea and Spears count dispositions toward physical attraction and physical cues as governing relational development and an emphasis on the oral exchanges among people in intimate relationships among these biases. Clearly, if the nonverbal qualities of physical presence and orality are unquestionable criteria for what can and cannot be defined as a relationship, then those initiated online clearly fall short. However, if our explanation of what constitutes relating is broadened to move beyond these biases, it may well be that theories for defending the legitimacy of online relationships are possible.

Not surprisingly, then, Lea and Spears are part of a team offering one such theory that helps explain why genuinely felt relationship bonds seem to emerge online. Tom Postumes, Spears, and Lea (1998) assert that they can predict the conditions under which relationships will emerge through their **social identification/deindividuation (SIDE) model**.

The SIDE Model

In order to understand the SIDE model, we must first review our understanding of identity. As suggested in chapter 3, our identities are defined by the tensions between our culture's desire to have us conform to particular roles and our own desire to resist this pressure and establish a unique sense of self. Noting the lack of nonverbal markers that could serve to pigeonhole any one of us, many argue that the Internet is the ultimate liberating channel, freeing us to be the persons we always wanted without the stifling restrictions that culture enforces because of our gender, race, physical attractiveness, and so on. However, the SIDE model suggests that just the opposite is true. People online seem to rely even more on group-based discriminators.

According to Postumes et al. (1998), it is exactly because there are so few nonverbal cues to process in online environments that people more actively seek out norms of behavior in order to find acceptance among the other participants. A **norm**, as you might know, is an accepted social behavior. Using a fork to eat a salad is a norm, and people who comply with norms generally tend to find acceptance among others who practice the same. Let's say you enter a chat room in which you observe the other contributors using a lot of abbreviations in their messages, such as BTW for "by the way" and LOL for "laugh out loud." The SIDE model predicts that you are likely to pick up this norm for yourself. In doing so, you are likely to appear more attractive to those around you and thus have a better chance of initiating relationships.

As you can tell, the SIDE model asserts that you are more likely to comply with a social role than worry about asserting your individual identity. This is not to say that people become cardboard cutouts in the process. Instead, it is to say that people learn to play by the rules, as it were, and in doing so increase their attractiveness to other players in this social game.

Interestingly, the foundations of the SIDE model are built on psychological investigations into mob mentality. If you have seen news footage of a crowd in the midst of a riot, you may have questioned how people could ever behave so outrageously, smashing windows, setting fires, and looting stores. Clearly, these are all antisocial behaviors, yet they are committed in a very social moment. Psychologists call this process **deindividuation** because personal identity is decreased in favor of one's social identity. This social identity reacts to the situation and correspondingly takes its cues for appropriate behavior from others in the same situation. Thus, although looting a television set from a store window display might seem like an outrageous act to commit in the context of an everyday stroll down Main Street, in the midst of a riot, where others are making off with all kinds of home electronics, taking the TV appears to be the appropriate thing to do.

Of course, Internet communicators are not engaged in a crime, but the same psychological conditions seem to govern interaction and attraction online. In text-based interaction, there is less individuating information available to communicators. In lieu of relying on distinctions to mark us as attractive, the SIDE model argues that it is our similarities that foster attachment among people online.

Over the last decade, Postumes et al. have conducted a series of experiments with group interaction to establish the power of the SIDE model to predict human behavior. These studies have suggested two important qualities to this processes. First, visual anonymity among participants in a group seems to foster stronger SIDE effects toward conformity and group norms than in groups where participants saw one another face to face. Second, anonymity also seems to encourage stronger self-categorization among users. In one experiment where the participants were made aware of one another's gender, the communicators tended to behave along the lines of their gender roles more than those to whom this information was not disclosed.

In summary, the SIDE model predicts that people will set aside personal identity and adopt the appropriate social identity in order to find acceptance among others. We can observe this same subversion of the personal self in favor of social self on a typical playground. Imagine that a child, Pat, arrives at the park only to find all the other children playing basketball. Pat might have no particular knowledge of basketball but wants to find social acceptance among these peers. Provided that Pat picks up the rules of the game and makes the effort to dribble, pass, and shoot like the others, the rest of the children are likely to accept Pat as one of their own. Likewise, when one enters an online social setting, one must put forth an effort to play along with one's peers.

The other side of the SIDE model is, of course, that of the receivers. Even as the individual must struggle to figure out the norms of a group, the group must struggle to figure out whether or not the individual has the qualities to be "one of the gang." This results in a reliance on stereotyping in order to define who this other is. One individual actively attributes a great deal of meaning to the evident behaviors of the other during their interactions. Quite often then, one will turn to stereotypes to help decode this behavior. Stereotyping is one way in which we try to make sense of the world by focusing on what we might believe to be certain patterns of behavior exhibited by members of a group. Thus, if an individual introduces him- or herself as a hacker, your stereotype of hackers might lead you to conclude that the person is technically proficient with programming and prompt in you a favorable evaluation of the individual.

Perceived similarity has long been held to be a strong predictor of individual attraction (Trenholm & Jensen, 2000), and it seems to be a key in explaining the SIDE model's effects in cyberspace. More recently, researchers have found support for the SIDE model in fostering resistance against certain outgroups. For instance, they found that students were more likely to find support among their peers and consequently express opinions deemed unacceptable by faculty when communicating through computer-mediated channels (Spears, Lea, Cornelliussen, Postumes, & Harr, 2002). From the SIDE perspective, people who conduct relationships online must communicate enough common ground with one another that the parties involved are interested in sustaining relational ties. How commonly and effectively this is accomplished is the focus of the next section.

Frequency of Interpersonal Relationships

In further support of the notion that interpersonal communication can, and does, take place in online media, Malcolm Parks and Kory Floyd (1996) conducted survey research among users of various Usenet BBSs to see to what degree personal relationships are formed online. Almost two thirds of the people responding

HYPERLINK: TASK AND SOCIAL FUNCTION OF E-MAIL AMONG UNDERGRADUATES

When instructors ask students in their classes to communicate with one another using e-mail, they expect that the students will use the network to discuss course topics or perhaps collaborate on assignments. According to the research findings of Naomi McCormick and John McCormick (1992), students will indeed use e-mail to exchange task-related comments, but they will exchange a lot more social messages throughout the term. In a study aimed at discovering what undergraduates in a computer science course wrote about in their e-mail, McCormick and McCormick found that a good deal of the communication was work-related (41.1%), but a majority of the messages served social functions (51.7%).

Of the messages they categorized as fulfilling social functions, 50% displayed less intimate content and the rest more intimate content. The less intimate content consisted of salutations ("Hellllllloooooooo"), crude flirtations ("I'm looking forward to your slobbering kisses!"), humor ("Old Geologists never die, they just weather away"), and put-downs ("You are trully [sic] the scum of the earth . . ."). Although we might think of put-downs as being more antisocial than social, McCormick and McCormick (1992) explain that "rather than being a sign of dislike or alienation, such threats and put-downs may be an adolescent sign of affection and trust among some male, undergraduate, computer users" (p. 390).

Although such superficial communication might be expected among the messages of people interacting in a public forum, it surprised the researchers to find that almost one fourth of the messages collected in their survey displayed deeper relational sentiments. More intimate content was expressed in messages that functioned as sharing ("I wish that I was [sic] graduating this year though!"), refined flirtation and establishment of relationships ("I realize that we don't know each other, but how does dinner and a movies [sic] sound to remedy that situation?"), work on relationships and love messages ("I just wanted to say I had a great weekend and I Love You very Very Much."), and social planning ("I will bring your notes on Wed. Se [sic] you then!!"). Overall, sharing was the second most popular type of message (21.2 %), right after work comments (26.4%).

Other findings in their survey suggest that students seemed more likely to write messages to one another at times when their academic demands were less, that they sent more flirting and relationship establishment messages early on in the semester when people do not know one another as well, and that "C" students were more likely to use the system than "A" and "B" students were.

McCormick and McCormick conclude that students use e-mail to support one another through both task and social messages. Although it might be preemptive to consider closing down the traditional student center just yet, it does appear that e-mail opens another channel for students to accomplish the important tasks of being a college student, from exchanging assignments to exchanging phone numbers.

reported that they had initiated a personal relationship with someone they had met online. The people who tended to have personal relationships seemed to be those who used the newsgroups with more frequency and with greater duration in contrast to those who did not feel any personal attachment achieved through this channel. In looking at relational qualities such as interdependence, breadth and depth of information exchanged, and commitment, Parks and Floyd found that relational partners reported statistically moderate levels of these qualities, indicating that despite the boundaries between them, these people shared a connection to one another.

Furthermore, one half of those with personal relationships (about 30% of the survey) had high enough scores in these areas that they could be considered to be in highly developed relationships. As such, they are likely to migrate to other channels as well. In this survey, a majority of those with some kind of personal relationship followed up with their online interaction by contacting their partner through some other channel, be that telephone, snail-mail, or face-to-face meetings. Even though this extension into other channels hints at a shortfall in maintaining relationships through only one channel, it still provides support for the ability of people to initiate relationships in cyberspace.

Of course, those relationships initiated online are for many people only a small fraction (if indeed any fraction) of the relationships that they maintain using Internet technologies. Sarah Birnie and Peter Horvath (2002) point out that for many people, the Internet is a tool for complementing or extending their efforts in maintaining preexisting relationships. In a study they conducted on a wired campus (where each student and faculty member was equipped with a laptop computer and Internet connection), they found that people participating in this campuswide network used it as a supplement for conducting social activities within their exisiting social network. In other words, friends were likely to chat with friends about their evening plans, classmates would discuss assignments with one another, and so forth. Interestingly, their study suggests "that online social communication is more likely to be an outlet for the sociable person than a compensatory mechanism for the shy or socially anxious individiual with infrequent or superficial social contacts." Thus, the study could be used as evidence for an interpersonal perspective on relating online, as it suggests that there is meaningful interaction—in contrast to the impersonal perspective—and it fails to support the notion that shy people have greater social abilities online than off—a claim supported by the hyperpersonal perspective, which we turn to next.

In short, despite the earlier reservations expressed by those favoring the impersonal perspective, research suggests that there is enough information for some people to find that they can connect with others in personally meaningful ways even without as much information as they would find face-to-face. In fact, there is support for the lack of nonverbal cues being more helpful than harmful to some people in connecting with others. As shown in the next section, characteristics of this context could make communication more conducive to communication.

HYPERPERSONAL COMMUNICATION: TRANSCENDING RELATIONAL LIMITS THROUGH CMC

Different people shine in different conditions. Consider José, a junior whose soulful poetry has won him numerous awards. And yet when people meet José, they are often surprised by how quiet he is. Because he has such a powerful way with words in his writing, people expect him to show equal skill in his speaking. We all know people like José, individuals who find their voice in one channel rather than another. Those who find their voices through CMC engage in **hyperpersonal communication**. In short, hyperpersonal communication occurs when individuals find that they are better able to express themselves in mediated environments than they are in face-to-face interaction.

According to Walther (1996), author of this theory, hyperpersonal communication can be attributed to four interdependent factors: the sender, the receiver, the channel, and feedback. Let us take a look at how each of these four elements contributes to a potentially hyperpersonal experience. As an example, let us imagine Ling, a first-year student at a small, state-run college who is having difficulty relating with the other women in her dorm and has begun to frequent a chat room seeking support.

The first factor that can contribute to a hyperpersonal experience is the sender, who possesses greater control of self-presentation to others. Thus, one can be highly selective in what one chooses to reveal about oneself. Because one is not handicapped by many nonverbal characteristics outside one's control, one is able to create an even more idealized self-image. For example, Ling has always been very self-conscious about a large mole on her right cheek. When talking with friends in face-to-face situations, she swears that she can sense their eyes wandering over to this disfiguring "beauty mark." Needless to say, she has chosen not to mention this feature in her dialogues with online contacts. Instead, she has described herself as musically gifted, a talent she is most proud of, but something, unlike the mole, that people wouldn't immediately notice about her in real life. Having her musical talent forefronted as a distinguishing quality, rather than her blemish, boosts Ling's confidence in her online interactions.

Second, the receiver can overestimate the qualities of a conversation partner in a hyperpersonal experience. The previously discussed SIDE model supports the notion that people can overattribute qualities to the people on the other end of a message. In her online conversations, Ling has been interacting with Scooby-Snak, a self-professed sophomore at a Big Ten institution. From early on in their interactions, Ling feels a kinship with Scooby-Snak because they both report having received some verbal abuse from seniors in their schools. Even though she doesn't know that much about Scooby-Snak, she begins to infer certain similarities between them and decides that this is a likable person.

Third, characteristics of the channel itself, most notably its asynchronous aspects, factor into the hyperpersonal experience. As noted previously, asynchronicity means that communication is occurring nonsimultaneously. In face-to-face interaction, not only must partners be physically co-present, but also they are expected to exchange messages back and forth in a process akin to a tennis match. Asynchronous communication allows individuals to overcome the limitations of co-presence and to construct messages in a more deliberative manner. Case in point, Ling returns from her 10 a.m. class to find an e-mail from Scooby-Snak asking her the latest question in a music trivia contest the two have initiated between them. Ling is stumped by the question, so she walks across campus to the music library, finds the answer, and then returns to write back to her partner. In a face-to-face interaction, Ling would have been at a disadvantage. The nature of their asynchronous exchange, however, allowed her the freedom to construct a suitable reply, one that no doubt made her feel more confident about herself and thusly the relationship.

And, finally, feedback between the partners can intensify the experience. According to Walther (1996), feedback within CMC can lead to "an intensification loop" where the confirming messages of each partner reinforce the behavior of the other. Feedback is, of course, an important part of many communication interactions. Without feedback, we would be left to wonder whether or not our messages made any impact on our audience. The contributions of feedback in an electronic encounter seem to reduce the uncertainty about whether or not the message was received and interpreted in the way it was intended. Replies would seem to be particularly important sources of feedback in such instances because information gathered by nonverbal channels (say, a confirming smile, for instance) is not immediately accessible.

In Ling's case, she and Scooby-Snak continue to exchange messages pertaining to their musical trivia contest for some time. Each time Scooby-Snak issues another question, Ling is encouraged to respond with an answer, issue her own question, and keep the process flowing. Ling perceives Scooby-Snak's continued feedback as a confirming sign for the continuation of the relationship, especially because this partner's demonstrated interest in the topic shows more attention to her interests than she has received from the people who share her dorm.

The hyperpersonal perspective is a provocative explanation for why some people are intensely attracted to networked conversations. The promise of greater control over the nonverbal elements of your self-presentation, of interaction with someone predisposed to reading a favorable impression of you, of more time to create more thoughtful and articulate messages, and of affirming feedback creates a situation that many cannot experience in real life. For Ling, and others like her, online interaction may provide a forum to find a voice that might otherwise remain silent.

Whether communication via networked channels is found to be impersonal, interpersonal, or hyperpersonal, the research discussed here collectively suggests that it is not the nature of the technology that determines the evaluation of the communication experience as much as it is one's perception of that experience. Thus, this body of research suggests a counterpoint to the technological determinism discussed in previous chapters. Accordingly, individual perception, rather than the qualities of the medium itself, once again reasserts its dominance in human interaction in this context as in all others. Our interpretive lenses lead us to look on network interaction as distant, immediate, or extraordinary. All three perspectives view interaction as relevant but the quality as divergent. As you think about your own opinion on this debate, we turn now to a consideration of issues that have emerged in the wake of online relationships.

MANAGING ONLINE RELATIONSHIPS

Just as we experience different kinds of relationships in our real lives, we are likely to develop different kinds of relationships online as well. If you have not already experienced them, you may well develop some working relationships and, perhaps, even some friendships or romances in cyberspace. In order to manage these relationships effectively, competent communicators need to attend to some issues that are even more salient in online relationships than in real-life relationships. In particular, we think that you should pay close attention to the challenges of depersonalization in working relationships and emotional detachment in romantic relationships.

Working Relationships

According to a survey conducted by the International Telework Association & Council, more than 28 million people, or one fifth of the workforce, telecommuted for their jobs, spending at least part of their time working outside of traditional offices and using networking technologies to link to their employers (Fetto, 2002). Engineers, artists, designers, programmers, sales people, and writers are just some of those in career fields that are moving toward telecommuting. As you might imagine, the nature of telecommuting requires that employers communicate their directives and that employees submit their products over electronic communication systems. Even if you don't find yourself engaged in a telecommuting job, you are still likely to find yourself interacting with employers and clients through e-mail and other communication systems. (More is discussed about telecommuting and the role computer technologies play in professional life in chapter 7.)

As these systems become increasingly more common as part of the working experience, it becomes easier to take for granted the effect they have on human communication. As the impersonal perspective suggests, however, there is a temptation to forget many of the rules that govern civil face-to-face interaction. Although sufficient evidence exists that CMC is not inherently depersonalizing, people can still behave in manners that are injurious to others.

This is most obvious in the act of **flaming**. A message can be considered a flame when it is intended and/or interpreted to be hostile in nature. Take a look at the following hypothetical exchange:

```
ArchEE:   I think that the client really appreciates my
          contribution.
JuggHed:  ALL the clients at Riverdale appreciate you.
ArchEE:   What's THAT supposed to mean?!?!
```

JuggHed might have intended to compliment ArchEE (if he really does think that ArchEE's that well liked), or he might have intended to mock him. It is difficult to tell what his comment intended to communicate without the accompanying vocal qualities that distinguish awe from sarcasm. However, ArchEE's exclamatory reply suggests that he perceived it to be an attack.

Philip Thompsen (1996) claims that the confrontational nature of flaming can best be understood by a **social influence model** of technology use (originating in the work of Fulk, Steinfield, Schmitz, & Power, 1987). Accordingly, "a social influence perspective on flaming thus considers both the behavior of flaming and the social negotiation of what that behavior means . . . flaming is both a media use and a media evaluation—a [CMC] behavior and an interpretation of that behavior" (pp. 303–304). Several components contribute to a deeper understand of flaming.

Thompsen lists direct statements, vicarious learning, group behavioral norms, social definitions of reality, media experience and skills, media evaluations, task evaluations, situational factors, media features, and prior use of other media as potential contributors to the creation and interpretation of flames. From the user's perspective, social influence and media experience seem to be the key factors in leading to flaming. Social influence comes in many forms, including vicarious learning. If JuggHed has observed others flaming in the chat room where he and ArchEE meet, then he is more likely to know how to flame but also to infer that it is okay to flame.

HYPERLINK: MATCHMAKER, MATCHMAKER, MAKE ME A MATCH

In the popular musical *Fiddler on the Roof*, the young women of Reb Tevia's village croon, "Matchmaker, Matchmaker, make me a match," longing for the matronly matchmaker to choose them husbands. The role of third parties in establishing romantic relationships is long and lasting, despite the more recently romanticized vision of true love appearing spontaneously.

American literature and film have popularized the spontaneous vision, making stories about people meeting the love of their life online seem unusual. The meetings of couples because of chat rooms, MUDs, and Web sites may make it seem like technology introduces something unnatural to a relationship. However, in lieu of matronly matchmakers to find them love, people have used various communication technologies throughout the past century to find a mate.

For example, take the consistent popularity of newspaper personal ads. As an aid to relationship initiation, they not only allow one to advertise one's best attributes, but because they specify qualities sought in a partner, they help to reduce the uncertainty and awkwardness of face-to-face interaction (Parrott, Lemieux, Harris, & Foreman, 1997). An even more "scientific" approach was popular in the middle of the last century. Computer dating services had singles fill out questionnaires that then electronically matched them with persons with highly similar answers. The success of this method can be attested to by one of the authors of this book. His parents met and married thanks to computer dating. Arguably, every technological development of the electronic era, from the telephone to the television, has played a role in courtship.

Recently, the popularity of online dating services has soared. According to Michael McCarthy (2003), more than 8 million people use Match.com, the site used to unite the couple in this chapter's opening anecdote. Many of those people are paying subscribers and contributing to the $302 million spent on online personal ads in 2002. Of course, Match.com is not alone, and a number of sites contribute to the phenomenon, including those sites that cater to particular segments of the population such as BlackPlanet.com for African Americans and JDate.com for Jewish singles.

Finding a romantic partner can be a difficult process, one that many find is best not left to happenstance or fate. In due course, it seems that many people are turning to technology in order to narrow the odds in their favor. Yet there is a persistent doubt in the minds of those who question the authenticity of such tactics, preferring human intervention to technological intervention. Ultimately, the question comes around to, What difference does it make if your matchmaker is dowdy or downloaded?

As for media experience, if JuggHed is new to the online experience, he might have inadvertently flamed without intending to. His novice status might have led him to make an online faux pas.

From an evaluator's perspective, social influence and media experience continue to affect our perceptions of a message. Here, again, our perceptions of what is appropriate in the setting and our own familiarity with the conventions of the technology will lead to our interpretation of a given message. ArchEE's heavily punctuated response certainly suggests that he has negatively interpreted JuggHed's message. His own perception of the online environment might suggest that JuggHed has issued a personal innuendo inappropriate to this context. As such, he sees a flame where his partner might or might not have intended one to be.

Intentionally or unintentionally, flames can cause turmoil in a relationship. The challenge for communicators is twofold as well. From the message creation side, one must know the norms of a given setting and practice reading a message from the other person's point of view. Asking yourself, "In what ways could ArchEE misread this message?" before you send it could lead you to make some subtle, yet meaningful revisions to the text. Had JuggHed intended his comment as a compliment, he might have elaborated further, adding, "ALL the people I have spoken with at Riverdale have told me just how much they appreciate you."

On the other end, receivers could benefit from an accounting of their own interpretation and bracket that within the realm of possible interpretations. Had ArchEE been open to the possibility of multiple meanings, he might have replied with a question that engaged in more perception-checking than inquisition, "Do you mean to say that you've heard a positive response?" Although it is entirely possible that people will be intentionally caustic at times, it is a shame when unintended interpretations lead to a series of hurtful messages, a "flame war" in the online vernacular, when there are ways to quench the sparks. We now turn our attention to another kind of spark, the romantic kind, and challenges communicators face in these online relationships.

Romantic Relationships

When it comes to romantic relationships, many people like to think that they are mutually beneficial. Ideally, both parties have their needs for affection, inclusion, and control met through the arrangement (Schutz, 1958). Yet experience has taught most of us that romantic relationships are rarely ideal. For one reason or another, most of them are complicated by shortfalls. When it comes to relating online, relationships can be no less perfect. In particular, research centered on romantic relationships has been characterized by some degree of emotional detachment between partners. As the following two cases demonstrate, this detachment suggests that a game-playing type of love is displayed and results in a lack of commitment to the online relationship.

In the first case, Lynn Schofield Clark (1995) found that dating in online contexts is more likely an exercise in self-fulfillment than in building relational bonds. She studied teens who participate in chat rooms to determine the character of their dating relationships. What she found was a degree of emotional detachment that seemed to contrast sharply with that of face-to-face interactions. Summarizing the teens' responses, Clark asserts that the primary motivation for dating online is to have "fun" rather than to establish strong emotional ties or lasting commitments. In fact, although the relationships practiced in cyberspace offered each participant a strong sense of emotional gratification, participants often failed to follow up these relationships in offline contexts.

Removed from the constraints imposed by physical appearance and one's social groups, teens, most especially girls, reported a stronger sense of emancipation and power in online dating than they had encountered in real-life dating. Girls said that they described themselves as meeting the imagined "ideal" of the desirable female, thus garnering more attention from boys and competing with other girls on the basis of their personality and wit rather than their physical attributes. Other reasons girls reported for finding the medium emancipatory included the option to avoid unwanted sexual advances (seeing as how it is much easier to avoid a pursuer who inhabits a chat room than one who is seated in a classroom) and to express themselves verbally. As one of Clark's (1995) respondents explained, "I act a lot more aggressive on the Internet. I just express my feelings a lot more in the chat rooms and stuff, so if somebody talks about something that I don't like, then I'll say it. And I would probably never do that in class, in school and everything" (p. 165).

As such, the disembodied relationships that can emerge in teen dating scenarios in chat rooms offer their participants fewer "emotional hazards" than face-to-face inter-actions. With the resulting decreased emotional attachment, one might wonder why teens bother to engage in such "dating" encounters at all. In Clark's (1995) estimation, the answer can be found in self-gratification. Experimenting with others in an exercise of imagined intimacy contributes to the development of one's own self-concept. Finding acceptance from a suitor who is not a threat to one's physical well-being or one's social standing (which can be risked by dating beneath one's socioeconomic group under the watchful eyes of one's socially sensitive peers) can be rewarding, especially to persons who might be less competent in other social settings. But, as they lack the consequences that romantic relationships with personal contact introduce, these relationships should be assessed with some caution. Although they might serve as strong contributors to the construction of self-identity, they seem to fall short in equipping teens to deal with people in more enduring, more immediate interactions.

Consequently, our real-life relationships seem to involve greater emotional attachment than those thus far documented online. This would explain why one party in a real-life relationship like a marriage can be harmed if another turns to the computer rather than to the spouse to meet needs for identity affirmation and sexual gratification.

Table 4.3
Three Perspectives on Working and Romantic Relational Issues

Perspective	Depersonalization Through Flaming	Emotional Detachment Through Self-Gratification
Impersonal	Limited cues encourage disinhibited behavior such as letting one's temper flare.	Because the other is unknown, it is easy not to think of this conversation partner as a feeling individual.
Interpersonal	Conflict is a natural part of interpersonal relationships.	Both parties know what they want to get out of this relationship.
Hyperpersonal	The freedom that comes with expressing yourself sometimes means that people will express themselves in negative ways.	These folks aren't constrained by convention; they're able to experiment with their own identities and relationships.

Although researchers have yet to conclude that there is anything inherently harmful with establishing ties via the Internet, there is evidence that online channels can help manifest problems in an existing real-world relationship. For example, the Internet may provide an avenue that enables one or more parties to retreat from a real-life relationship and seek emotional support from their online relationships. Kimberly Young (1998), a clinical psychologist, shares accounts of couples who have suffered strain and undergone divorce because of one partner's "online addiction." (This is discussed in greater depth in chapter 5.)

Certainly at the extreme of this type of behavior is a so-called **cyberaffair**, where one partner in a relationship carries on an interpersonally, but not necessarily physically, intimate relationship with someone online. Some have doubted the viability of a cyberaffair, likening it to the reading of a romance novel. However, the key distinction of interactivity seems to suggest infidelity in the perception of a partner (Sullivan, 1997). The root of cyberaffairs, however, might rest outside the medium. According to one physician's commentary:

> This is a marital-dysfunction problem, not an Internet problem. The Internet has simply made the problem manifest. It can't be very flattering to be replaced by a machine, and the natural response is to blame the machine instead of examining the relationship and the part that you are playing—or not playing—in it. (p. 1618)

In the case of both flaming and emotional detachment, it seems that a common theme threads these implications together. The evidence presented here points to people behaving in ways that are more self-centered than not. Expressing one's anger or fulfilling one's own emotional gratification are, after all, self- rather than other-centered activities. As illustrated in Table 4.3, each of the three perspectives explained earlier in this chapter might view the inclination of these behaviors differently.

Ethical Inquiry

People going online should certainly be mindful of the fact that not everyone they meet online may be acting in their best interest. However, people seem all too willing to develop bonds of trust over time rather than operate in suspicion in perpetuity. Although these people may commit trust in such relationships willingly, what responsibility do those who are "playing" online have to disclose either their motives (as with the teen daters) or their marital status (as with those having a cyberaffair)? Who should be responsible for the broken hearts that follow these online romances, those who view them as online fun or those who fall too far?

CHAPTER SUMMARY

This chapter has reviewed several perspectives and implications of online relationships. Research has suggested that there are three relevant perspectives in examining online relationships: the impersonal, the interpersonal, and the hyperpersonal. Early work in the field of CMC suggested that interaction there was task-oriented and, consequently, impersonal in nature. It was argued that the lack of nonverbal and social cues handicapped communicators interacting in this context. However, it might be that online relationships simply take longer to deepen than those in face-to-face settings. Indeed, evidence suggests that people do form interpersonal bonds. The SIDE model argues that there are enough cues for individuals to adopt social roles enabling them to fit into these relationships. Moreover, some find the reduction of cues empowering, leading them to perceive online relationships as hyperpersonal in nature. Certainly, there are some implications in building relationships online, whether they are working, friendly, or romantic in nature. Competent communicators need to be wary of the potential self-serving bias that comes from disregarding the implications of flaming and emotional detachment.

In the future, scholars have much to learn about the nature of online relationships. There are a number of questions that still need to be answered. For instance, communication scholars theorize that interpersonal relationships develop in stages. Do online relationships develop in a parallel or unique fashion? We also know that people involved in face-to-face relationships use a number of compliance-gaining strategies in order to persuade their partners to do things for them. Are there now unique strategies that have emerged among online communicators? Finally, how and why do these relationships terminate? Although there are certain processes that are quite similar across contexts, we cannot take for granted that what we know about face-to-face interaction is necessarily the case in cyberspace. Although there are many unanswered questions about online relationships, there are many people whose curiosity about these issues will propel the search for understanding them forward.

ONLINE COMMUNICATION AND THE LAW

Although we would like to think that most people initiate or maintain relationships online with the best of intentions and mutual consent, the reality of the Internet is that just as perfectly normal human behavior gets translated, so too does aberrant behavior. One of the dark sides of romance is stalking; so, too, one of the dark sides of online relationships is **cyberstalking**. According to the U.S. Attorney General's Office (1999), cyberstalking occurs when someone is the target of repeated harassing or threatening electronic communications. Most stalking cases are the result of previous relationships gone sour, as one partner attempts to become reinstated in the other's life; on average, 2% of men and 8% of women experience some form of stalking in their lifetimes (Tjaden, Thoennes & Allison, 2000). It is against the law to stalk, offline or online, but the crime continues to victimize many.

Research by Brian H. Spitzberg and Gregory Hoobler (2002) found that almost a third of college students had experienced some type of online harassment. Although the majority of the harassment was relatively benign, consisting mainly of stalkers repeatedly professing their aspirations and making disclosures about themselves, this study suggests that cyberstalking has the potential to affect more and more of the people online. Perhaps this is because stalkers have much greater access to their targets, being able to instant message them, e-mail them, appear in a chat room they frequent, etc., all with the relative ease of conducting their stalking from the perceived safety of their home computers. Because cyberstalkers have such access to their victims, they may be more of a threat to individual liberty and security than any abstract government surveillance might be: "The fear that the common person may need to be most concerned about may not be 'Big Brother' so much as each other" (p. 87).

Glossary

Cues-filtered-out approach: A perspective on CMC that says the Internet is inferior as a channel for communication because of a lack of nonverbal cues.

Cyberaffair: A perceived infidelity that occurs when one partner in a real-life relationship maintains a romantic relationship with a different partner online.

Cyberstalking: The repeated sending of harassing or threatening electronic communications.

Deindividuation: The psychological process of surrendering personal identity in favor of the dominant social identity; the so-called mob mentality.

Emoticons: Text-based cues designed to reveal the emotional intent of a message.

Flaming: The practice of sending intended or perceived hostile messages in mediated contexts.

Functional alternatives: A perception that one channel accomplishes the same task just as well as another.

Hyperpersonal communication: A perspective on mediated communication suggesting that greater control over self-presentation by the sender, overestimations by the receiver, the asynchronicity of the channel, and confirming messages offered through feedback allow some people to express themselves better in mediated rather than in face-to-face interactions.

Nonverbal cues: All the nonlanguage elements of communication, including vocal qualities, facial expressions, posture, movement, and eye contact.

Norms: Behaviors accepted among members of a social group.

Social context cues: A perspective on human behavior suggesting that actions are governed by subtle indicators in the social environment.

Social identification/deindividuation (SIDE) model: A perspective on mediated communication suggesting that interpersonal attraction and acceptance come from identification with group norms.

Social influence model: A perspective on mediated communication suggesting that a media use results from a negotiation between the features of the medium and the social conditions.

Social information processing: A perspective on mediated communication suggesting that it takes more time to develop relationships in mediated interactions than in face-to-face interactions given the presence of fewer nonverbal cues.

Social presence theory: A perspective on mediated communication suggesting that people perceive differing degrees of substance to others they interact with over mediated channels and to their relationship to them.

Specialized channels: A perception that each medium is particularly well suited to accomplishing a particular task.

Topics for Discussion

1. In addition to those mentioned in the text, make a list of five other nonverbal cues by which you interpret meaning during your face-to-face interactions. In what ways do you see these cues compensated for in online interactions? Does

the absence of any of them make communicating easier or more difficult in the online environment?

2. According to the SIDE model, people are willing to give up their personal identities and assume social identities in order to find acceptance online. Write a paragraph in which you identify situations, online and in real life, in which there are advantages to choosing one over the other. How can one avoid being swept up by deindividuation in these situations?

3. In the explanation of hyperpersonal communication, we focus on an example of how it could explain a positive encounter. Explain how a negative encounter could be accentuated by the hyperpersonal factors of sender, receiver, channel, and feedback?

4. Cite five criteria you use to determine if a message is a flame. Print out a message that you have interpreted as flaming in nature. What response would you typically follow up with? How are your interpretation and response affected by social influence and media experience?

5. Make a list of the qualities that you think lead people to seek out romantic relationships online. Is it fair to compare the standards for relating in face-to-face relationships with those in mediated relationships?

REFERENCES

Birdwhistle, R. L. (1970). *Kinesics in context*. Philadelphia: University of Pennsylvania Press.

Birnie, S. A., & Horvath, P. (2002). Psychological predictors of Internet social communication. *Journal of Computer-Mediated Communication, 7*(4). Retrieved June 10, 2003, from http://www.ascusc.org/jcmc/vol7/issue4/horvath.html

Clark, L. S. (1995). Dating on the net: Teens and the rise of "pure" relationships. In J. T. Wood & S. Duck (Eds.), *Under-studied relationships: Off the beaten track* (pp. 159–183). Thousand Oaks, CA: Sage.

Culnan, M. J., & Markus, M. L. (1987). Information technologies. In F. M. Jablin, L. L. Putnam, K. H. Roberts, & L. W. Porter (Eds.), *Handbook of organizational communication: An interdisciplinary perspective* (pp. 420–443). Newbury Park, CA: Sage.

Fetto, J. (2002, February). You can take it with you. *American Demographics, 24*, 10–11.

Flaherty, L. M., Pearce, K. J., & Rubin, R. R. (1998). Internet and face-to-face communication: Not functional alternatives. *Communication Quarterly, 46*, 250–268.

Fulk, J., Steinfield, C. W., Schmitz, J., & Power, J. G. (1987). A social information processing model of media use in organizations. *Communication Research, 14*, 529–552.

Kiesler, S., Siegel, J., & McGuire, T. W. (1984). Social psychological aspects of CMC. *American Psychologist, 39*, 1123–1134.

Lea, M., & Spears, R. (1998). Love at first byte? Building personal relationships over computer networks. In S. G. Jones (Ed.), *Cybersociety 2.0: Revisiting CMC and community* (pp. 197–233). Thousand Oaks, CA: Sage.

Match.com. (2003). *Match.com success stories* [Online]. Available: http://www.matchnewscenter.com/success/index.php [June 10, 2003].

McCarthy, M. (2003, April 28). Consumers decide ads not a match. *USA Today*, p. 6B.

McCormick, N. B., & McCormick, J. W. (1992). Computer friends and foes: Content of undergraduates' electronic mail. *Computers in Human Behavior, 8,* 379–405.

Mehrabian, A. (1972). *Nonverbal communication.* Chicago: Aldine.

Metz, J. M. (1994). Computer-mediated communication: Literature review of a new context. *Interpersonal Computing and Technology: An Electronic Journal for the 21st Century.* Retrieved from http://www.helsinki.fi/science/optek/1994/n2/metz.txt

Parks, M. R., & Floyd, K. (1996). Making friends in cyberspace. *Journal of Communication, 46,* 80–97.

Parrott, R., Lemieux, R., Harris, T., & Foreman, L. (1997). Interfacing interpersonal and mediated communication: Use of active and strategic self-disclosure in personal ads. *Southern Communication Journal, 62,* 319–332.

Postumes, T., Spears, R., & Lea, M. (1998). Breaching or building social boundaries? Side-effects of CMC. *Communication Research, 25,* 689–716.

Reid, E. (1991). *Electropolis: Communication and community on Internet Relay Chat.* Unpublished master's thesis, University of Melbourne. Available: http://www.ee.mu.oz.au/papers/emr/electropolis.html

Rice, R. E. (1987). CMC and organizational innovation. *Journal of Communication, 37,* 65–94.

Schutz, W. C. (1958). *FIRO: A three-dimensional theory of interpersonal behavior.* New York: Holt, Rinehart & Winston.

Schwartz, P. (1996, June). R-tech. *Wired, 4.06.* Retrieved from http://www.wired.com/wired/archive/4.06/rtech.html

Short, J., Williams, E., & Christie, B. (1976). *The social psychology of telecommunication.* London: Wiley.

Spears, R., Lea, M., Cornelliussen, R. A., Postumes, T., & Haar, W. T. (2002). Computer-mediated communication as a channel for social resistance: The strategic side of SIDE. *Small Group Research, 33,* 555–574.

Spitzberg, B., & Hoobler, G. (2002). Cyberstalking and the technologies of interpersonal terrorism. *New Media & Society, 4,* 71–92.

Sproull, L., & Kiesler, S. (1986). Reducing social context cues: Electronic mail in organizational communication. *Management Science, 32,* 1492–1512.

Sullivan, P. (1997). Physicians debate Internet-related marital problems on CMA's online service. *Canadian Medical Association Journal, 156,* 1617–1618.

Thompsen, P. A. (1996). What's fueling the flames of cyberspace? A social influence model. In L. Strate, R. Jacobson, & S. B. Gibson (Eds.), *Communication and cyberspace: Social interaction in an electronic environment* (pp. 297–315). Cresskill, NJ: Hampton Press.

Tjaden, P., Thoennes, J., & Allison, C. (2000). Comparing stlaking victimization from legal and victim perspectives. *Violence and Victims, 15*(1), 7–22.

Trenholm, S., & Jensen, A. (2000). *Interpersonal communication* (4th ed.). Belmont, CA: Wadsworth.

U.S. Attorney General (1999). *Cyberstalking: A new challenge for law enforcement and industry* [Online]. Available: http://www.usdoj.gov/criminal/cybercrime/cyberstalking.htm [June 26, 2003].

Walther, J. B. (1992). Interpersonal effects in computer-mediated interaction: A relational perspective. *Communication Research, 19,* 52–90.

Walther, J. B. (1996). CMC: Impersonal, interpersonal, and hyperpersonal interaction. *Communication Research, 23,* 3–43.

Walther, J. B., & D'Addario, K. P. (2001). The impacts of emoticons on message interpretation in computer-mediated communication. *Social Science Computer Review, 19,* 324–347.

Wolf, A. (2000). Emotional expression online: Gender differences in emoticon use. *CyberPsychology & Behavior, 3,* 827–833.

Young, K. (1998). *Caught in the net: How to recognize the signs of Internet addiction and a winning strategy for recovering.* New York: Wiley.

CHAPTER 5

SEEKING THERAPY ONLINE

The Internet is so big, so powerful and pointless, that for some people it is a complete substitute for life.

—Andrew Brown

More than 400,000 people across the globe regularly log on to EverQuest. The online game, created by the online entertainment branch of the media giant Sony Corporation, creates a virtual environment where players not only engage in complex fantasy scenarios, but do so in real time with other players online. Like its MUD forebearers discussed in chapter 1, EverQuest is a highly interactive, social environment. Unlike most early MUDs, though, EverQuest is visually intensive, not limited to text-only interaction. It is a interactive environment that never shuts down and, theoretically, never ends, with the game continuing even when more than 1 or even more than 100,000 players log off. This never-ending quality has made some players label EverQuest as "EverCrack," for in the lure to keep on playing, some claim to have found the experience "addictive" (Patrizio, 2002). Whether or not a computer-similated experience can be addictive in the same sense as crack cocaine or any other chemical substance is a topic of substantial debate, but in terms of EverQuest having measurable negative effects on the lives of some of its players, even as a drug might, there is clear support. Among the consequences is the creation of a support group for EverQuest Widows, those who love the players but feel abandoned by them because of the time that they devote to the game. This loss of companionship is regrettable, but accusations that EverQuest might have led someone to lose his life are even more serious.

That is the claim made by Elizabeth Wooley of Wisconsin. Her son, Shawn, committed suicide in the fall of 2001, and Elizabeth claims that EverQuest contributed to the decision Shawn made to end his life. Just prior to his death, Shawn had been ignoring his family, had lost his job, and had taken to playing the game up to 12 hours a day. Although his mother acknowledges that Shawn had other problems in his life, she still holds Sony responsible for creating a product that, in her opinion, addicted her son. "It's like any other addiction. Either you die, go insane or quit. My son died" (S. A. Miller, 2002). Like Elizabeth, some scholars and therapists have argued that case studies like Shawn's and the results of survey research support their claims that for some people, overreliance on online interaction can have detrimental effects, little different than if one were suffering from any other behavioral disorder. Although some surveys place the number of affected people at a high of 6% (Donn, 1999), conservative estimates place 3.5% of the Internet's population in the group of addicts

(Whang, Lee, & Chang, 2003). Translated into the worldwide number of users, this means that millions of people are in this group. Even so, other scholars and therapists raise questions about this phenomenon and, for reasons that we discuss shortly, cast doubt on the viability of "addiction" as an explanation for these dilitorious outcomes.

This chapter examines the effects that online communication can have on users' well-being, both negatively and positively. We begin by examining the alleged problem itself by reviewing the symptoms of online addiction. In the course of examining the effects of this phenomenon, we focus particular attention on human sexuality as a contributor to this life-altering behavior. However, we also want to acknowledge that although some people suffer detrimental effects because of their online affiliations, others can reap rewards. Thus, we conclude this chapter with a look at the ways in which people benefit from online therapy sessions and support groups.

INTERNET ADDICTION DISORDER

The results of one of the most widely cited studies of Internet usage suggests that greater use of the Internet has a detrimental effect on one's well-being. According to a research team from Carnegie Mellon University, the more that participants used the Internet, the less likely they were to communicate with members of their household; moreover, their social circles were likely to grow smaller, and they experienced increases in depression and loneliness (Kraut et al., 1998).

Likewise, the Stanford Institute for the Quantitative Study of Society (2000) reported findings that the Internet has detrimental effects on people's lives. The poll indicated that 13% of the respondents reported spending less time with family and friends, 26% talked less with family and friends on the telephone, and 8% attended fewer social events. According to Norman Nie, a Stanford University political scientist, "The Internet could be the ultimate isolating technology that further reduces our participation in communities even more than did automobiles or television before it" (O'Toole, 2000). Although evidence we present later in this chapter contests these findings, such conclusions lend support to the notion that the Internet indirectly reduces the quality of life enjoyed by some people, leading in some cases to an extreme condition that psychiatrist Ivan Goldberg dubbed **Internet Addiction Disorder** (IAD).

Like other psychological disorders, IAD has distressing implications for one's psychological, physical, and social well-being. For some people, the addiction is to the applications made available through the Internet, and they find themselves caught up in the lure of online gambling, competitive auctions, and stock trading (Young, 1998b). For others, however, the appeal is interpersonal. The case of Sandra Hacker received national attention when she was discovered neglecting the care of her children because she was preoccupied with the Internet. Her obsession with online interaction allegedly led her to lock her children in a filthy room for up to 12 hours a day (Bricking, 1997). Cases like Hacker's demonstrate that communication can be just as addictive as any other behavior. Affirming this notion is Pavel Curtis, creator of the social MUD, LambdaMOO, who noted a warning in the following statement:

> I am concerned about the degree to which people find virtual communities enchanting. We have people who use LambdaMOO who are not in control of their usage who are, I believe, seriously and clinically addicted.... These people aren't

addicted to playing video games. It wouldn't be the same for them. They're com-munication addicted. They're addicted to being able to go out and find people twenty-four hours a day and have interesting conversations with them. We're talk-ing about people who spend up to seventy hours a week connected and active on a MUD. (cited in Rheingold, 1993, pp. 151–152)

Certainly, one of the presumptions held about online addicts is that they are repressed, socially awkward, inwardly focused individuals. However, Curtis counters that pre-sumption by arguing, "If someone is spending a large portion of their time being so-cial with people who live thousands of miles away, you can't say that they've turned inward. They aren't shunning society. They're actively seeking it. They're probably doing it more actively than anyone around them" (p. 152). Thus, it is the interpersonal connection made through communication, rather than the novelty of the technology itself, that contributes to the Internet's allure.

Symptoms of IAD

Having a problem and recognizing that one has a problem are often two different things. Take the case of "Jamie," a 16-year-old living in the United Kingdom. Jamie spends 40 hours a week online, often in discussion groups, and even when he isn't online, he reports thinking about logging on for his next session. Yet despite his inabil-ity to regulate how long he stays online and other compulsive behaviors associated with his Internet use, Jamie denies having any kind of problem, much less being an "addict" (Griffiths, 2000a). In order to help people like Jamie identify when their behavior has changed from casual to addictive levels, the American Psychiatric As-sociation has recommended attending to the following indications (Ferris, 1997). If people suffer three or more of the following symptoms within a 12-month period, they may be experiencing IAD.

1. They build a **tolerance** for the Internet. That is, they require more exposure to the Internet in order to feel the same amount of satisfaction as with previous amounts of exposure.
2. They experience **withdrawal** symptoms when they stop using the Internet. Withdrawal symptoms can include feelings of anxiety or obsessive thinking about what they are missing online.
3. They find themselves accessing the Internet more than they intend to or they access it for longer periods of time than they intend to.
4. They have a desire to reduce, or have been unsuccessful in reducing, their Internet use.
5. They spend a good deal of time with activities related to the Internet (e.g., buying Internet-related books).
6. They neglect to attend to social, occupational, or recreational activities because of the Internet.
7. They continue to use the Internet despite an obvious problem with their health, relationships, job, or mental health caused by their Internet use (e.g., insomnia, marital conflict, neglect of occupational duties, or anxiety).

In short, these criteria imply that use of the Internet becomes a problem when it comes to occupy a disproportionate amount of one's life, as it has in Jamie's case. But what attracts people to the Internet, per se?

According to Kimberly Young (1998a, 1998b), founder of the Center for Online Addiction and author of *Caught in the Net*, one explanation for the attraction to the Internet is found in her **ACE model**. This acronym stands for *accessibility, control,* and *excitement*. In Young's view, these qualities of the communication context make it particularly attractive to some people. For many, the Internet is readily accessible. If they have a connection at home or work (or both), they can log on many times a day and seek the personal gratification that comes with indulging in conversation, gambling, or whatever particular reward one is seeking. Control is also a major attractor. People like to feel that they have control over what they will do, when they will do it, and how they will do it. Finally, excitement contributes to the attraction. There is a mental "high" that is associated with good conversation, winning a bet, or discovering something one does not know or has never seen before. The ACE model thus suggests that the rewards one perceives from interaction with the Internet are, at least initially, a strong lure for people getting caught up in addictive behaviors.

Interestingly, Young also suggests that the reasons leading people to addiction may be gender-based. In her research, Young found that men tend to gravitate toward online interaction because it offers them the opportunity to exercise power and dominance. In particular, MUDs are known for both their creative and their combative characteristics. One exercises control over the creation of identities, tools, and stories in these forums. Men also seem to enjoy the domination they can exercise in sexually explicit chat (which is discussed in greater depth later). Young also found that women, on the other hand, seem attracted to the absence of judgment of their physical appearance and the company of others that the context provides. Thus, even though women will participate in romantic dialogue, for them it is a matter of being appreciated for their personalities rather than for their bodies. Given that human sexuality contributes to the attraction of IAD, we focus some attention in the next section on a particular form of the disorder and one that has certainly garnered much attention in the popular media, the type based on sexuality.

HYPERLINK: OBSCENITY IN CYBERSPACE

If you have ever made the error of typing in www.whitehouse.*com* instead of www.whitehouse.*gov* (as a senior colleague of ours once did while trying to show his mother how to find information on the presidency), then you are probably aware, at least in part, of the vast repository of pornographic material available online. Whitehouse.com is just one of the countless sites featuring sexually explicit materials that many people consume on a regular basis. Media measurement service Nielsen-NetRatings estimates that 27.5 million Americans visit pornographic web sites (Elias, 2002).

The proliferation of erotica online has been one of the thornier issues over which legislators and Internet advocates have tussled. On one hand, authorities have sought to protect children from literature and images of an adult nature. On the other hand, cyberculture enthusiasts have vehemently objected to any kind of government regulation of online speech. The problem of regulating obscene material and protecting free speech is not a new one, and the Supreme Court established some guidelines for what materials would fall into the category of the "obscene" and thus within the bounds of regulation. In its 1973 decision on *Miller v. California*, the court established a three-part test, each part of which must be met in order for material to be considered obscene:

1. the material, taken as a whole appeals to prurient interests, that
2. the work depicts or describes, in a patently offensive way, sexual conduct, and that
3. the material lacks serious literary, artistic, political, or scientific value. (cited in Birsch, 1996)

As you can tell, even these guidelines themselves are somewhat ambiguous. Initially, when Congress attempted to reduce that uncertainty by prohibiting "indecency" on the Internet in the Communication Decency Act of 1996, its far-reaching restrictions on free speech met with the disapproval of the courts (Bilstad & Godward, 1996). However, the more clearly defined prohibitions of the Children's Internet Protection Act of 2000 (CIPA) met with Supreme Court approval and require schools and public libraries to use filtering software in order to prevent children from accessing sites that meet the criteria for obscenity. As this text went to press, CIPA was once again up for review before the courts, further underscoring the uncertain legal territory that such material traverses.

Given the difficulty that government has had with regulating the morality of certain messages within this new medium, a better solution to coping with obscenity online might rest with private entities rather than legislative agencies. One possible solution would be to have local service providers censor materials that fail to meet community standards (Birsch, 1996). For years, CompuServe monitored and blocked the flow of objectionable material through its commercial system. Another possible solution is for households to control this material through the use of software programs like CyberPatrol, Cyber Sentinel, or NetNanny, each of which filters out obscene sites on the Web (Bilstad & Godward, 1996). Although such alternatives are not foolproof, they do provide a less constitutionally questionable solution to coping with the bounty of obscene material online.

Addiction to Sexual Content

According to their testimony in the *Columbus Dispatch*, one Franklin County, Ohio, couple had a healthy and happy relationship until the husband logged onto the Internet. Shortly after buying a home computer, the husband began to explore the darker side of the Internet, visiting pornographic Web sites, exchanging pornographic images with other users, and participating in more risqué chat rooms. Gradually, his compulsion led him to spend increasing amounts of time online, at home and on the job, until as much as three fourths of his work day was spent chatting. Eventually, he connected with a woman who lived in Philadelphia and began exchanging increasingly flirtatious messages with her, culminating in a weekend drive to meet her face-to-face. Shortly after that trip, the husband could bear the guilt no longer and confessed his unfaithfulness to his wife. Coincidentally, his employers discovered that he had embezzled $300 to finance his weekend in Philadelphia. They fired him. Within just 6 months, this man had gone from being upright to downtrodden (Fiely, 1999).

This midwestern fellow is not alone. Al Cooper, director of the San Jose Marital and Sexuality Center, estimates that up to a quarter of Internet users engage in some form of sexual activity, or **cybersex** (Kelleher, 2002), ranging from visiting erotic Web sites to sending suggestive e-mail to joining sexual chat rooms. Throughout the Internet's rapid growth, people have found numerous ways to experiment with sexuality online. Beyond the presentation of graphic material on the World Wide Web, the Internet is also home to a library of erotic literature as well as a forum for the posting of bulletin board messages and real-time exchanges in which conversants describe sexual activity to one another. Called "cybersex chat," "hot chat," and "tiny sex," among other things, such interactive messages seem to be attractive for three reasons. According to Cooper, online sexual content owes its popularity to the affordability, accessibility, and anonymity of the Internet (4.6 million, 1999).

Because of these "AAA" factors, consuming "XXX" sexual content on the Internet is a lot different than visiting the local adult bookstore. Beyond the expenses charged by one's ISP, a great deal of this material is free to the consumer. Moreover, wherever one has an Internet connection, at work or at home, one can easily access this material. There is no store one has to drive to in order to consume it. And, of course, one is less likely to have one's pseudonym recognized during a visit to an adult chat room than one's face recognized when walking out of the adult bookstore on a busy city street. Thus, the conditions of affordability, accessibility, and anonymity suggest logical explanations based on convenience and security for why sexual content is so popular online.

However, a healthy curiosity about human sexuality does not indicate abnormality. As Cooper explains:

> We have this myth that people go online in an uncontrolled way and cybersex takes over their lives. But those who use the Internet as a recreational tool rather than in a sexual way demonstrate no significant problems. It's like watching *Baywatch* or looking at Victoria's Secret catalogs. (4.6 million, 1999)

Problems arise, of course, when one's interest in cybersex interferes with the rest of one's life, leading to the neglect of one's professional responsibilities and personal relationships, as was the case with the Ohio man.

Recognizing the implications that such behaviors pose to one's professional and personal reputation, Diane Witmer (1997) sought to understand why people would engage in such risky CMC. After all, electronic forums are certainly not secure channels for interacting. Although the Electronic Communications Privacy Act of 1986 makes breaking into someone's account a criminal offense akin to wiretapping, the fact is that most people are more vulnerable to intrusions on their privacy than they may think. For instance, a system's administrator, such as a university's director of computer services, has access to the accounts in a given organization. E-mail messages with potentially embarrassing or inflamatory content ("Our boss is a cheesehead!") can easily be forwarded to any number of recipients with a mere click of the mouse by the original recipient. And certainly, a skillful hacker can break through security measures and access a person's files. Given that anything they say or forward on an electronic platform is stored somewhere and can be recalled and made public, why would people risk making contributions to discussion groups such as alt.sex, alt.sex.bestiality, and alt.sex.bondage?

Interestingly, the results of Witmer's survey found that a majority of respondents perceived that their participation had little bearing on their reputations. In fact, 57.7% said that their privacy was unimportant or extremely unimportant and an additional 25% reported neutral feelings about privacy. As Witmer (1997) notes, "Respondents tended to feel personally and technically secure in their CMC, and felt that they had little or nothing to lose if their activities were discovered by unintended others." Thus, even though a number of cases testify to the negative impact that such participation can have on one's life, this survey's results demonstrate how many people do not perceive the detrimental possibilities until they are made manifest in their lives.

Indeed, further research suggests that people perceive "the other guy" as more likely to be negatively influenced by sexual material. Ven-hwei Lo and Ran Wei (2002) explain this through the **third-person effect hypothesis**. The hypothesis states that people see media messages as having a greater impact on others than on themselves (Davison, 1983). Lo and Wei tested this hypothesis in terms of people's perceptions of online pornography and found, indeed, that most people perceived that it would negatively impact others more than themselves. (Not surprisingly, females in the study reported that they thought men would be more negatively impacted by consuming it than they themselves would be. Even individual males in the study thought that other males were more susceptible to negative impacts than they as individuals would be. Curiously, neither men nor women in the study thought that the effects of pornography would be as severe for females.) Such rationalizing may further explain why people are willing to participate in cybersexual activities.

Mental health professionals have spoken to the need for people to cope with compulsions such as obsessive cybersexual behaviors. The first step, as with any problem, is to recognize that one has a dependency on the Internet. Once this basic premise is acknowledged, one can begin to explore the underlying problems that have led to the addiction. Thereafter, one can construct and enact a plan to cope, rather than escape, from the addiction (Ferris, 1997). Young (1998b) points out that one need not go "cold turkey" to overcome Internet addiction. The Internet is, after all, a useful tool, and one should learn to use it wisely, not recklessly. The key to healthy Internet use, as seemingly with all things in life, is moderation.

> **Ethical Inquiry**
> Recent popular sentiment holds that you can do whatever you want until or unless you are caught. Certainly, we may wonder whether many Internet users would hold such carefree attitudes about their online sexual activity if those behaviors were announced at their workplaces, their Thanksgiving dinner tables, or their places of worship. Such cavalier attitudes suggest that moral boundaries are fluid, achieving definition only when individual behavior is scrutized by society. Are the moral boundaries long observed in real life justifiably more open online? How would you argue for observing or loosening moral guidelines for people, such as those used in sexual behavior, when going online?

Is IAD Real?

Cases of people whose lives have been negatively affected by the presence of the Internet—including the Carnegie Mellon and Stanford studies—can serve as evidence for why society should be aware of IAD. However, a study by the UCLA Center for Communication Policy contradicts these conclusions.

> According to respondents' reports, concerns that the Internet reduces household time together appear to be nearly groundless. Nearly all users (91.8 percent) say that since being connected to the Internet at home, members of the household spend about the same amount of time together or more time together. (Cole et al., 2000, p. 29)

Given that the medium itself might not be inherently capable of inducing a disorder, we might ask if problematic behaviors are indicative of a bona fide mental disorder or merely instances where people with bigger problems found an outlet or excuse through the Internet? Some critics have stepped forward to question the validity of claims suggesting IAD as a distinct affliction. For one, Sherry Turkle notes, "Compters and communication networks are not drugs...X amount of heroin use is never a good thing; this same amount of Internet activity can be helpful or a hurtful thing, depending on the content of the messages and the role of the activity in the life of the person doing it" (quoted in Rheingold, n.d.).

Joseph Walther and Larry Reid (2000) also point out the scant amount of research that supports the notion that these cases are indicative of a psychological disorder. They would like to see more scrutiny of people's activities on the Internet. The presumption that seems to support a number of the present arguments "is that offline activities are better—healthier, or more natural—than online behavior, but we haven't examined whether that is so" (p. B4). Also, at present no evidence exists that people engaged in compulsive online behaviors would not engage in the same activities offline. Moreover, the increased amounts of time people seem to spend online may not necessarily stem from an addiction as much as a characteristic of the medium. Because most people type much more slowly than they can talk, a conversation that takes 1 hour offline could run 4 hours online.

Walther and Reid (2000) also note that research exists to suggest that spending increased amounts of time online is nothing unusual for participants to experience and is not necessarily indicative of an addiction. Scholars have studied how chat room participants seem to go through phases during their online tenure. A participant's initial exploration is typically followed by "obsessive enchantment," but that in turn is followed by a disillusionment phase and decreased usage thereafter. "Rather than ongoing addiction," it seems that this period of enchantment "represents a stage of intense usage of the Internet as the individual comes to terms with what appears to be an alternative reality, and integrates the...experience into their lives" (Roberts, Smith, & Pollock, 1996).

Another objection asserts that "addiction" may be simply too strong a term to apply to this phenomenon. Some have suggested categorizing IAD as an impulse control disorder rather than an addiction, as it lacks the physical withdrawal symptoms associated with chemical addiction (Beard & Wolf, 2001). Indeed, critics contend that many of the subtypes of IAD are not disorders unique to the Internet—including cybersexual addiction, cyberrelationship addiction, and net compulsions—and that many of these are made manifest offline in real-life gambling, shopping, and stock trading (Griffiths, 2000b). Because people can become compulsive about these activities in real life, they simply seem to migrate online rather than being prompted by the technology itself. Yet, that a simple semantics change would satisfy critics seems doubtful.

Other critics have argued that attention focused on addictive behaviors is exaggerated. Maia Szalavitz (1999), who has experienced substance addictions in the past, is

HYPERLINK: COMPUTER-ASSISTED THERAPY PROGRAMS

As you know from your experience with various software packages, computer programs can be highly interactive tools. You may have experience turning to Quicken to order your finances, to GroupWise to consult your daily calendar, and to the latest version of *Final Fantasy* for entertainment. But would you turn to your computer for mental health advice?

Engineer Joseph Weizenbaum (1976) stressed that computer programs were good for a number of tasks, but he did not advocate that they be used for human counseling. In order to make his point, he wrote ELIZA, a program that could recognize and respond to natural language. An exchange with ELIZA could go something like this:

User:	Men are all alike.
ELIZA:	IN WHAT WAY
User:	They're always bugging us about something or other.
ELIZA:	CAN YOU THINK OF A SPECIFIC EXAMPLE
User:	Well, my boyfriend made me come here.
ELIZA:	YOUR BOYFRIEND MADE YOU COME HERE
User:	He says I'm depressed much of the time.
ELIZA:	I AM SORRY TO HEAR YOU ARE DEPRESSED. (p. 3)

Counter to Weizenbaum's intent, ELIZA turned out to be the first in a generation of computer-assisted therapy (CAT) programs. Today, there are programs available to help people deal with depression, dilemma, and lifestyle problems. Although Weizenbaum intended to use ELIZA as a demonstration of the limits of the computer's ability to interact successfully with people, many responded favorably to the program (Mainville & Valerius, 1999). His collaborator, Kenneth Colby, a psychiatrist, contended that ELIZA's positive reception rested in the fact that a human being had written the original codes that ELIZA used and thus the program still conveyed a human ethos (Turkle, 1995). Nonetheless, Weizenbaum argued that successful psychotherapy depended on the relationship between the patient and the therapist, and many in the psychology field have agreed, viewing ELIZA and her progeny with a suspicious eye.

suspicious of IAD, noting, "People can and do use everything from methamphetamine to mountaineering to avoid doing what they should. If you can't face the world, you'll always find somewhere to hide" (p. 11). Moreover, she wonders if the hype over IAD has been publicized by a bunch of pundits who may well be promoting the disorder in order to lay claim to the profits and notoriety that come along with the media attention.

Such opposition suggests that the introduction of the Internet has caused some discomfort about and suspicion of the technology. A natural reaction to dealing with new technology is to use it as a scapegoat when it appears to be the cause of life's problems. Indeed, history has shown that the introduction of any new communica-tion medium into society has met with some suspicion. Alarmists have objected to the influence of everything from the printed book to the television. Even comic books, despite their conservative avocation of American values, were once accused of con-tributing to juvenile delinquency (Wertham, 1954). With the widespread influence of the Internet in recent years, Jim Clark, founder of Netscape, reminds us that all new media are attacked as something dangerous at first (cited in Doyle, 1996). Thus, discussions about IAD, whether or not the disorder itself is real, may well be indica-tive of society's suspicion about this complex new factor being introduced into our lives.

Despite indictments against the Internet's viability as a beneficial communication tool, a number of scholars, and far more practitioners, see personal and social benefits to CMC. In contrast to the view that the Internet is detrimental to personal well-being, the next section examines ways in which people have used the networks of the Electronic Age to promote their mental health through various forms of online therapy.

ONLINE THERAPY

Despite the potential for self-destructive behavior, many people turn to the Internet for support and guidance in coping with life's problems. The American Psychological Association (2000) claims that some 60 million people look to the 15,000 available sites to find health-related information on the Internet. Among these sources are sites such as HelpHorizons.com, which allows visitors to chat with a licensed professional or search for a counselor who seems to match their particular interest. Others function as clearing houses for therapists, such as the site for the International Society for Mental Health Online (ismho.org) and Metanoia.org. These sites, and many other reputable ones, offer a mental health alternative to those who might not otherwise seek or have access to such services.

Several studies have demonstrated the possible mental health benefits that people can gain through the use of CMC. For example, in a study of senior citizens, Jasmin McConatha found that after 6 months of Internet use, the participants in the study improved their scores on the Geriatric Depression Scale by 14% (Sorenson, 1997). On the other end of the age spectrum, a separate study found that severely disturbed ado-lescents were more comfortable expressing their thoughts and feelings in computer-mediated rather than face-to-face settings (Zimmerman, 1987). Such findings suggest that mental health can benefit from the presence of mediating technologies in peo-ple's lives. In fact, research has shown that people actively seek out online interaction to improve their psychological well-being. In this section, we review some of that research, tracing the emergence of online therapy, its methods of support, and its potential shortfalls.

Coming to Online Therapy

Many people who go online in search of help are searching for some kind of **therapy**. To mental health professionals, therapy is "a series of contacts between a profession-ally trained person and someone seeking help for problems that interfere with his or her emotional well-being" (Binik, Cantor, Ochs, & Meana, 1997, pp. 71–72). Thus, tra-ditional therapy consists of a meeting between a trained therapist and a client or group of clients. In recent years, a precedent for more distant contact has been established by so-called "self-help" books and cassette tapes that purport to provide the same content that a therapy session would. However, such products clearly lack the vital relationship between therapist and client that many mental health professionals would insist is crucial to the process. Because this connection is perceived as fundamental to the success of any treatment program, a common concern is expressed among scholars considering the implications of online therapy. Even those who celebrate the potential benefits of online therapy note that it should function as a complement to, rather than a replacement for, personal interaction with a trained therapist.

Another move away from traditional therapy has emerged in the form of social support groups, also called "self-help groups," such as Alcoholics Anonymous. The key feature of these therapy programs is that people suffering from the same concern provide guidance and support to one another. In this way, they help not only themselves, but one another at the same time (King & Moreggi, 1998). The popularity of this type of therapeutic interaction has gained considerable momentum, and there are now programs to help people coping with other addictions, including gambling and sex, among many others. Estimates place between 8 and 10 million Americans in some sort of face-to-face social support group (Kessler, Mickelson, & Zhao, 1997).

Both forms of nontraditional therapy can be found online. On one hand, a number of psychotherapists offer their services through mediated channels by providing their clients with e-mail, chat, or telephone consultations. On the other hand, **virtual support groups** have been founded on topics ranging from anorexia to cancer to help people who have these conditions communicate with one another. Several factors contribute to the attraction of seeking therapy online.

The first of these factors is *anonymity*. There is, unfortunately, a good deal of social stigma still attached to seeking professional help when it comes to mental health. E-mailing a concern to an online psychologist or visiting an electronic bulletin board discussing a particular concern allows people to seek out the help they may need without exposing themselves to the potential embarrassment that comes with visiting a mental health facility or attending a social support group meeting. Coincidentally, participants in online exchanges have been found to disclose more about their conditions, probably because they do not sense being as readily judged by the recipients of their messages, given the lack of nonverbal cues to indicate disapproval or disappointment. The presence of fewer status cues (such as dress and jewelry) also seems to level the playing field for participants who may be from different socioeconomic groups. For these reasons, online therapy might be especially helpful in treating people who experience apprehension in social settings (King & Moreggi, 1998).

The second attractive quality of online therapy has to do with its ability to *transcend distance*. People who live in rural areas, the physically disabled, and those with no transportation have difficulty getting access to mental health care through traditional means. Thus, forms of online therapy have the potential to reach people who otherwise might not be able to get access to this kind of help. Additionally, the comfort of being able to experience therapy in the security of one's own home was highly rated by participants in one survey (Dublin, Simon, & Orem, 1997).

In the case of virtual support groups, more than one-on-one therapy sessions, a third attractor is the *opportunity to find others* who share one's same concern. Research has shown that many people who frequently participate in these groups come to perceive the network of social support built through them as valuable (Wright,

Table 5.1

Selected Usenet Newsgroups

Newsgroup	Topic
alt.support.depression.seasonal	Seasonal affective disorder
alt.support.schizophrenia	Schizophrenia
alt.support.big-folks	Fat acceptance
alt.abuse.recovery	Abuse recovery
alt.support.eating-disorder	Eating disorders

2000). This seems to be particularly true in cases where real-life support was low (Turner, Grube, & Meyers, 2001). Kristen Mickelson (1997) followed Usenet groups like alt.education.disabled in order to better understand the reasons why parents with mentally challenged children went online. In her research, she found that parents turned to the virtual support groups because they felt misunderstood by traditional support networks like their spouses, parents, and casual friends. They needed to talk with others who were experiencing the same reactions. Finding others who share their experience is particularly relevant for those who suffer an uncommon problem and may not be able to identify and associate with any social support group in their area.

Communicating Support in Online Therapy

People are attracted to online therapy for a number of reasons, then (see Table 5.1 for a sampling of some virtual support groups). These groups offer people both informational support (e.g., links to useful Web sites, experiences of other participants) and emotional support (e.g., messages of comfort or encouragement) (Wright, 2002). Either form of support, though, relies on interpersonal communication. A number of scholarly investigations have examined the kinds of communication that go on in the public setting of virtual support groups. The findings of these studies indicate that the two most common types of communication occurring in virtual support groups are actually statements of support and self-disclosures.

John Miller and Kenneth Gergen (1998) found that the participants in an electronic bulletin board focused on suicide survivors demonstrated a great deal of support for one another. In fact, statements of empathetic understanding were the most frequently used during the 11 months the researchers followed messages. An example statement of this type is, "I really do feel and share your pain. I understand where you are coming from" (p. 196). Such statements were complemented by expressions of gratitude, including the following:

> Thank you for your support. . . . I really appreciate your notes and e-mail. As I've said before, this is the group therapy I've been looking for. One can count on the caring and trust and, most of all, understanding and belief that is found here. (p. 197)

In addition to statements of support, people who posted to the BBS also engaged in frequent self-disclosures. In these statements, participants shared their experiences with the topic. Intimate details and emotional energy were frequently incorporated into such disclosures, which unto themselves have therapeutic value. As other scholars point out, "The energy and time a person takes in the very act of formulating and expressing his or her distress may provide at least some release from tension and

HYPERLINK: ONLINE MEMORIALS AS THERAPEUTIC COMMUNICATION

The impact of the terrorist attacks of September 11, 2001, will endure in the collective memories of a generation, but the losses of that day are felt most deeply by those who knew people on the hijacked planes and in the twin towers of the World Trade Center. In some cases, the bodies of those loved ones were never recovered from the rubble, leaving those who mourned without a traditional burial site to commemorate the life of their friend, coworker, child, parent, or lover. Whether or not they buried their loved one, many of these mournful people have channeled their grief into the creation of online memorials. These sites serve to commemorate the lives of their loved ones in a way that is at once very personal and yet obviously public. The sites often recount intimate details about the victim's life and the effects that the person had on the lives of those around him or her. Yet they are also virtual places for people to gather, for friends, family, and even strangers to record their condolences in a guest book. As one report put it, these sites give the living somewhere to go and remember their departed (Harmon, 2002). With scores of these sites scattered about the web, www.911digitalarchive.org serves as a portal to many of the tributes (Fig. 5.1).

Taking grief online is certainly poignantly portrayed in the aftermath of 9-11 and in the losses experienced by those touched by the AIDS crisis. The AIDS Memorial Quilt is an ever-growing patchwork of tributes to those who have lost their lives to this disease. Although the Memorial Quilt exists in the real world, tens of thousands of its individual panels are accessible online thanks to archiving by the NAMES Project (www.aidsquilt.org). One can view these panels and either read or leave messages associated with the project at the site as well.

Online memorials offer mourners an opportunity to express their grief and for visitors to participate in ceremonial tribute to the departed. Andrew Wood and Tyrone Adams (1998) note that these sites are reminiscent of old-time quilting bees, where a number of quilters would gather to create ornate projects, each individual sewer contributing a small piece to the larger design. Historical quilts have often depicted subjects of interest to particular communities, and online memorials seem to do this as well, particularly in the cases of the 9-11 and AIDS tragedies. Among the results of this modern version of quilting, Wood and Adams count the creation of a community of caring and a sense of safety fostered by "a miniature world of connections and hidden spaces—to be seen or to hide" (p. 227). Online memorials thus have the potential to function both as monument, albeit an electronic one rather than one of granite or marble, and as wake, a gathering to commemorate and to comfort through acts of communication.

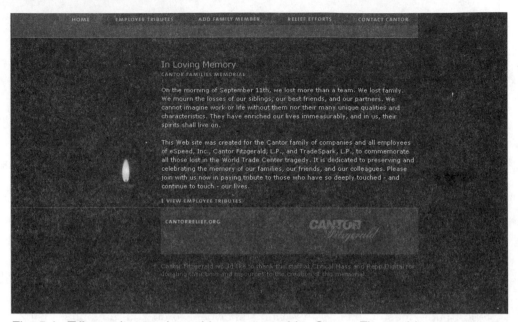

Fig. 5.1. Tribute sites such as this one posted by Cantor Fitzgerald commemorate the victims of September 11, 2001.

anxiety" (Binik, Cantor, Ochs, & Meana, 1997, p. 89). Given these qualities, virtual support groups seem to assist people in coping with their problems, but as J. Miller and Gergen (1998) point out, they may be less successful in helping people move beyond their problems. In their review of messages, they found very few statements directed at growth or transformation. In traditional therapy, the therapist might suggest alternative interpretations of events or offer new plans of action for the client to adopt. In the substantial lack of such suggestions, Miller and Gergen indicate one limitation of online therapy, although other scholars have suggested more.

Shortfalls in Online Therapy

In addition to the shortfalls in helping people grow beyond the problems cited by Miller and Gergen, several other criticisms have been issued by concerned professionals. In particular, Jay Lebow (1998) worries that virtual support groups might make some conditions worse rather than better:

> Take, for example, ideas about helplessness in relation to depression. Learned helplessness is often integral to depression, and most therapy for depression today is aimed in some way at reducing the client's sense of helplessness. What happens when people with the same difficulty merely share their feelings? Might one person's helplessness reinforce another's? (p. 204)

Other critics have objected to the very premise that effective therapy can occur online. These observers worry that the lack of nonverbal cues diminishes a therapist's ability to read and ultimately relate to a client. As such, they harbor doubts about the ethics of some commercial, Internet-based therapists (Hamilton, 1999; Nakazawa, 1999).

Despite these objections, people are still turning to online therapists and virtual support groups for aid. Given that trend, perhaps a practical warning is more imperative for those who elect to seek help in the forums. People who use the Internet for therapy should be cautious consumers of the information and advice they receive. According to the Pew Internet & American Life Project, as many as 55% of Americans with Internet access have looked for medical information online (Fox et al., 2000). Although many reputable agencies and practitioners post authentic information, there is always the possibility that inaccurate information can be downloaded. The BBSs used by many virtual support groups seem to be especially vulnerable to misinformation, given that someone with inaccurate or even harmful information could post a message to the board just as easily as anyone else. Even a well-meaning poster could communicate some erroneous facts. For these reasons, Irene McDermott (1998) warns that one can use newsgroups for expressing frustration, asking questions, or offering support, but one should never rely on them as sources of factual information without confirming that information with a doctor. Clearly, even in times of pain, grief, and suffering, we must still be critical consumers of information. McDermott's remedy is readily agreed on by many health care professionals: Online therapy works best when used as a complement to professionally supervised care.

The American Psychological Association (2000) echoes McDermott's call for caution. In an online pamphlet, they have advised potential clients to be aware of the distinct challenges presented by searching for advice online. Among their suggestions, they warn people to:

- Guard your privacy—Consumers should look for a privacy policy statement on any Web site that asks you to disclose personal information. When consulting a BBS or chat room, you should consider using a pseudonym. In any forum, you should be careful about what you disclose, as anything offered online may be forwarded, collected by a database, or otherwise used without your knowledge or express permission.
- Watch for commercial influences—Looking to a site's "About" or even "Investor Information" links could provide information that the site is actually a paid advertisement or unduly influenced by a sponsor. Increasingly pharmaceutical companies are creating sites to market their products in the form of help centers. Information on such sites may lack objectivity because of the profit motive involved in the sponsor's involvement.
- Exercise caution—In order to assess the usefulness of a site, you should check for frequent updates, review the licensing credentials of the author, and get a second opinion whenever information offered in an online forum raises concerns.

These warnings remind us that even though most of the information and services offered online may be offered for our benefit, the ability of some to perpetrate fraud and others to operate unchecked in the medium means that we must approach all information with some degree of suspicion, or as the APA cleverly put it, "dotCOMsense."

Thankfully, recent research indicates that people do view the health-related information available online with some degree of skepticism. In focus group interviews, a group of researchers found that although people were willing to turn to the Internet for health-related information, they retained concerns about their privacy, the credibility of the source, and the accuracy of the information available, all seemingly in-line with the American Psychological Association's warnings (Bernhardt, Lariscy, Parrott, Silk,

& Felter, 2002). Respondents noted that they took information gathered from health-related sites with the proverbial "grain of salt." With increasing efforts to educate the public in media literacy, perhaps even more consumers of online information will express the same healthy skepticism.

CHAPTER SUMMARY

This chapter has examined how CMC plays a role in one's well-being. For some people, the combination of accessibility, convenience, and excitement creates a trap with serious ramifications on their lives. In some cases, the trap is made all the more alluring by the sexual "bait" within. Whether or not the deleterious use of the Internet constitutes a distinct psychological disorder is open to debate, but it is clear that there are negative effects associated with disproportionate use of the Internet. On the other hand, people are also discovering ways to improve their well-being through use of the Internet. Online therapy and virtual support groups evidence positive contributions to the lives of those who might otherwise not receive the advice and recognition that they need. At present, however, experts contend that any use of online therapy works best in conjunction with qualified professional interaction.

ONLINE COMMUNICATION AND THE LAW

One evening in December 1999, aspiring actor Michael Campbell of Cape Coral, Florida, found himself in a chat room, exchanging messages with Erin Walton of Littleton, Colorado. Walton was a survivor of the Columbine High School massacre earlier that year. Campbell, using the pseudonym "Soup81," wrote to Walton, alias "Gingerhrts," warning her not to attend school the following day.

```
   Soup81:  Listen, I can't tell you who I am
            because you know me.... Do me a favor,
            don't go to school tomorrow.
Gingerhrts:  Why?
   Soup81:  Please, I trust in you and confide in
            you.
Gingerhrts:  I have to go. I can't miss school.
   Soup81:  I need to finish what begun and if you
            go I don't want blood on your hands.
Gingerhrts:  Please don't do this. You are really
            scaring me.
   Soup81:  There is nothing to be scared about,
            just don't go to school and don't tell
            anyone. If anyone finds out, you'll be
            the first to go.
```

Horrified by the exchange, Walton reported the threat to Columbine's principal and the authorities. Columbine closed its door 2 days early for the winter break, Walton decided to switch schools after this incident, and the FBI tracked Soup81 back to Campbell. They arrested him for making a threat across state lines.

Campbell would later profess regret for the seriousness with which Walton reacted to his statements but maintained that he had never intended to hurt anyone. Rather, he claimed to be caught up in the role he perceived himself as playing within the chat room. His lawyer, Ellis Rubin, subsequently attempted to capitalize on this notion, offering a defense of "Internet addiction" on his client's behalf (Janofsky, 2000).

Although Campbell later changed his plea to guilty, the attempt to displace responsibility for his statements using addiction to the Internet as an excuse was a legal first. As with other instances discussed in this chapter, Campbell's case is another example of how people can jeopardize everything, from their jobs, their families, and their health to the well-being of others, and blame it on too much use of the Internet. Whether or not Campbell's criminal actions can be attributed, at least in part, to the communication context rather than solely his own poor judgment is certainly an issue for debate.

Glossary

ACE model: A theoretical explanation for the allure of the Internet that suggests that the qualities of accessibility, control, and excitement lead to IAD.

Computer-assisted therapy (CAT) programs: Software that provides an interactive, conversational experience with alleged mental health benefits (e.g., ELIZA).

Cybersex: Textual descriptions of sexual behavior exchanged between two partners in an online encounter.

Internet addiction disorder (IAD): A psychological condition associated with Internet use that leads to adverse effects on one's psychological, physical, or social well-being.

Therapy: Traditionally, a series of contacts between a trained professional and a client seeking emotional well-being; also broadly taken to include similar interactions with a group of people.

Third-person effect hypothesis: A theory that suggests that individuals perceive mass mediated messages as having greater effects on other people than on themselves

Tolerance: The condition of being able to endure the effects of a stimulus; in particular, being able to endure increasing amounts of exposure to the Internet with decreasing effect or satisfaction.

Virtual support group: A type of social support group that meets online and provides participants the opportunity to give and receive positive feedback to and from one another.

Withdrawal: The moving back from a stimulus that typically results in adverse mental or physical effects.

Topics for Discussion

1. The individuals involved in this chapter's first anecdote (Shawn Wooley) and its final one (Michael Campbell) were claimed to be "under the influence" of the Internet when they did the things that they did. Write a paragraph in which you analyze these defenses from the perspective of those who believe that IAD

is a legitimate disorder. Then write a second paragraph about these cases from the perspective of those who say that IAD is not a disorder. Which side do you believe offers a more credible explanation?

2. Reflecting on the material covered in the Hyperlink "Obscenity in Cyberspace," what role would you prescribe for government intervention in the future of the Internet? Adopt a position in which you call for either national regulation or limited/no regulation of content. In your response, consider how you will answer critics from the other extreme.

3. The results of Witmer's research on risky CMC suggest that people hold a perception that it is harmless to engage in disreputable behavior. Is this symptomatic of a larger social belief that it is okay to do anything unless you get caught? Write a response in which you provide three reasons supporting the majority's position in that study or three reasons the people should reconsider their position.

4. Visit a Usenet newsgroup focused on a particular ailment and read through several dozen postings. In what ways can you see a virtual support group functioning on this electronic bulletin board? In your response, record examples of supportive and self-disclosive statements. How do you think these statements may have helped or hindered the well-being of visitors to the BBS?

5. McDermott, among others, advises users to be wary of the factual information they find about medical conditions online. Why is this a wise recommendation? In your response, recall a situation in which you received allegedly factual information (online or in real life) that proved to be untrue. How can people avoid falling prey to misleading information?

REFERENCES

American Psychological Association. (2000). *Dotcomsense: Common sense ways to protect your privacy and assess online mental health information.* Available: http://helping.apa.org/dotcomsense/[July 14, 2003].

Beard, K. W., & Wolf, E. M. (2001). Modification in the proposed diagnostic criteria for internet addiction. *CyberPsychology & Behavior, 4*, 377–383.

Bernhardt, J. M., Lariscy, R. A. W., Parrott, R. L., Silk, K. J., & Felter, E. M. (2002). Perceived barriers to internet-based health communication on human genetics. *Journal of Health Communication, 7*, 325–340.

Bilstad, B. T., & Godward, C. (1996, September). Obscenity and indecency on the Usenet: The legal and political future of alt.sex.stories. *Journal of Computer-Mediated Communication, 2*. Retrieved February 29, 2000, from http://www.ascusc.org/jcmc/vol2/issue2/bilstad.html

Binik, Y. M., Cantor, J., Ochs, E., & Meana, M. (1997). From the couch to the keyboard: Psychotherapy in cyberspace. In S. Kiesler (Ed.), *Culture of the Internet* (pp. 71–100). Mahwah, NJ: Lawrence Erlbaum Associates.

Birsch, D. (1996, January). Sexually explicit materials and the Internet. *CMC Magazine.* Retrieved February 29, 2000, from http://www.december.com/cmc/mag/1996/jan/birsem.html

Bricking, T. (1997, June 16). Internet blamed for neglect. *The Cincinnati Enquirer.* Retrieved February 29, 2000, from http://enquirer.com/editions/1997/06/16/loc_hacker.html

Cole, J. I., Suman, M., Schramm, P., van Bel, D., Lunn, B., Maguire, P., Hanson, K., Singh, R., Aquino, J., & Lebo, H. (2000). *The UCLA Internet report: Surveying the digital future.* Retrieved November 1, 2000, from http://www.ccp.ucla.edu/newsite/pages/internet-report.asp

Davison, W. P. (1983). The third-person effect in communication. *Public Opinion Quarterly, 47,* 1–13.

Donn, J. (1999, August 23). Can't resist the online pull. *ABC News.* Retrieved February 29, 2000, from http://www.abcnews.go.com/sections/tech/DailyNews/netaddiction990823.html

Doyle, M. W. (Producer). (1996). *Cyberspace: Virtual unreality?* [Videocassette]. Princeton, NJ: Films for the Humanities and Sciences.

Dublin, J., Simon, V., & Orem, J. (1997). *Analysis of survey results.* Paper presented to New York University School of Social Work, New York.

Elias, M. (2002, February 25). Cybersex follows Mars, Venus patterns. *USA Today,* p. 9D.

Ferris, J. R. (1997). *Internet addiction disorders: Causes, symptoms, and consequences.* Retrieved February 29, 2000, from http://www.chem.vt.edu/chemdept/dessy/honors/papers/ferris.html

Fiely, D. (1999, February 28). Web junkie. *The Columbus Dispatch,* pp. 1G–2G.

4.6 million could become addicted, cybersex study says. (1999, April 14). *San Francisco Examiner.* Retrieved February 29, 2000, from http://dispatches.azstarnet.com/joe/1999/cybersex.htm

Fox, S., Rainie, L., Horrigan, J., Lenhart, A., Spooner, T., Burke, M., Lewis, O., & Carter, C. (2000). *The online heath care revolution: How the web helps Americans take better care of themselves.* Washington, DC: Pew Internet & American Life Project. Retrieved July 15, 2003, from http://pewinternet/reports/toc.asp?Report=26

Griffiths, M. (2000a). Does internet and computer "addiction" exist? Some case study evidence. *CyberPsychology & Behavior, 3,* 211–218.

Griffiths, M. (2000b). Internet addiction—Time to be taken seriously? *Addiction Research, 8,* 413–418.

Hamilton, A. (1999, May 24). On the virtual couch. *Time, 153,* 71.

Harmon, A. (2002, September 11). Real solace in a virtual world: Memorials take root on the web. *The New York Times,* p. 39.

Janofsky, M. (2000, January 13). Defense sites an addiction to the Internet in threat case. *The New York Times on the Web.* Retrieved February 29, 2000, from http://www.nytimes.com/library/tech/00/01/biztech/articles/13colo-school-threat.html

Kelleher, K. (2002, September 30). Internet draws the prying eyes of the voyeur. *Los Angeles Times,* p. E2.

Kessler, R. C., Mickelson, K. D., & Zhao, S. (1997). Patterns and correlates of self-help group membership in the United States. *Social Policy, 27*(3), 27–47.

King, S. A., & Moreggi, D. (1998). Internet therapy and self-help groups—The pros and cons. In J. Gackenbach (Ed.), *Psychology and the Internet: Intrapersonal, interpersonal, and transpersonal implications* (pp. 77–109). San Diego, CA: Academic Press.

Kraut, R., Patterson, M., Lundmark, V., Kiesler, S., Mukopadhyay, T., & Scherlis, W. (1998). Internet paradox: A social technology that reduces social involvement and psychological well-being? *American Psychologist, 53,* 1017–1031.

Lebow, J. (1998). Not just talk, maybe some risk: The therapeutic potentials and pitfalls of computer-mediated conversation. *Journal of Marital & Family Therapy, 24*, 203–207.

Lo, V., & Wei, R. (2002). Third-person effect, gender, and pornography on the Internet. *Journal of Broadcasting & Electronic Media, 46*, 13–33.

Mainville, S., & Valerius, L. (1999, May). Nothing but Net: Therapeutic recreation and the web. *Parks & Recreation, 34*, 86–93.

McDermott, I. E. (1998, June). Informed consent: Disease and ailment information on the Web. *Searcher, 6*, 50–55.

Mickelson, K. D. (1997). Seeking social support: Parents in electronic support groups. In S. Kiesler (Ed.), *Culture of the Internet* (pp. 157–178). Mahwah, NJ: Lawrence Erlbaum Associates.

Miller, J. K., & Gergen, K. J. (1998). Life on the line: The therapeutic potentials of computer-mediated conversation. *Journal of Marital & Family Therapy, 24*, 189–202.

Miller, S. A., II (2002, March 30). Death of a game addict: Ill Hudson man took own life after long hours on web. *Milwaukee Journal Sentinel Online.* Retrieved July 14, 2003, from http://www.jsonline.com/news/state/mar02/31536.asp

Nakazawa, L. (1999). Virtual therapy. *Psychology Today, 32*(2), 11.

O'Toole, K. (2000, February 16). *Study offers early look at how Internet is changing daily life* [Press release]. Stanford Institute for the Quantitative Study of Society. Available: http://www.stanford.edu/group/siqss/Press_Release/press_release.html

Patrizio, A. (2002, April 3). Did game play role in suicide? *Wired.* Retrieved July 14, 2003, from http://www.wired.com/news/games/0,2102,51490,00.html

Rheingold, H. (1993). *The virtual community: Homesteading on the electronic frontier.* New York: HarperPerrenial.

Rheingold, H. (n.d.). *Mind to mind with Sherry Turkle. Brainstorms.* Retrieved July 2, 2003, from http://www.well.com/user/hlr/texts/mindtomind/turkle.html

Roberts, L. D., Smith, L. M., & Pollock, C. (1996, September). *A model of social interaction via computer-mediated communication in real-time text-based virtual environments.* Paper presented at the annual meeting of the Australian Psychological Society, Sydney.

Sorenson, J. (1997). *Seniors in cyberspace.* Retrieved February 29, 2000, from http://192.211.16.13/individuals/sorensoj.home.htm

Stanford Institute for the Quantitative Study of Society. (2000). *SIQSS Internet study.* Retrieved February 29, 2000, from http://www.stanford.edu/group/siqss/Press_Release/Internet Study.html

Szalavitz, M. (1999, December 6). Can we become caught in the Web? *Newsweek, 134*, 11.

Turkle, S. (1995). *Life on the screen: Identity in the age of the internet.* New York: Simon & Shuster.

Turner, J. W., Grube, J. A., & Meyers, J. (2001). Developing an optimal match within online communities: An exploration of CMC support communities and traditional support. *Journal of Communication, 51*, 231–251.

Walther, J. B., & Reid, L. D. (2000, February 4). Understanding the allure of the Internet. *Chronicle of Higher Education, 46*, B4–B5.

Weizenbaum, J. (1976). *Computer power and human reason: From judgment to calculation.* San Francisco: Freeman.

Wertham, F. (1954). *Seduction of the innocent.* New York: Rinehart.

Whang, L. S., Lee, S., & Chang, G. (2003). Internet over-users' psychological profiles: A behavior sampling analysis on internet addiction. *CyberPsychology & Behavior, 6,* 143–150.

Witmer, D. F. (1997, March). Risky business: Why people feel safe in sexually explicit on-line communication. *Journal of Computer-Mediated Communication, 2.* Retrieved February 29, 2000, from http://www.ascusc.org/jcmc/vol2/issue4/witmer2.html

Wood, A. F., & Adams, T. L. (1998). Embracing the machine: quilt and quilting as community-building architecture. In B. Ebo (Ed.), *Cyberghetto or cyberutopia? Race, class, and gender on the internet,* pp. 219–223. Westport, CT: Praeger.

Wright, K. (2000). Computer-mediated social support, older adults, and coping. *Journal of Communication, 50,* 100–118.

Wright, K. (2002). Social support within an on-line cancer community: An assessment of emotional support, perceptions of advantages and disadvantages, and motives for using the community from a communication perspective. *Journal of Applied Communication Research, 30,* 195–209.

Young. K. S. (1998a). *Caught in the net: How to recognize the signs of internet addiction and a winning strategy for recovery.* New York: Wiley.

Young, K. S. (1998b). *The Center for Online Addiction* [Online]. Available: http://www.netaddiction.com/

Zimmerman, D. P. (1987). A psychological comparison of computer-mediated and face-to-face language use among severely disturbed adolescents. *Adolescence, 22,* 827–840.

CHAPTER 6

COMMUNICATING IN VIRTUAL COMMUNITIES

> *Without a sense of caring, there can be no sense of community.*
> —Anthony J. D'Angelo

Once upon a time, when people spent their evenings chatting on their front porches, folks knew what made a community. The romanticized community consisted of tree-lined roads like "Main Street," buildings like "McNamara's Drug Store," and, most importantly, people like your next-door neighbors, the "Daileys."

In more recent times, chatting is still a popular pastime, but many people's conception of what makes a community has changed. A community might now consist of a data-laden Information Superhighway, pharmaceutical advice is dispensed on an electronic bulletin board, and the neighbor you feel closest to could be half a world away in Australia.

Despite the distances that can separate them, people have an intrinsic need for community. Consider the invention of the Walt Disney Company's idealized community of Celebration in central Florida or a film such as 1998's *Pleasant-ville*. Both of these nostalgic re-creations are reminiscent of a simpler time, when community was easier to define. Yet the introduction of computer-mediating technologies has challenged many of the concepts and definitions people have long taken for granted, including that of community. As such, people who use CMC technologies and people who study them are aware that the Internet fosters relationships not just between two individuals, but among many, many more people.

The desire for community seems to be particularly relevant in recent years, as civic engagement has been on the wane. In *Bowling Alone: The Collapse and Revival of American Community*, Robert D. Putnam (2000) outlined how over the last third of a century people living in the United States have grown less likely to participate in civic organizations like service groups, churches, and bowling leagues. This shift away from the more substantial amounts of participation just a generation earlier can be explained in part by urban sprawl (people are moving farther and farther away from their communities) and in part by television's privatization of leisure time, as well as other factors. In sum, it leads to a climate where people feel detached from their geographic communities and leaves them searching for a sense of belonging in other forums.

DEFINING VIRTUAL COMMUNITIES

Take, for example, the community of common interest that has emerged at the online auction site eBay (www.ebay.com). Whereas other dotcoms have risen and fallen in recent years, eBay has proven to be one of the true commercial successes of the Internet age, helping tens of millions of users trade everything from new car parts to rare antique collectibles. According to Josh Boyd (2002), a large part of eBay's success has been built on the way it has employed community as a metaphor for building and sustaining trust among those participating in the auctions. This is no small feat, considering the range of threats posed against that trust. Even if we discount instances of outright fraud and the sale of counterfeit merchandise, eBay buyers still have to overcome the obvious hurdle of committing to purchase an item that they cannot inspect in person. Rather, they must rely on the fact that the seller is disclosing honest information about the merchandise's condition.

Boyd explains that a number of factors help to reinforce eBay's ideal of community to counteract buyer misgivings. Among these he counts the use of feedback forms to influence one another. When a sale has been completed through eBay, both seller and buyer are invited to comment on one another. These comments then become an ongoing part of the individuals' profiles on the site. If a seller or buyer has received a good deal of negative feedback (for doing things like not honoring a bid or hocking damaged merchandise), then others may be wary of entering into a transaction with this individual. It's important to note here that it's not eBay assigning value to participants' conduct, but participants bearing reciprocal influence on one another. Presumably, then, good behavior is rewarded and bad behavior is punished through such collective actions.

Of course, beyond the mutual influence that people have on one another in this forum, eBay also demonstrates one of the key draws of online communities: mutual interest. Whether it is the movie poster collector in Iowa and her buyer in Idaho or the quilter in Maine and his buyer in Mississippi, persons who might never have met face-to-face can connect with one another and interact online. That the motivation for their interaction is commercial would seem to make it no less of an authentic reason for community to emerge. As Boyd (2002) explains, "This commercial orientation is not peculiar to eBay, however. Other 'communities' have been commercially grounded as well; even the quintessential American community, the small town, typically has a commercial district at its center." Indeed, commerce is but one of the factors that draws people to virtual communities.

Communities of common interest, such as that observed in the milieu of eBay, are examples of how CMC interaction questions the assumption that a community is geographically bound and that the people who share a community must interact face-to-face. After all, the relationships among participants in eBay's community of commerce exist solely in cyberspace, and for the vast majority their association is begun and sustained without the benefit of any face-to-face initial meetings. Unlike cities in Idaho or Maine, their community is not a physical place you can pack up your belongings and move to. eBay, like many other communities we discuss in this chapter, exists not as a physical presence but as a shared understanding of interrelatedness among its participants.

These communal constructs have become popularly known as **virtual communities**. In *The Virtual Community: Homesteading on the Electronic Frontier*, Howard

Rheingold (1993) introduced his often-quoted definition of this phenomenon: "Virtual communities are social aggregations that emerge from the Net when enough people carry on those public discussions long enough, with sufficient human feeling, to form webs of personal relationship in cyberspace" (p. 5). Note that Rheingold's definition does not account for the need for structures or the proximity of participants to one another or even the necessity for face-to-face interaction, all features long associated with traditional communities. Instead, his definition asserts that community is based in ongoing communication.

Unlike many traditional communities, virtual communities are not bound together by economics or the need for mutual protection. Why, then, do people join them? As psychologist William Schutz (1966) explained, all people have a need for inclusion, a desire for the company of others. Virtual communities provide individuals with a means for acquiring that feeling of inclusion, especially among those individuals who seek the company of like-minded people. At the heart of the concept of community, then, is the quality of commonality (Fernback, 1999). After all, you might be the only person in your small town who collects Elvis Presley memorabilia, but there are many such collectors located across the country that you can meet online. Virtual communities thus allow people to transcend geographic boundaries and unite with others who share their common interests, whether that's watching a particular television series, promoting a social cause, or collecting original vinyl recordings of "Love Me Tender."

HYPERLINK: WHAT A *DIvI'*!

One of the many virtual communities that have thrived on the Internet is the one existing among practitioners of the invented language Klingon. Originally developed by linguist Marc Okrand for use in Paramount Pictures' *Star Trek* franchise, Klingon, or HolQeD, as it is called in its own language, became even more popular among fans after Okrand published *The Klingon Dictionary* in 1985. Linguists and other academics interested in this phenomenon formed the Klingon Language Institute (KLI) to study it in 1992.

Now with members in more than 45 countries, the KLI perpetuates its work through an academic journal (catalogued by the Modern Language Association), its Web site (http://www.kli.org/), and its e-mail discussion group (Shoulson, 2003). KLI serves as a good example of an organization that transcends geographic-bound definitions of community. With members on all seven continents (including Antarctica), it took their common interest to unite them, and it seems evident that CMC is playing a significant role in helping to expand their membership and sustain their mission to share their love of language play with like-minded individuals.

(Oh, and just in case your Klingon is a bit rusty, *DIvI'* translates loosely into "community.")

This chapter explores the concept of the virtual community as a prominent metaphor in both people's experiences with the Internet and within the study of CMC. What follows, then, is an examination of some historical precedents for contemporary virtual communities, the common features they share, the ways in which members are regulated through norms, and some objections to the viability of the virtual communities themselves.

PRECEDENTS FOR VIRTUAL COMMUNITIES

Although the Internet represents the latest medium to facilitate the construction of community, it is certainly not the first. Benedict Anderson (1983) supposes that newspapers were an earlier medium used to help establish what he termed **imagined communities**. Anderson explains that, like virtual communities, imagined communities emerged because of the intervention of mediated communication. As he elaborates, the national identity that led the British colonies to form the United States was due, in part, to the communication fostered by colonial newspapers. Given the strength of the union today, it is hard to imagine the differences that separated the colonies in the 18th century, but the differences among the 13 separate colonies made unity a problem that had to be addressed if any of them were to free themselves from British rule. The newspapers, with their messages of uniting against a common foe, helped create an imagined community of Americans and fostered ideals that could be adopted by people living in such geographically disparate places as Maine or Georgia. Today, we recognize this once-imagined community as a nation, and newspapers—such as *USA Today*—continue to serve as a medium for uniting an even more geographically dispersed population by fostering a common identity among them.

Another example of media's ability to unite people in communal bonds can be found in the early 20th century, when print media gave rise to other imagined communities whose participants used self-publication and networking innovations to come together. Fan magazines, which eventually became known as *fanzines* and then simply as **zines**, were at the root of modern-day fan cultures. Beginning with the printing of the first fan letter to the editor in a 1926 edition of the science fiction magazine *Amazing Stories*, publications have served as vehicles for fans to build "communities based upon the exchange of ideas and recounting of events instead of immediately shared experience and pressing of the flesh" (Moskowitz, 1994, p. 27). In following the precedent established by *Amazing Stories*, fans began to self-publish their commentaries and original works in their own homespun periodicals. Historically, zines have had small press runs, limiting the number of fellow fans one could reach. However, fans attempted to improve the diffusion of their publications by establishing networks called amateur press associations (**apas**). In an apa, one member receives and then redistributes a collection of fanzines to each contributing member across the country (Bosky, 1994). The continuation and variety of apas over the years, covering everything from monster movies to soap operas, testified to their ability to unite and sustain another breed of imagined community. Once again, a participant's sense of belonging to such a community was based on mediated communication and not immediate interaction.

Certainly, the emergence of community on the Internet goes hand in hand with the development of the medium itself. As discussed earlier in this text, the Internet began as a network of computers linked for military communication but increasingly used

In chapter 3, we presented a Hyperlink about a "virtual rape" committed by a lewd character named Mr. Bungles. However, when we were discussing that incident and the meaningful impact it had on a number of people, we only told you half the story. Julian Dibbell's (1993) ethnography of the MUD known as LambdaMOO tells an interesting tale not only of how individuals are affected by online communication but also of how societies are formed through their interactions.

According to Dibbell's account, after Mr. Bungles had used a "voodoo doll" program to force a number of characters to commit demeaning sexual acts, a number of his victims, several eyewitnesses, and various interested parties who participate in the LambdaMOO forum began to discuss punitive actions against Mr. Bungles. Several people proposed that Mr. Bungles be "toaded" for his actions. In the Dungeons and Dragons forebearers to more contemporary MUDs, a wizard could change a character into a toad, divesting that character's on-screen description of all individual markers and replacing them with those of a common toad (green complexion, warts, etc.). In LambdaMOO and other MUDs, toading had evolved into a process that resulted in the characters being barred from entering the database and thus being forbidden from participating henceforth in the online discussion. Some participants perceived this to be the equivalent of banishment from the tribe, whereas others contended that it was so severe that it could be likened to a death sentence.

Dibbell recounted how participants of various opinions and various political persuasions first exchanged bulletin board messages and then met in a LambdaMOO chat room to decide what kind of action should be taken. Amidst these debates, no clear consensus emerged as to what punishment Mr. Bungles should suffer or, perhaps more importantly, how that punishment should be decided. Some argued that it was time for LambdaMOO to develop a judicial system to hear and try cases such as this. Others suggested that the wizards, those master programmers who had originally written the codes to create the MUD, should take a more active role in policing their creation. Still others, including, interestingly enough, Mr. Bungles himself, said that no action at all should be taken.

Ultimately, Mr. Bungles' fate was unilaterally decided by a lone wizard named JoeFeedback, who toaded Mr. Bungles right out of the system. But that's not the end of the story, for when the founder of LambaMOO, another wizard, named Haakon, discovered the whole messy affair, he decreed that a system of petitions and voting be put in place to handle any future sanctions against objectionable behavior.

The Mr. Bungles incident served as a catalyst to hasten LambdaMOO's development as a community. Although it clearly was possible for LambdaMOO to function without formalized social rules until this incident, it became clear that an "anything goes" attitude wasn't going to work as increasing numbers of participants demanded a reprisal for Mr. Bungles' behavior. Sustaining bonds that unite people, that make a community, seem to call for some amount of formal regulation.

by academics to share research information. Although much of the early messaging was carried out in a one-to-one fashion, much like an individual sending a postcard to a colleague, eventually the number of channels expanded to include the one-to-many communication of BBSs. Your campus is likely to have any number of bulletin boards filled with flyers posted by various people trying to get rides home, to sell old computers, or to encourage you to attend a campus event such as a speaker or club meeting. Anyone can read such messages and get a sense of what is going on in the campus community. In like manner, the sharing of these messages electronically among the early research scientists helped to foster the sense that these contributors were a part of some communal experience. As different discussion groups began to break off and form new bulletin boards around specific areas of interest, new communities arose.

Finally, initiatives like the Freenets have continued to increase both the diversity of and access to virtual communities. The Freenet, introduced by Case Western Reserve University in the mid-1980s, originally provided people living in the Cleveland area with free access to an interactive computer system. Its successors in the metropolitan and rural areas of more than 40 states offer bulletin boards for messages of local interest (such as the city schools) and e-mail for messaging capabilities to the rest of the world. In many ways Freenets are like other Internet service providers (ISPs) such as AOL and Earthlink, but they offer their services for free so that people who cannot afford the cost of commercial ISPs can participate online. With thousands of subscribers, Freenets offer people the opportunity to better connect to the community in which they reside and to discover a community beyond that of their immediate face-to-face experience.

QUALITIES OF VIRTUAL COMMUNITIES: WHAT MAKES A COMMUNITY?

Being part of a virtual community means more than merely having a group of people communicating online. Even in the tangible world, it is understood that the quality of community takes more than mere presence. Consider sharing a crowded elevator with a group of strangers. Although everyone onboard shares a common experience in a common space, few would label this assembly a community. Elevator rides are all too brief and all too impersonal. (In fact, the norms of American culture dictate that passengers do not look at one another and rarely speak in an elevator.) What, then, makes a group of people into a community?

At the heart of it, community is based on a sense of belonging. Individuals rarely feel as if they belong with a group of strangers on an elevator in the same way that they belong with their classmates in school or with their coworkers on the job. The German social theorist, Ferdinand Tönnies (1957), makes this distinction clear in his classic comparison between society and community. The detached, happenstance gathering of people he called *gesellschaft*, but the sense of belonging, a sense of "we-ness" he called *gemeinschaft*. The distinction is a subtle but important one, for it helps define the virtual communities forming online. Therein, the feeling of belonging to a fellowship reflects the bonds experienced in a state of *gemeinschaft*.

Quentin Jones (1997), writing in the *Journal of Computer-Mediated Communication*, establishes four qualities that he feels characterize these virtual communities.

Interestingly, these qualities could just as easily define a geographically bound community. According to Jones, virtual communities distinguish themselves from a simple online gathering when they feature

(1)   a minimum level of interactivity,
(2)   a variety of communicators,
(3)   common public space, and
(4)   a minimum level of sustained membership.

Let's explore each of these qualities by examining how each might function within a claimed virtual community. We use the example of **webrings**. Webrings form when different people link together a series of sites, each of them typically addressing a shared theme. For instance, there are a Yu-Gi-Oh! WebRing, a Missing Children's WebRing, and an Audrey Hepburn WebRing, to name but a few. Greg Elmer (1999) suggested that webrings could serve as a "grass-roots" approach to building connections online as individual web page creators worked to link themselves together. Webring, Inc., certainly promotes itself as providing community for its nearly 60,000 rings and almost 1 million active sites. It provides people interested in establishing a webring with a centralized directory and some technology to facilitate the exchange of links. Its home page boldly cries "WebRing: We Bring the Internet Together!" and offers participants the chance to "Use WebRing to participate in highly focused and rich online communities" (WebRing, 2003). Although most participants in these webrings have never met, their fulfillment of Jones' (1997) criteria suggests that many nonetheless share a communal identity.

A Minimum Level of Interactivity

In order for a virtual community to exist, there must be a flow of messages among the participants. If one individual were to post a Web site and no one were to comment on it, there would be no basis for a virtual community. However, when a poster gets a comment and responds to it, and then the original sender responds again, we have interactivity among participants. In most cases, people do not create webrings for their own collection of sites but rather to connect with others who share their interest. In order to have one's site join an existing WebRing community, one must apply to the existing decision maker(s) for admittance, affording some initial interactivity. Of course, there is also the possibility of interaction occurring among any number of web masters and visitors via e-mail (as many include an e-mail address right on the site) or other channels once they've met via the webring.

A Variety of Communicators

Of course, interactions among two individuals can establish a relationship, but more contributors need to join the conversation for a virtual community to arise. The richness of different virtual communities is enhanced by the variety of people who participate and the contributions they make. For example, the Yu-Gi-Oh! WebRing, focused on the popular manga cartoons and card game, features nearly 100 distinct contributions from people living as far apart as the United States and Singapore.

meet that desire, then a sense of belonging may follow. Likewise, if one's motive is to gather news about a topic, but the participants are more often discussing issues unrelated to the topic, then the community will lack attractiveness. As Baym found, the purposes she observed for her group included interpretation of the shows but also the opportunity to process personal matters, as the contributors found voice to give to their own experiences in relationship to events on the serials and in response to things said by their fellow participants.

Characteristics of the Group and Its Members

Finally, the idiosyncrasies of each person involved play a role in determining each individual's suitability for a virtual community. These qualities might range from the similarities of one's interests to that of other members in the community to one's skill with the computer. Clearly, there must be some commonalities among these members in order to sustain community. Some people might be deeply devoted to a topic but not join in on the virtual community simply because they do not enjoy CMC. In Baym's analysis, the members clearly were devoted both to the topic and to the medium through which they communicated. Their interest and their forum might not appeal to everyone but did serve to unite them.

As you can see, Baym's (1998) model suggests that a number of factors need to work in harmony in order for a sense of community to emerge. For instance, if individuals who were characteristically unskilled with computer systems found their way onto a listserv with a complicated infrastructure, that would be two strikes against their discovering a sense of community. Although there are some obvious differences between virtual and immediate communities, there are several significant similarities. In the next section, we look at one such parallel, the question of citizenship, and examine what it means to be a valued participant in the social setting of an electronic village.

Hyperlink: Commercialized Community

When the earliest "homesteaders," like Howard Rheingold, migrated to the Web, they described the experience of connecting with others in metaphorical terms. That metaphor of community was initially so accessible that it served as a means for many other newcomers to interpret the experience. It ultimately became so potent that commercial interests coveted it, co-opting the community metaphor into what has become a repeated, and often exaggerated, marketing strategy.

In its earliest years of operation, GeoCities (http://geocities.yahoo.com/) made ample use of the community metaphor, employing it in both the language and the visual imagery of its Web design. GeoCities provides subscribers with free computer storage space for their personal Web pages. In exchange, they post advertising banners on the site whenever it is downloaded. In its formative years, GeoCities welcomed each "homesteader" to choose a

"neighborhood" for the personal Web page. There were over 40 of these desig-
nations, and the site encouraged subscribers to select the neighborhood best
reflecting their individual interests, including those designated for science fiction fans and alternative lifestyles. It even attempted to perpetuate an illusion
of proximity among its clients visually. While choosing an address to register
one's page, one would tour a virtual suburb along a two-lane street, looking for
images of homes marked "vacant." Although GeoCities has scaled back on the
use of the metaphor in more recent years, the image of the cozy cottage, smoke
rolling out of its chimney, still invokes a sense of hominess and is still a part of
the service's logo.

In an analysis of how the wider business community viewed the community
metaphor, Chris Werry (1999) points out that business texts were initially dis-
missive of the community-building possibilities of the online experience but that
they soon changed their opinion. In the mid-1990s, when commercial interests
were beginning to turn increasingly to the Internet with increasing interest, the
rhetoric of the advisory texts concluded that community was contradictory to
commerce. But by the late 1990s, authors realized that communities not only
captured attention, but promoted loyalty (usually in the form of return visits to
a site). Accordingly, "commercial sites began to add chatlines, bulletin boards
and games, forms for people to enter personal information, and celebrity guests
to host discussions" (Werry, 1999). Perhaps one of the most extreme examples
of this community-building attempt was conducted by pharmaceutical manufacturer SmithKline Beecham. In an effort to promote their products for the control of genital herpes, they created "Café Herpé." Based loosely on the idea of
a coffee house, the café included information on SmithKline Beecham products, links to support groups, and a host of interactive features such as games.
Although people suffering from sexually transmitted diseases certainly seek out
information and support for their condition, the idea of doing so in a virtual coffee
house presents a dissonant combination (Fig. 6.1).

Commercially sponsored virtual communities may present the familiar trappings of community, but they do not necessarily exercise the egalitarianism of
earlier, noncommercial sites. The reality is that these sites are controlled by the
commercial interest and thus everything posted is under its control and dedicated to its best interest. Commercially sponsored virtual communities raise the
specter of another metaphor, that of colonization, where richer more powerful
entities seek to take control of native territories. If we are not vigilant about these
interests, then the dominant images and ideals of corporate culture may super-
sede the homespun values of the original virtual homesteaders (Riley, Keough,
Meilich, & Pierson, 1998).

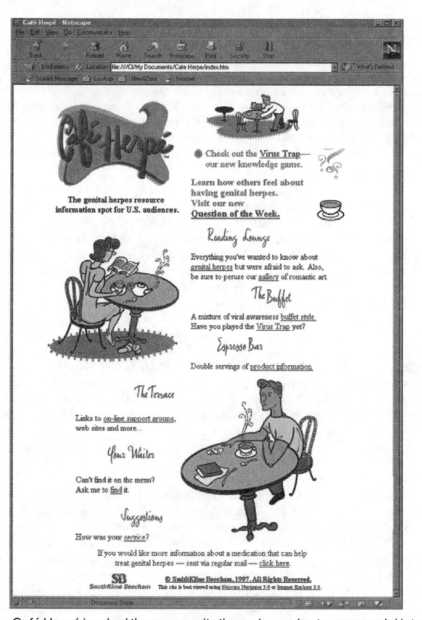

Fig. 6.1. Café Herpé invoked the community theme in service to commercial interests.

NETIZENSHIP: RESPONSIBILITY AND REGULATION IN THE VIRTUAL COMMUNITY

Although being a member of a virtual community suggests a number of privileges, it also seems to imply a number of responsibilities. People who self-identify with a virtual community are referred to as **netizens**, and these "Internet citizens" are presumed to shoulder responsibilities to the larger community. Writing about the nature of netizenship in *CMC Magazine*, Michael F. Hauben (1997) qualifies that true netizens distinguish themselves through active contributions to the development of a sustained community:

> Netizens are the people who actively contribute online towards the development of the Net. These people understand the value of collective work and the communal aspects of public communications. These are the people who actively discuss and debate topics in a constructive manner, who e-mail answers to people and provide help to new-comers, who maintain FAQ [frequently asked questions] files and other public information repositories, who maintain mailing lists and so on. These are people who discuss the nature and role of this new communications medium. . . . Netizens are people who decide to make the Net a regenerative and vibrant community and resource.

Although Hauben praises the selfless contributions of many participants, he argues that not everyone visiting a virtual community is necessarily a netizen. He cites some specific terminology to designate nonparticipants, including the **surfer** (an infrequent and detached visitor), **lurkers** (who are present but offer no comment or contribution), and **privateers** (people using the net for profit), who do not qualify as netizens in his conception of the term because of their selfish, rather than selfless, use of the technology. Accordingly, netizens help to build the virtual community, not with brick and mortar per se, but with contributions of ideas and information.

Like other cultures, those emerging online need new members to perpetuate their ideals. Among the functions of good netizens, Hauben notes the importance of maintaining Frequently Asked Questions (FAQ) files. FAQ files serve to explain the culture of any given virtual community by providing the basic information a newcomer, or **newbie**, needs to function competently within the virtual environment. They might answer questions associated with accessing the technology at use in the environment, observing norms of engagement among members, or learning the history of the organization. Certainly not every virtual community has created such a code to govern itself, but even in the well-intentioned social worlds shared by netizens, it sometimes helps to know what rules everyone has agreed to follow.

Clearly, any competent communicator will want to learn and then operate within the social norms established by a given community. Like any other society, virtual communities establish rules that they expect their members to observe. Any number of the rules governing accepted behavior have been codified as Internet etiquette, or **netiquette**. It should come as little surprise that such rules may seem comparable to the rules of good behavior that people are expected to observe in other contexts, especially face-to-face interaction. In fact, Laurel A. Sutton (1996) suggests that netiquette, true to its name, is a reworking of the classic rules of common etiquette, such as that espoused by Emily Post or Miss Manners. Consider the following comparison offered by Sutton.

> *Etiquette:* Those with vivid imaginations are often unreliable in their statements. (Post, 1955, p. 46)

> *Netiquette:* Make yourself look good online: Know what you're talking about and make sense. (Shea, 1994, p. 33)

Although the words have clearly changed between 1922 and 1994, the intent of the advice still holds true: Know something before you speak.

Although advice varies among the sources recording just what netiquette one should follow, Virginia Shea (1994) constructed a widely regarded list of 10 rules that help form a general outline of effective netiquette. Like many other forms of etiquette, these guidelines can be summarized with one simple rule, "Do unto others as you would have them do unto you."

1. **Remember the human**—People, with feelings, are on the other side of the screen, and it behooves us to be sensitive to them.
2. **Adhere to the same standards of behavior online that you follow in real life**—Behave in both ethical and legal fashion online, even as you are expected to in real life.
3. **Know where you are in cyberspace**—Because netiquette varies from forum to forum, it is advisable to observe silently prior to contributing, or as Shea puts it, "Lurk before you leap."
4. **Respect other people's time and bandwidth**—Messages take time to read and use computer resources (i.e., **bandwidth**); consider other people's time in constructing your contributions.
5. **Make yourself look good online**—Express yourself in quality writing, including standard grammar, and know what you are talking about before you contribute.
6. **Share expert knowledge**—It is helpful to share insight that you have gained with others.
7. **Help keep flame wars under control**—Although an occasional sharp comment may appear, prolonged personal attacks are disruptive and wasteful of bandwidth.
8. **Respect other people's privacy**—Consideration of others includes not reading their personal e-mails.
9. **Don't abuse your power**—Those in authority, such as system administrators, should not abuse their power by taking advantage of it (say, by reading someone's e-mail).
10. **Be forgiving of other people's mistakes**—Everyone's a newbie sometime, so if you feel that you must point out an error to someone, do so politely.

Again, the netiquette suggested here may not be the only rules one needs to learn in order to function effectively within a given virtual community. In fact, there may even be communities where one or more of the above suggestions are contradicted in common practice. However, if you are first and foremost attentive to the practices of those already a part of the community, you will probably adapt to their standards given sufficient observation.

In a survey of netiquettes, Uta Pankoke-Babatz and Phillip Jeffrey (2002) found that in the posted rules for e-mail, listservs, chat rooms, and MUDs, three common themes emerged. The lists tended to cite desired behavior (such as those rules advocating politeness), undesired behavior (such as those rules prohibiting personal attacks), and the sanctioning mechanisms available to punish those violating netiquette. Certainly, there are those who do not play by the rules. In fact, when participants have behaved in ways that are unacceptable to the virtual community's standards, others have enforced certain regulations to counter, curb, or eliminate the offender. Tamir Maltz (1996) catalogs the mechanisms used to sanction offenders in Table 6.1. As you might expect, the distance and anonymity associated with CMC make it difficult to punish an offender in customary ways, such as levying fines

HYPERLINK: GROUP DECISION SUPPORT SYSTEMS

Not all group interaction using computer-mediated technology is necessarily as socially oriented as the examples in this chapter suggest. In fact, as you enter the professional world you may find yourself directed to use communication technology in certain task-oriented situations as well. Small-group and organizational communication scholars have been intrigued by the introduction of computer systems to enhance workplace communication. Marshall Scott Poole (1995) provides a description of one of these Group Decision Support Systems (GDSSs), called SAMM:

> Developed at the University of Minnesota, SAMM is intended to promote participative, democratic decision-making in 3- to 16-person groups. Designed to be operated by the group itself, SAMM provides public and private messaging and a number of decision tools such as problem definition, idea or solution evaluation, stakeholder analysis, and nominal group technique. The group assembles at a horseshoe-shaped conference table with a terminal and keyboard for each group member.... At the front of the room is a large screen for display of group information (such as vote tallies or idea lists). Any member of the group may call and use any procedure in SAMM and it is up to the group to manage usage. (p. 91)

Teams working with GDSSs like SAMM have demonstrated a number of improvements in group processes. Research indicates that groups equipped with GDSSs can process more information, more quickly, with greater participation among its members than in traditional meetings (Poole, 1995).

It is that third quality that is among the most intriguing, for in traditional group processes, members seem to gravitate toward dominant and subordinate roles. Recall the student council, fraternal, or any other brainstorming meeting you have attended, and you probably can remember various people who contributed more than their fair share and those from whom you never heard an utterance. Nonverbal status cues help to explain why this occurs: A person who stands up and shouts during a meeting is difficult to challenge. However, GDSSs do not allow interactants to shout over one another (unless, we suppose, they do so in ALL CAPS!). Studies have shown that GDSSs promote a greater degree of equity among participants using the systems than they experienced before they were introduced (Scott & Easton, 1996). Such findings certainly promote the notion that people can improve aspects of goal-directed behaviors like decision making using new technologies.

Table 6.1
Methods of Sanctioning Online Offenders

Mechanism	Meaning	Example(s)
Harassment (reception)	Forced reception of unwanted information	Flaming
Silencing (transmission)	Interfering with either current or future transmission of information or destroying past archives of transmissions	Canceling current messages; deleting stored messages from public database
Capture (transmission)	Controlling transmissions	Posting offensive messages under another user's name
Interference (reception)	Obstructing ability to receive information	Mail-bombs and mass flaming; denying access by administrator

Source: From Maltz (1996).

or imprisonment. The community's remaining recourse, then, is to sanction the individual through communication. They can do so by chiding the offender through harassing responses, obstructing the offender's access to information, or interfering with the offender's ability to use the medium effectively.

As you can see, participation in a virtual community is not unlike participation in a physical community. Despite the lack of physical contact, such communities can thrive. The key to making them work, as the theories discussed here suggest, lies in the reliance of these communities to define and to regulate themselves through communication.

> **Ethical Inquiry**
> Whenever someone joins an online community, even one as large as AOL or MSN, how much responsibility do they assume in contributing to the quality of communication within that community? Is it adequate to simply behave well oneself by not inflicting harm to others? Or do people have an obligation to be their "brother's keeper," reporting violations of posted rules, such as those against spamming, posting pornography, or advocating bigoted positions? How active should we expect each netizen to be in order to have a communication environment that is hospitable to all?

CRITIQUES OF THE COMMUNITY METAPHOR

Despite the fact that a number of people have embraced the metaphor of community as an explanation for their online networks, others are critical of this analogy, suggesting that the label is inaccurate on a number of counts. These criticisms include concern for the limitations imposed by access to these communities, their potential to foster narrowed rather than expanded views of the world, and the inherent shortfalls present in establishing rapport without face-to-face contact.

In terms of access, Mihaela Kelemen and Warren Smith (2001) argue that "the cyberspace seems to create a tribal environment that controls membership through highly effective powers of inclusion and exclusion. Membership, therefore, is not simply a matter of individual choice" (p. 382). They note that in order to even be a participant in a virtual community, one must first have the money to purchase computer equipment and Internet service, the time to devote to the Internet, and the ability to read and write a language. These qualities are not universally shared, so the liberating qualities that some praise virtual communities for fall short of delivering to all people. Indeed, many have questioned the suitability of the community metaphor in a world where access is still limited to a privileged few. Although access to the Internet continues to grow at a steady rate, economically depressed people in the United States and across the globe do not have access to the technology and thus cannot become contributors to this online community. The ideals of community cannot be achieved as long as this inequity persists. (We explore these inequalities in greater detail in chapter 8.)

Critics also note that the disparity manifests itself not only in a bifurcation between those online and those not, but also among those already online. Marshall Alstyne and Erik Brynjolfsson (1996) point out that in some cases people elect to spend increasing amounts of time with others who share in their special interests, at the expense of being exposed to all types of people, particularly those with views different from their own. They call this process **cyberbalkanization**, intending to invoke memories of the breakdown of the nation of Yugoslavia into various Balkan states. In the process of breaking up the ethnically diverse Yugoslavia, a number of the Balkan states strove for independence from one another, resulting in distance and, ultimately, bloody war among them. Alstyne and Brynjolfsson warn us that cyberbalkanization may lead to increasingly fragmented virtual communities, populated by ignorant, if not intolerant, people who have indulged in their own interests, opinions, and creeds and who have consequently sheltered themselves from diversity. We revisit the issue of cyberbalkanization in chapter nine.

An additional line of argument questions whether or not the exchange of information is enough to establish a community. As one critic put it, "Virtual community is the illusion of community where there are no real people and no real communication. It is a term used by idealistic technofiles who fail to understand that authentic community cannot be engendered through technological means" (Wilbur, 1997, p. 14). Thus, some scholars insist that community can only exist where face-to-face interaction can occur. As evidence, Frank Weinreich (1997) followed the progress of a number of BBS. In one survey he conducted, with several hundred participants, 62% of the respondents reported that they had met other users. These face-to-face follow-up meetings, Weinreich suggests, are indicative of the claim that mediating communication is simply not enough to establish meaningful relationships among individuals. Indeed, participants often can and do seek one another out for face-to-face interaction (Rheingold, 1993), lending some support to Weinreich's indictment.

Certainly, like any other metaphor, that of the virtual community can be useful in explaining part, if not the whole, of what it seeks to compare itself to. As these criticisms suggest, we must continue to refine our understanding of how this online experience will emerge without assuming its impact will be benign or without consequence.

CHAPTER SUMMARY

Virtual communities have challenged our conception of what a community can be. The Internet has allowed people to relate to groups of people who live beyond the borders of their small towns or outside the wall of their tenement apartments. For those who chose to involve themselves in the lives of others through mediating technologies rather than in face-to-face encounters, the virtual communities they inhabit represent a widespread movement into a manner of relating that defies the limitations of physical space.

Certainly, such distance transcending communities have been constructed before, among the American colonialists, among science fiction fans earlier last century, and among the developers of the early Internet. Such communities share some similar characteristics, including interactivity, variety of participants, common space, and sustained membership. As we saw within webrings, such characteristics are evident in virtual communities. Moreover, we saw that the appeal of joining the virtual community is a complex set of factors, including external factors, the temporal structure of the forum, the infrastructure of the computer system, the purposes for CMC's use, and the characteristics of the group and its members. As responsible netizens, participants are expected to make contributions to the community and respect others in it. When they fail to do so, virtual communities regulate their members through sanctions. Although the metaphor can help to explain some aspects of online behavior, it is not immune from criticism. Limited access, close-mindedness, and the desire for face-to-face follow-ups suggest some limitations to the metaphor that we should weigh along with its virtues.

Virtual communities remain fascinating arenas for further exploration. People seem to be attracted to these outlets for three reasons. First, like other CMC venues, they allow people to experiment with, and in many cases transcend, identity. Second, they provide interaction for those who might not otherwise be able to do so. Third, they allow individuals to make a contribution to the creation of something greater than themselves. For these and many other reasons, these self-identified settlements on the electronic frontier deserve our attention.

ONLINE COMMUNICATION AND THE LAW

E-mail in your inbox with subject lines such as `RE: Free adult site passwords`; `RE: Get out of credit card debt`; `RE: Copy DVDs in one click`, can indicate only one thing: You've got spam! Spam is the annoying commercial messages that quickly fill up mailboxes with offers hocking everything from insurance to pornography. If you have an e-mail account, chances are that you are quite familiar with spam, and chances are that you don't like it. Many other people online don't like it either, as evidenced by the fact that 10 million complaints a day are logged by AOL subscribers (Kady & Anselmo, 2003). Legislators aren't fans of spam either, and that's why a number of states have already enacted measures to control the distribution of unsolicited mass e-mails. Even Congress has debated national legislation to handle the flood of spam.

Unfortunately, the problem of spam is likely to get worse before it gets better. Jupiter Research, which tracks Internet traffic, reported that in 2002 about 260 billion unsolicited e-mails were sent. By 2005, they project that the number will increase to 10.3 trillion messages (Taylor et al., 2003). It's little wonder that the amount of spam is likely to increase. Spam is relatively easy to produce. One person armed with an account, an e-mail list, and a product or service to sell can reach a large audience much more easily and inexpensively than through more traditional direct mailing. Of course, most spammers are a bit more sophisticated than this, taking full advantage of the technology at hand to gather large lists of e-mail addresses as ripe targets for their wares.

In fact, it is the nature of the technology that makes it so difficult to prevent spam, even where governments have labeled it illegal. For instance, Delaware prohibits the distribution of spam; however, this has not stopped residents of Delaware from receiving (or even those native spammers from sending) unsolicited e-mails. Part of the problem is that because the Internet is decentralized, a spammer doesn't have to be in Delaware to send spam to people there. One could do it just as easily from a neighboring state. In fact, even if spamming became illegal in the United States, spammers could still send their messages from other countries.

Of course, spam is so annoying in part because it is a clear violation of netiquette, showing disrespect for people's time and bandwidth. It is also a burden on the service providers who must store and process the unwanted messages. Moreover, one estimate calculates that spam costs business $8.9 billion a year because of the productivity lost to being distracted by and deleting spam (Taylor et al., 2003). Yet while we struggle to deal with spam in legal terms, we must acknowledge one disturbing truth. Someone somewhere is responding to these messages. If spam didn't work at all, then it would be unprofitable for the spammers to continue. Many people find the billboards, junk mail, and endless parade of commercial advertising in our physical communities to be irritating, and that tradition of assaulting the senses continues with spam in the online community. Until or unless we change the system that allows it to be sent, or alter the society that accepts its appeals, we are likely to be up to our in-boxes in spam.

Glossary

Apa: Amateur press association, an imagined community sustained by members who distribute self-published periodicals to one another.

Bandwidth: The resources (including others' patience) consumed by messages in online forums; originally bandwidth referenced the carrying capacity of media delivery systems, such as a cable line.

Cyberbalkanization: The fragmentation of virtual communities into potentially intolerant interest groups.

Gemeinschaft: A sense of community based on identification with the group.

Gesellschaft: A community based on proximity and circumstance.

Imagined communities: Aggregates of people who, thanks to forms of mediated communication, perceive themselves as part of a common social unit despite the geographic distances among them.

Lurkers: People who observe but make no contribution to a virtual community.

Netiquette: Internet etiquette; a code of accepted behavior for virtual communities.

Netizen: An active participant who contributes to the growth or maintenance of a virtual community.

Newbie: A newcomer.

Privateer: A person who uses the Internet for profit.

Spam: Unsolicited, and typically unwanted, commercial e-mail messages that annoy e-mailers by their collectively flooding in-boxes.

Surfer: An infrequent and detached visitor to a virtual community.

Virtual community: A shared understanding of interrelatedness among participants in computer-mediated environments.

Webring: A community formed by linked Web sites, each one typically addressing a shared theme.

Zines: Fan magazines; self-published periodicals that are circulated among people sharing a common interest.

Topics for Discussion

1. This chapter considered the past and present of virtual communities. What do you think the future holds for these organizations? Are they merely fads or will they play a role in future socialization? Respond by making three predictions about the state of virtual communities in 10 years. If applicable, identify a virtual community from the Internet that you think will still be thriving in the future.

2. In an autobiographical paragraph, recount an experience where you were a "newbie" in a community (first time attending a club meeting, moving to a new town, or joining a team). When did you feel like you were a part of the community? It might be helpful to think of when you first made a contribution to the others involved or felt (or spoke of) a sense of "we-ness."

3. Participate in a chat room or review the contents of an electronic bulletin board for the next several days. Make a list of what rules of netiquette you observe governing interactions among the participants in one of these forums. Write an ethnographic essay explaining what rules you observed and, more importantly, how they might have been enforced if someone broke them.

4. Visit http://www.webring.org/rw and explore one of the many webrings presented there. As you visit various sites associated with the ring, can you find evidence that the people perceive themselves as a community, or are they merely associates? Write a review of your chosen webring by noting what qualities the sites therein exhibit or lack that would support a perspective of these connections as community.

5. How would you address the objections to the metaphor of the virtual community given above (see Critiques of the Community Metaphor)? Take each of the arguments against the virtual community and offer support or counterpoints to it. Consider using a virtual community that you have found on the Internet in order to support your claims. Can you suggest an alternative metaphor to describe these ongoing group interactions?

REFERENCES

Alstyne, M. V., & Brynjolfsson, E. (1996). *Electronic communities: Global village or cyber-balkans?* Available: http://web.mit.edu/marshall/www/Abstracts.html [June 23, 2003].

Anderson, B. R. (1983). *Imagined communities: Reflections on the origin and spread of nationalism.* London: Verso Editions.

Baym, N. K. (1998). The emergence of on-line community. In S. G. Jones (Ed.), *Cybersocity 2.0: Revisiting computer-mediated communication and community* (pp. 35–68). Thousand Oaks, CA: Sage.

Bosky, B. (1994). Amateur press associations: Intellectual society and social intellectualism. In J. Sanders (Ed.), *Science fiction fandom* (pp. 181–195). Westort, CT: Greenwood Press.

Boyd, J. (2002). In community we trust: Online security communication at eBay. *Journal of Computer-Mediated Communication, 7.* Retrieved November 6, 2003, from http://www.ascusc.org/jcmc/vol7/issue3/boyd.html

Dibbell, J. (1993, December 21). A rape in cyberspace: Or, how an evil clown, a Haitian trickster spirit, two wizards, and a cast of dozens turned a database into a society. *Village Voice,* pp. 36–42.

Elmer, G. (1999). Web rings as computer-mediated communication. *CMC Magazine.* Retrieved June 24, 2003, from http://www.december.com/cmc/mag/1999/jan/elmer.html

Fernback, J. (1999). There is a there there: Notes toward a definition of cybercommunity. In S. Jones (Ed.), *Doing Internet research: Critical issues and methods for examining the net* (pp. 203–220). Thousand Oaks, CA: Sage.

Hauben, M. F. (1997, February). The netizens and community networks. *CMC Magazine.* Retrieved June 24, 2003, from http://www.december.com/cmc/mag/1997/feb/hauben.html

Jones, Q. (1997, December). Virtual-communities, virtual settlements & cyber-archaeology: A theoretical outline. *Journal of Computer-Mediated Communication, 3.* Retrieved June 24, 2003, from http://www.ascusc.org/jcmc/vol3/issue3/jones.html

Kady, M., & Anselmo, J. C. (2003, May 24). Is "There oughta be a law" a real answer to "spam"? *CQ Weekly.* Retrieved June 20, 2003, from http://www.cq.com

Kelemen, M., & Smith, W. (2001). Community and its "virtual" promises: A critique of cyberlibertarian rhetoric. *Information, Communication & Society, 4,* 270–387.

Maltz, T. (1996). Customary law & power in Internet communities. *Journal of Computer-Mediated Communication, 2.* Retrived June 24, 2003, from http://www.ascusc.org/jcmc/vol2/issue1/

Moskowitz, S. (1994). The origin of science fiction fandom: A reconstruction. In J. Sanders (Ed.), *Science fiction fandom* (pp. 17–36). Westport, CT: Greenwood Press.

Okrand, M. (1985). *The Klingon dictionary: English/Klingon, Klingon/English.* New York: Pocket Books.

Pankoke-Babatz, U., & Jeffrey, P. (2002). Documented norms and conventions on the Internet. *International Journal of Human-Computer Interaction, 14,* 219–235.

Poole, M. S. (1995). Decision development in computer-assisted group decision making. *Human Communication Research, 22,* 90–128.

Post, E. (1955). *Etiquette*. New York: Funk and Wagnalls. (Original work published 1922).

Putnam, R. D. (2000). *Bowling alone: The collapse and revival of American community*. New York: Simon & Shuster.

Rheingold, H. (1993). *The virtual community: Homesteading on the electronic frontier*. Reading, MA: Addison–Wesley.

Riley, P., Keough, C. M., Meilich, O., & Pierson, J. (1998). Community of colony: The case of online newspapers and the web. *Journal of Computer-Mediated Communication, 4*. Retrieved June 24, 2003, from http://www.ascusc.org/jcmc/vol4/issue1/keough.html

Schutz, W. (1966). *The interpersonal underworld*. Palo Alto, CA: Science & Behavior Books.

Scott, C. R., & Easton, A. C. (1996). Examing equality of influence in group decision support system interaction. *Small Group Research, 27*, 360–382.

Shea, V. (1994). *Netiquette*. San Francisco: Albion Books.

Shoulson, M. (2003, February 24). *The Klingon Language Institute* [Online]. Available: http://www.kli.org [June 24, 2003].

Sutton, L. A. (1996). Cocktails and thumbtacks in the old west: What would Emily Post say? In L. Cherny & E. R. Weise (Eds.), *Wired women: Gender and new realities in cyberspace* (pp. 169–187). Seattle, WA: Seal Press.

Taylor, C., Klarreich, K., Scully, S., Roston, E. Crittle, S., & Isackson, N. (2003, June 16). Spam's big bang! *Time*, 50–53.

Tönnies, F. (1957). *Community and society* (C. P. Loomis, Trans.). East Lansing, MI: Michigan State University Press. (Original work published 1887)

WebRing, Inc. (2003). *Webring: We bring the Internet together* [Online]. Available: http://dir.webring.com/rw

Weinreich, F. (1997, February). Establishing a point of view toward virtual communities. *CMC Magazine*. Retrieved from http://www.december.com/cmc/mag/1997/feb/weinstat.html

Werry, C. (1999). Imagined electronic community: Representations of virtual community in contemporary business discourse. *First Monday*. Retrieved June 24, 2003, from http://www.firstmonday.org/issues/issue4 9/werry/index.html

Wilbur, S. P. (1997). An archaeology of cyberspace: Virtuality, community, identity. In D. Porter (Ed.), *Internet culture* (pp. 5–22). New York: Routledge.

PART III

INTERNET CULTURE AND CRITIQUE

The effects of the Internet might be easier to ignore if they only affected the worlds that exist online. However, that is not the case. In August 2003, a dark side of online communication reminded us of the powers of this medium to affect "real life," when variants of an Internet worm slowed or disabled computer networks at the Federal Reserve Bank of Atlanta, the U.S. Senate, CBS in New York, and home offices across the nation (Krebs, 2003). The worm worked by installing itself in computers with weak firewalls or outdated security patches and using these compromised nodes to copy itself elsewhere. The result was an estimated $300 million in lost productivity and countless hours of frustration for workers worldwide. Add to that the innumerable viruses that course through the computer networks (some appearing to come from reputable companies asking you to install "antivirus" software) and suddenly the arcane codes and protocols of online communication become important to us all.

The economic costs of Internet worms and viruses offer one manifestation of the effects the Internet has on businesses and cultures around the world. The introduction of this technology has meant that we have had to adapt to new economic, political, and cultural challenges. In many instances, these challenges have also presented opportunities to question traditional assumptions about the way we as a society conduct ourselves. This third and final part of the book examines how we have adapted to the presence of the Internet as a factor in our lives and further suggests how people have critiqued those adaptations. Some of the issues raised herein are at the very core of what it means to function as interdependent people, especially now that our interdependence has expanded to a global scale. Yet as the next four chapters demonstrate, in our quest to cope with our complex new communication technologies, we have a long way to go before we understand the implications of online communication.

REFERENCE

Krebs, B. (2003, August 14). FBI looks for source of internet infection. *Washington Post*, p. E01.

CHAPTER 7

REBUILDING CORPORATIONS ONLINE

When Big Brother arrives, don't be surprised if he looks like a grocery clerk.
—Howard Rheingold

Charlie Chaplin hardly seems like a credible expert on the impact of computer technology on the workplace. For most folks, the most enduring memory of the "little tramp" is a bumbling, although well-meaning, goof. In fact, Chaplin was an astute social observer who used humor to make serious points about U.S. culture. In one of his most memorable movies, *Modern Times*, Chaplin (1936) offers a vivid depiction of the social impact of mechanization on workers (Fig. 7.1).

At one point in the film, representatives of an automatic feeding machine visit the boss of a plant whose employees make some sort of widget. Why waste hours of productivity as workers idle their time eating their lunches when the feeding machine can serve a hot bowl of soup right on the assembly line? Previously isolated activities like eating and working merge in Chaplin's vision of the modern factory. Even private activities in the restroom are subject to the all-seeing gaze of the boss, who can view his workers through a wall-sized telescreen. At one point, Chaplin's overworked, overstressed character gets sucked into the gears and cogs of the machine—blurring, ultimately, the distinction between people and their tools.

Is contemporary corporate life so far removed from Chaplin's nightmarish comedy? You might think so. Increasingly, scholars of the "information economy" report that knowledge work is replacing industrial work. The assembly line of old cannot churn out original ideas as quickly as it can turn out durable goods. However, in our increasingly computer-mediated society, corporate technology serves many of the functions described in *Modern Times*.

Think about how the machinery of today's workplace alters your habits and expectations. Formerly sharp divisions between home and office—illustrated by the vast differences built between suburban "bedroom communities" and urban corporate centers—are hard to differentiate as millions of Americans learn the art of telecommuting. Dining rooms and bedrooms make way for home offices filled with computers, scanners, and fax machines.

One way to understand this significant shift in how we live and work can be attributed to the emergence of the **information economy**. There was a time when the economic power of the United States was measured by its ability to build automobiles and sell washing machines. This was the age of the industrial economy, after Americans moved away from farms and filled the cities and factories in the 19th century. However, after World War II and the zenith of America's industrial might, the

Fig. 7.1. Charlie Chaplin struggles with the machine in *Modern Times*.

increasingly global economy made it difficult for the United States to compete in every field for industrial supremacy. At the same time, computer technology made it possible to envision an economy where knowledge, not durable goods, would constitute the nation's most important product.

In his germinal text, *The Control Revolution*, Beniger (1986) traces the emergence of the information economy and the more general **information society** to the 19th century and the growth of the railroads. The complexity of this undertaking—moving goods, services, and people across a continent—demanded a high degree of standardization, bureaucracy, and national-scale advertising. Modernization required more sophisticated mechanisms of control and feedback than had been acceptable to U.S. society before. As information became more broadly valued, it became more deeply embedded with the cohesion of national culture.

Although dating the emergence of the information economy and its corollary, the information society, is subject to historical interpretation, most economists have begun to argue that, at least since the 1960s, the United States has shifted its emphasis from the industrial to the information economy. Companies have begun to discover that information really is power. The U.S. Commerce Department seems to agree. In 1999, the department replaced a 60-year-old system designed to measure the strength of the U.S. economy that couldn't tell the difference between a computer and an adding machine. Only recently have important indicators such as the Gross Domestic Product begun to fully account for the impact of information technology on the strength of our economy. According to Robert Shapiro, former undersecretary for economic affairs at the Commerce Department: "In an information-based economy, the quality of information determines the quality of policy" (cited in Belton, 1999). From a more general standpoint, we suggest that for an astute understanding of the contemporary economy and corporate world, you must understand computer technology.

In this chapter, we explore the impact of Internet communication on the work world as corporations employ computer technology to improve the quality of information in their offices and throughout their industries. At the same time, we consider the corresponding implications of corporate influence on the Internet. Our approach calls for discussion of three approaches used to study these interlocking phenomena: *discipline*, *diffusion*, and *convergence*.

HYPERLINK: CHANGING CORPORATE CULTURES—TELEPHONY AND THE INTERNET

Telephone Tales

BY LONG DISTANCE

Says Bob Maguire
A noted buyer:

"I never worry, I never wait,
I never have to procrastinate.
I cover a multitude of firms
For quality, price and delivery terms.
I close the deal when I find the best
And I get the jump on all the rest.
This puts me in preferred position
Over slower competition.
How do I do it?" He cries emphatically,
"I use Long Distance systematically."
"And the other key men in our institution
Acclaim the telephone's contribution.
In sales and credit and traffic affairs,
It saves us all a lot of gray hairs."

The Saturday Evening Post (April 15, 1939, p. 40)

Throughout this book, we explore the relationship of technology, identity, and culture. Studying the emergence of the Internet as a social and cultural force is made easier when you consider the similarities between this medium and the growth of the telephone in early 20th-century America. Fischer (1991) argued that early telephone advertisements tended to stress corporate and professional uses of the electronic communications device, downplaying communal uses. Among the potential reasons for this orientation, Fischer argued, were economic and technical causes.

In terms of *cost*, phone companies were loath to allow what they perceived to be frivolous "chatting" on a device that was frequently rented on a flat-fee system. To understand this concern, place yourself in the position of a restaurant manager offering an all-you-can-eat special to someone who never leaves the premises. A second, *technical* concern emerges when you recall that many phone systems depended on party lines—telephone connections shared by two or more families. The phone company manager would hardly want one person to monopolize a line shared by many. Yet, Fischer argued that the primary reason for initial resistance to sociability was *corporate culture*.

The generation of phone company pioneers had come from the telegraph industry. According to Fischer (1991), this group was accustomed to understanding the medium primarily from the perspective of short messages serving a specific purpose: "In this context, industry men reasonably considered telephone 'visiting' to be an abuse or trivialization of the service" (p. 112). By the late 1920s and early 1930s, however, corporate advertising caught up with social uses of the telephone. Rather than merely selling the phone as a tool for business, advertisements extolled the product as a way to enjoy "voice visits with friends" (p. 99).

As you might imagine, the prescribed gender of telephone usage began to change as well. Women and men were encouraged to reach out and touch someone. Can you isolate parallels between the corporate conceptualization of early telephony and that of current Internet technology?

CMC AS CORPORATE DISCIPLINE

You might remember a film called *Enemy of the State* (Bruckheimer, 1998), starring Gene Hackman and Will Smith. In the film, Smith plays a lawyer who discovers a government conspiracy and flees for his life. Throughout the film, it seems that Smith's every move is monitored by listening devices, video cameras, and computer networks. In many corporations, employees can be forgiven for feeling that they too are under close surveillance. By the same token, many corporations might be forgiven for placing less trust in their employees, especially because job turnover at the turn of the century was at an historical peak.

Many theorists striving to understand this dynamic base their studies on the concept of **discipline**. In this chapter, we approach discipline as a network of strategies employed by a person or group to maintain a specific set of power relationships. In many ways, discipline is the mechanism of control. However, as seen here, corporate use of the Internet as a disciplinary tool can serve conflicting goals. Indeed, discipline and resistance often appear to form two sides of the same coin. It can liberate employees to pursue innovative solutions to complicated problems. However, the same technology can serve to limit their choices, particularly in how they relate to their company. The irony here is that technology is not a tool imposed on us, but one we willingly accept and use. Barker and Cheney (1994) explain that this tool (say, in the form of an e-mail network that helps us interact with one another at work) maintains inequitable and/or inhumane power relationships in a very subtle way. The subtlety of this power is its frequently hidden and ephemeral nature.

Let us consider an example in the form of online monitoring. Writing about network monitoring software that simultaneously blocks outside intrusion to the corporate network while it monitors employee actions, Blackburn (1999) provides a somewhat chilling example of how this power relationship might look:

> The software can scan every word employees write, every e-mail they send, and every Web site they visit. If the system detects an abnormality, it can instantly block the action. . . . The software also allows management to catalog employee misdemeanors for court and, if the need arises, to create a personal profile of each employee. (p. E13)

To understand this process, let's take a look at a disciplinary concept that communication researchers apply to contemporary corporations, the **panopticon**. The panopticon ("all-seeing place") was introduced in 1791 by English philosopher **Jeremy Bentham**. The first physical panopticon was designed to be an effective and humane penitentiary. In a series of letters, Bentham proposed that the building would be circular, with cells lining the perimeter. Each cell would be separated by walls on either side. A window on the wall facing the building's exterior and an iron grating facing the building's interior would allow light to pass through the cell. This light would ensure constant surveillance over the activities of each individual by an inspector who was located in a tower at the center of the panopticon (Fig. 7.2).

Fig. 7.2. The "humane penitentiary" designed by Jeremy Bentham illustrates much about today's workplace.

This surveillance was unidirectional, however. Bentham proposed that a set of blinders covering the windows in the inspector's tower would prevent prisoners from watching their captors. As Foucault (1979) writes in *Discipline and Punish*, "[The prisoner] is seen, but he does not see; he is the object of information, never a subject in communication" (pp. 202–203).

So, what does a panopticon have to do with Internet communication in corporate settings? A lot when you consider research from the American Management Association (2003) stating that 90% of employers have installed software to monitor incoming and outgoing electronic mail. In his book, *The Naked Employee*, Frederick S. Lane (2003), adds the story of a worker at a California porn company fired because he was surfing eBay and not watching enough porn. Of course, companies have gone far beyond Internet snooping to check on their workers' habits. Lane describes "smart uniforms" that keep tabs on employee whereabouts, GPS systems installed in company vehicles, and secretive testing of DNA to fire workers whose potentially life-threatening illnesses might cost company insurance policies millions.

> **Ethical Inquiry**
>
> One of the results of the Internet Economy is the emergence of the "permanent temporary" employee, who leaps from job to job in search of marketable skills. Similarly, many companies' hiring plans resemble accordions that expand and contract as the breeze blows. Suddenly, the myth of the "lifer" who remains loyal to one firm—and receives that loyalty in return—has been abandoned. Given that companies and employees have largely abandoned the lifelong relationships that marked the job market of the last generation, the rules of ethical behavior have surely changed. What remains to be determined is a clear sense of what you owe your employer in these days of rapid turnover. For example, Should your boss expect that you will never divulge the things you learn at one company when you move on to another?

This process of surveillance might be defined as a panopticon of sorts, one that inspires employees to discipline their actions for fear of being observed through the computer network. Remember, the panopticon, more specifically, the **electronic panopticon**, does not just impact that *percentage* of employees. It impacts *all* employees who imagine that they too are connected to a chain of electronic messages that can be deleted but never fully erased from company computers (to learn more, see Provenzo, 1992).

Botan (1996) conducted research on the impacts of electronic surveillance in the workforce. When surveying members of the International Brotherhood of Electrical Workers, he found that when workers perceive themselves to be under observation by their bosses, they feel less privacy, uncertainty about their role in the workplace, lower self-esteem, and a reduction in workplace communication. On this last finding, Botan notes, "This result is consistent with employees' being isolated within the virtual cells of an electronic panopticon and suggests that electronic surveillance may very well [reduce] workplace communication" (p. 309).

Electronic Surveillance and Anticipatory Conformity

An important implication of electronic surveillance in the workplace is defined by Lyon (1994) as **anticipatory conformity**—a practice in which an employee might adopt a docile and disciplined relationship to authority because of the potential rather than the practice of domination:

> Operators within the ubiquitous digital 'gaze' of such computer systems and with-
> out the more familiar face-to-face relationships with superiors, may seek modes of
> resistance, but compliance appears more common. . . . In workplaces where workers
> as well as management have access to the personal data collected on the systems,
> workers exhibit "anticipatory conformity," showing that the standards of manage-
> ment are internalized by workers. (p. 70)

HYPERLINK: MICROSERFS

You might find a parallel between this form of surveillance and that described
by Douglas Coupland in his description of life at Microsoft. In *Microserfs*, Coupland (1994) portrays Bill Gates as a formless, faceless presence—unseen by
most Microsoft employees. According to at least one character in the book,
Bill used his powers to see but not be seen to both inspire and discipline his
employees.

> Bug believes that Bill sits at his window in the Admin Building and watches
> how staffers walk through the Campus. Bug believes that Bill keeps note of
> who avoids the paths and uses the fastest routes to get from A to B, and
> that Bill rewards devil-may-care trailblazers with promotions and stock, in
> the belief that their code will be just as innovative and dashing.

The position of Bill's office as a site of surveillance is reminiscent of a panopticon. Through architectural technology, Bill's mechanism of control is mediated
by corporate culture—the myths and legends about a man who is rarely seen
by his employees.

Thus far, we have examined discipline as a network of strategies employed by a
person or group to maintain a specific set of power relationships. To understand the
role of computer technology in the disciplinary process, we examined some tools of the
electronic panopticon. We have also explored a result of this **disciplinary technology**:
anticipatory conformity. But the question may still remain: Why would companies
engage in the use of electronic surveillance to monitor the habits of their employees?
Among the reasons is a trend defined by Naughton (1999) as **cyberslacking**—using
corporate information technology for personal ends: "With the Internet morphing
into the virtual Mall of America, day trading, Quake playing, vacation planning and
hard-core porn (not to mention gateways to exciting new career opportunities) are all
just a click away" (p. 62).

CORPORATIONS AND CONSUMERS ONLINE

To this point, we have focused on the corporate use of computer technology to observe the behaviors of employees. However, many corporations also use sophisticated

computer technology to keep tabs on the habits and practices of consumers (Gandy, 1989). Their techniques range from innocent sounding devices called **cookies**, to voluntary sharing of personal information, to the somewhat more troubling practice of *data mining*.

Cookies

Every time you visit a Web site, you are not just viewing the contents of a document, you are retrieving that document from a server and displaying it on your own computer. This is a transactional process. In other words, your computer and the distant server must share information with each other to establish and maintain communication with one another. Fairly sophisticated Web sites use this connection to transmit more than the text, images, and other files you request; they also send **cookies**—files that place themselves on your hard drive. Cookies are not as nefarious as they might sound. They are most commonly used to identify you and store your Web preferences. A recent concern that has emerged with the use of cookie technology is the potential for companies to identify particular users who visit specific Web sites. Imagine, for instance, that you anonymously explored a site dedicated to mental health. Although the site maintainers might simply employ cookies to customize the page to meet your preference, they could also use the cookie to identify your computer (and potentially you) to prospective companies, insurers, employers, or other entities. For this reason, the use of cookies raises substantial privacy concerns.

Voluntary Data Submission

Think about every free service you might enjoy on the Web. Free e-mail, calendars, database management tools, and news clipping services. Certainly, you put up with banner advertisements when you access these sites. But you pay another price as well. Almost every one of these services requests personal information from you. Typing in your name and selecting a password are hardly the limit of these requests, as you surely know. Frequently, you are invited to note your age, employment, hobbies, and even income. This data, in the context of a specific Web site, might be necessary and appropriate. The question of privacy emerges once more, however, when that data is collected and sold to a third party who might employ it in ways you never intended. Both cookies and voluntary data submission play a role in the third practice: data mining.

Data Mining

Like most technologies, **data mining** is not so radically new, when you think about it. What's unique about the contemporary practice, however, is how companies use computer software to develop patterns out of apparently random facts. Imagine that you are standing at the checkout line, holding a pair of jeans, a plastic container of hair color, and a DVD player. Individually, none of these purchases would necessarily provide useful insight into your personality. Even when collected, these purchases do not ensure that someone could construct a psychographic profile of you. However, some companies have developed powerful software networks that comb through multiple purchases, data entries, Web site visits, and other online choices you have made to guess your next purchase and even tell if you can afford the one you are making. This raises important ethical questions (Marx, 1998; see Ethical Inquiry, right). Yet he admitted that he cannot impose an ethical "Rosetta Stone of clear and consistent... categorical imperatives" on any of these practices (p. 182). He argued, instead, that one must consider the contextual issues that range from whether a particular practice may cause physical harm to whether those participating in data collection would wish for the same practices to apply to them.

Having explored corporate use of disciplinary technology, you might wonder how this approach helps you analyze corporate use of Internet communication. We propose that a disciplinary framework encourages people to study more than the functional practices of CMC. This framework insists on a critical reading of the interlocking networks of power shaped and maintained by computer networks. As a critic, you might employ this approach to reveal this subtle relationship of computers and corporate power in several ways. You can study the interplay of technology and narrative to observe how the narratives we tell to confirm or contest allegiance to a particular firm are mediated through computer networks. You might instead choose to study the impact of data collection on the marketplace of goods, services, and ideas—considering whether information has fundamentally shifted power away from persons and toward corporations. Whatever approach you take, the study of disciplinary networks in corporate settings is less a method than a framework for a critical revelation of practices that we might otherwise take for granted.

Ethical Inquiry

Corporate use of cookies, voluntarily shared information, and data mining raise a host of ethical issues. Marx (1998) poses seven specific risks faced by individuals whose data is collected by corporations.

1. Unfair advantage: Companies may take advantage of information they have received about a consumer's desires or concerns. This would have added significance where information is key to bargaining (e.g., buying a car).
2. Restricted social participation: Companies or other organizations may employ information to discriminate against an individual seeking medical coverage, employment, or housing.
3. Unwarranted public embarrassment: Companies may publish or communicate information that could defame or humiliate a person.
4. Betrayal of confidence: Companies or employees may fail to maintain promised protections of privacy, illustrated by phone companies revealing an unlisted number through Caller ID.
5. Intrusions into solitude: Companies may publish or communicate information that would result in an individual becoming the recipient of unwanted telephone calls, e-mail, or other solicitations.
6. Individualized propagandistic appeals: Companies may tailor persuasive messages to individuals. Although not illegal in itself, a risk emerges from the possibility of manipulation.
7. Waste of communication resources: Companies may use personal data to send messages via fax, e-mail, and other media that incur costs and service disruption.

CMC AND THE DIFFUSION OF INNOVATION

Organizational communication scholars, who study the integration of computer technology and our workplace, often focus on the diffusion of innovations through social systems. In this approach, the theoretical emphasis is less on the maintenance of power and more on the ways in which companies confront and seek to manage change. In his landmark book on the topic, Rogers (1995) defines the **diffusion of innovations** as communication about new ideas through certain channels over time among members of a social system. The following examines this definition more carefully.

Communicating New Ideas

At its heart, the diffusion of innovations is a process of communication. Rules, standards, technologies, and other factors exist and are understood within the common frame of reference generated by human sense making. This idea may seem strange at first. After all, it appears that tools are tools because of the functions they possess. However, the connotative meaning we attach to our tools—how we *feel* about them—cannot truly be separated from their denotative functions—what they *do*.

Consider the American car and its necessary counterpoint, the highway. You might remember when the Internet was called the "Information Superhighway." Long before the popularity of this cliché, however, the real highway and its vehicles illustrated best the means through which innovations become diffused throughout a community.

The automobile—an object designed to move persons great distances at high speed—emerged as a potent social force because of the narratives that surrounded it. Even though the American "frontier" had been officially closed in the 1893 Columbian Exposition, travelers still faced rugged territory beyond the towns and cities of the turn-of-the-century United States. Most Americans never ventured farther than 40 miles away from their homes. The automobile served as a vehicle of innovation, as it communicated an ideology—a prescription for how people should live—of limitless horizons and tamed frontiers.

Communicating Through Channels

The channels of this innovation were not simply the roads, bridges, and highways of America's physical infrastructure. They were also the travelogues, foldout maps, radio plays, postcards, and other means through which motorists and corporate boosters shared their enthusiasm for this radical change of how people could travel the country. Many women, for example, discovered that they could use the technology of automobiles and highways to flee 19th-century expectations about how they should live their lives. Accounts of women motorists such as Effie Price Gladding taking to the unknown outdoors inspired countless readers to try this risky innovation themselves. The channels of discourse through which stories about the automobile were told and retold provide necessary context to any analysis of the ideology of the American roadside.

Communicating Over Time

It may seem obvious, but one must remember that the emergence of the automobile did not occur all at once. It took decades for car companies to decide whether to choose electricity or gasoline as the fuel for their creations. During those decades, city and state officials wrestled with the government over who should pay for the roads, bridges, and other infrastructural improvements necessary for mass-scale driving. Time provides a dimension to study the unfolding of events in various contexts. Yet it cannot be defined monolithically; in other words, this dimension is not experienced in the same way or punctuated at the same moments for all participants. Studying the diffusion of innovation is a practice in which one must correlate multiple, overlapping, and even contradictory perceptions of time.

Communicating in a Social System

One cannot separate the contexts of community and culture from the study of diffusion. To be sure, not every American could afford or operate an automobile in the early part of the century. The previous example of Effie Price Gladding is an exception that proves the rule of those days: Driving was primarily an activity for men. Women motorists were perceived by most auto enthusiasts and "good roads" boosters as a contradiction of terms. Moreover, the cost of purchasing and maintaining the cranky automobiles of the day all but ensured that the social system through which this innovation would be diffused according to the rigid distinctions and expectations of class.

From this perspective, the automobile illustrates the diffusion of innovations. Studying its technology demands careful attention to its unique idea, the channels through which that idea is communicated, the multiple histories in which that communication takes place, and the social systems that shape that discourse. As a theory, diffusion of innovations provides a set of questions and a necessary context to understand the management and implications of change.

The computer—the vehicle of the Information Superhighway—has also served as a conduit of diffusion. But there is no assurance that computers ensure that a company can successfully adapt to change. To illustrate this point, Rogers describes the challenges faced by researchers at the Xerox Palo Alto Research Center (PARC). Working among some of the brightest minds in the computer industry, PARC researchers were free to envision solutions to problems that did not yet exist. During the late 1960s and early 1970s, few people imagined that the average person would need personal access to a computer; fewer still thought that "head-in-the-cloud" researchers hired by a company that made copy machines could offer society anything much of substance. But PARC revolutionized computing by developing the laser printer, the mouse, and the Graphical User Interface.

Why isn't Xerox a key player in the computing industry today? Among the answers to this question, Rogers noted the *physical distance* between decision makers in the Xerox corporate headquarters, the excessive *rapidity* of change overtaking the industry as innovation outpaced most managers' wildest expectations, the *opposing internal cultures* of Xerox employees living and working on opposite coasts, and the *inflexible corporate identity* of Xerox—a copy machine company, not a computer company.

Think about factors that have slowed the diffusion of innovation in any industry: solar power in the automobile industry, standardization in the hotel industry, online stock management in the financial industry. You'll probably find a combination of two or more of these factors responsible for the paralysis that affects managers and other "experts" as old ideas give way to new ones.

Drawing from Rogers' work, Papa (1990) conducted research in two insurance companies that introduced new computer systems to their employees. He found that about one third of computer systems introduced to corporate settings fail to improve efficiency. So what are the factors necessary for computer-mediated diffusion of innovations? According to Papa, they are *interaction* and *diversity*. These two factors are more important than employees' previous experience with technology: "Put more simply, the more diverse an employee's network was, the more coworkers he or she talked to about the new technology, and the more frequently he or she talked about the new computer, the more productive that employee was likely to be using the new system" (p. 361). This should remind you of Jones' four qualities of virtual communities, described in chapter 6.

Here a question emerges: Is it possible for a diverse and active network of employees to maintain the corporate status quo? The role of diversity becomes central to this issue. Papa found that employees who interact across traditional functional lines of division—chatting in the hallway among members of different corporate departments, for example—are more successful in finding new and improved ways to utilize the technology than they would in networks of close colleagues. Might not these networks provide the means for isolated individuals and groups to find common interests in their relationship with the company? On the other hand, does technology as a motivator of human interaction serve merely to allow a more efficient transmission and maintenance of corporate discipline?

When studying the diffusion of innovations from the perspective of corporate Internet communication, you are challenged to reveal the functional relationships between persons and groups in a corporate setting and to analyze the restrictions and flow of human communication as mediated by computer technology. This approach might best be served when you assume the position of an auditor rather than a critic. Your primary goal is to observe practices at the level of lived and functional experience and to analyze how persons make sense of the machines in their midst. There is room for your individual response to the ideological implications of a corporate environment, but the ultimate goal of the diffusion perspective is to bring to sharp relief the ways in which discourse and change are channeled or blocked in a social setting.

CMC AND CORPORATE CONVERGENCE

A third perspective concentrates on *corporate convergence*. Here, one studies the ways in which computer technology in general (and Internet communication, specifically) blurs existing relationships and creates new ones. From the perspective of the corporate "bottom line," *convergence* appears to be the watchword in Internet communication. In this case, convergence refers to a process in which industries, formerly considered to offer distinct services, merge their products and distribution networks.

Schiller (1999) explains how Internet convergence mirrors a larger economic trend that began in the 1980s:

> In a cascade of huge mergers and acquisitions, multibillion dollar media properties—film studios, broadcast networks, program packagers, cable systems, satellite channels—changed hands like marbles. Such vertically integrated mega-media as TimeWarner, Disney, and News Corporation were created to fulfill the strategic goal of cross-promotion and cross-media program development. In their search for profit maximization, these powerhouse firms typically try to design and move program products across individual media boundaries. (p. 99)

This trend toward media convergence spells out important changes in how you'll be entertained, informed, and connected. We are referring not merely to the Internet, but to a convergence of all kinds of data: local phone calls, cable television shows, dial-on-demand movies, Web documents, and other forms of mediated communication, even the merger of information and entertainment into **infotainment**.

Of course, something strange happened on the way to that bright future. During the boom years of 1998 to 2000, young Internet companies eyed older, more established traditional media companies as likely targets in takeovers, both friendly and unfriendly. The newer companies with their paper profits would cherry-pick the ripe "content" from the older companies and spin off the remains. Although certainly convergences did, indeed, reap profits, the failure of one reflects the changing culture of the Internet Age.

Consider the example of AOL Time Warner, a result of the merger between two corporate behemoths in 2000 at the height of the dot-com boom. AOL, with its millions of subscribers and high-flying brand name, viewed the venerable conglomerate of Time Warner, with its incoming media outlets, magazines, book imprints, and other properties, as just spoils of war between so-called new media and old media. During a high-flying season of giddy market watchers proclaiming the advent of Dow 30,000, AOL poised itself to become the largest and most successful example of corporate convergence in human history. However, the explosion of Internet stocks fizzled once financiers began to expect profits from their venture capital investments. Moreover, consumers continued to find ways to get their news and entertainment for free, by-passing the central portals and fee-based systems created by converged companies to turn their plans into payments. Two years and $100 billion poorer, the merged company sheepishly dropped AOL from its name; the two corporate leaders who brought two companies together had long ago quit (Wilbert, 2003, p. 1B).

In a larger sense, we find that the problems faced by those seeking to profit from corporate convergence reflect the overall "reality check" endured by the Internet economy. Fast-growing regions that promised millions of high-tech jobs responded to the plunge of Wall Street support with layoffs and retrenchments. In the section that follows, we explore the status of one such region, Silicon Valley, before considering the factors necessary for a high-tech cluster to survive the post–dot-com boom era.

Convergence and Clusters of High-Tech Jobs

Like most nicknames, **Silicon Valley** is based on an historical reference more than a contemporary reality. Although you won't find Silicon Valley on most maps, most people agree that it is composed of a cluster of cities stretching south from the San Francisco Bay that include Menlo Park, Palo Alto, Cupertino, San Jose, and Campbell, California. Of course, as Winner (1999) wrote, Silicon Valley is "less a specific geographical location than a state of mind" (p. 36). Certainly, semiconductors and hardware are still manufactured in the Valley thanks to companies like HP, Sun Microsystems, and Cisco Systems. However, some of the fastest-growing companies like eBay, the online auction firm, and Yahoo!, the popular search engine company, illustrate how the Valley has begun to face a global economy that allows cheaper wages than can be paid in the United States.

The open question is whether Silicon Valley can sustain itself. Once the gathering place for billions of dollars of venture capital, the Palo Alto/San Jose array of businesses and allied services has settled into a funk best illustrated by the fact that the once unending traffic jams have become reduced to mere "rush hours." Corporate towers that sold for sky-high rents per square foot now go begging for tenants. Most tellingly, schools that once seemed to serve only as temporary incubators for "the next big thing" have become long-term holding patterns for students unsure of their next move beyond college. The jobs that powered Silicon Valley, once plentiful, now have become hard to find. Can Silicon Valley—and the dozens of similarly situated **high-tech clusters** around the world—survive?

What Are the Factors Necessary for the Development of High-Tech Clusters?

Here, the notion of convergence takes a predictive tone. As a researcher in this framework, you are encouraged to define parameters that shape and constrain the emergence of new clusters and analyze the passing of existing ones. Management consulting firm A. T. Kearney (1999) surveyed more than 100 executives for Internet-based firms searching for high-tech clusters—sites that draw highly educated workers, inspire technological innovation, and concentrate venture capital (seed money to grow businesses). They found four components that must converge for a high-tech cluster to be successful: access to talent, proximity to other industries/support services, access to capital, and high quality of life.

ACCESS TO TALENT. Three fourths of surveyed executives state that well-educated, motivated employees are essential for a high-tech cluster to thrive. This explains why so many clusters form in the intersection of several top-notch universities. Access to talent is particularly critical in an age of increased demand and decreasing supply of labor. In Silicon Valley, for example, too many jobs chase too few viable workers in most fields, resulting in escalating salaries and perks—and declining loyalty to the boss.

PROXIMITY TO OTHER INDUSTRIES AND SUPPORT SERVICES. High-tech clusters cannot survive on brainpower alone. They need access to good airports, media firms, advertising agencies, warehouses (data and physical), and other business-essential sites. Beyond the obvious support system necessary for a cluster to thrive, high-tech industry cannot endure without a secondary network of teachers, police officers, fire fighters, mechanics, and the other people who keep a community going. Turning once more to our Silicon Valley case study, rising salaries and limited housing have contributed to a struggle to keep secondary support services. For many folks who aren't awash in Internet-related earnings, it's just too expensive to live where they work. The result is a threat to this cluster's ability to endure.

ACCESS TO CAPITAL. Entrepreneurs with big plans and workers willing to turn the visions into reality may be the heart of a high-tech cluster, but funding is the circulatory system. This is particularly true when Internet businesses incur huge costs in rent, equipment, and (of course) talent but do not plan to make money for several years. Thus, clusters thrive near investment centers and investors who don't fear risking millions on a new idea. Returning to Silicon Valley, we see a partial explanation for success given that an estimated one fourth of venture capital invested in the United States comes to the land of Apple Computer, Cisco, and Yahoo!.

QUALITY-OF-LIFE ISSUES. A high-tech cluster cannot endure on work, support, and money alone. Other somewhat more intangible factors play into their success. Flush with cash, many Internet-age workers seek a combination of outdoor activities, cultural opportunities, and luxury items. On the same token, a cluster will suffocate in traffic, escalating housing costs, and stress. For this reason, many Internet business watchers cast a wary eye on the potential for Silicon Valley to dominate the computer and software industries for another 20 years.

The study of corporate convergence is the analysis of how disparate forces and personalities form networks. The method of your study stems less from ideology or auditing than your ability to analyze systems whose members do not necessarily plan their interactions. Certainly, some forms of convergence are organized in the forms of mergers and portals. However, convergence is frequently the study of serendipity and unplanned synchronicity as commercial, educational, and political entities align themselves. We highlight this approach here because of the increasing role of Internet communication in the emergence of these corporate networks that blur apparently insurmountable obstacles. As a student of Internet-inspired convergence, your primary goal is to invoke constellations where other people see random stars.

CHAPTER SUMMARY

This chapter has examined the impact of Internet communication on the corporate world as the United States shifts from an industrial economy to an information economy. We examined the roles of control and feedback mechanisms that precipitated this change and contextualized this revolution in light of changes that occurred after the World War II. To examine the cultural implications of this new economy, we proposed three theoretical approaches: discipline, diffusion, and convergence.

An emphasis on discipline mandates a critical approach that asks how computer technology serves to render docile the bodies and habits of employees and consumers in response to powerful corporations. Studying the use of hardware and software to monitor the activities of employees and consumers, we proposed the electronic panopticon as a metaphor to illustrate the process through which people are disciplined through individuation and disembodied influence, resulting, ultimately, in anticipatory conformity. The techniques we examined through which consumers are monitored are the use of cookies, voluntary data submission, and data mining. We concluded this section with a review of ethical issues that arise from the use of disciplinary technology.

We explored diffusion of innovation theory as a means to study the ways in which new technology reflects and inspires social and cultural change within corporations and other cultures. After defining diffusion as communication about new ideas through certain channels over time among members of a social system, we examined factors that can hinder this process such as physical distance, excessive rapidity of change, opposing internal cultures, and inflexible corporate identity. Then we described two factors linked to the effective diffusion of innovation: interaction and diversity.

The third section of this chapter identified corporate convergence as a standpoint for the study of Internet communication. In terms of method, corporate convergence calls on researchers to interpret historical and economic forces with an eye on the social impacts of these new megafirms. In this section, however, we concentrated on recent struggles of corporations to converge previously distinct information and entertainment businesses, particularly in light of the "Dot Bomb" era. We concluded with a discussion of four major factors necessary for the endurance of high-tech clusters: access to talent, proximity to other industries/support services, access to capital, and high quality of life.

In this chapter, we identified three frameworks for the study of how power is concentrated, diffused, and networked. What has been lacking is a careful analysis of how Internet communication might reflect and amplify social distinctions and inequities throughout U.S. culture. In the next chapter, we take on this issue directly.

ONLINE COMMUNICATION AND THE LAW

Is it legal to download free music from the World Wide Web? In Fall 2003, the Recording Industry Association of America (RIAA)—an umbrella group for the five largest music companies—weighed in on that question with hundreds of lawsuits against file sharers around the country, some with penalties in the billions of dollars for the songs they allowed millions of people to access. Reminiscent of our discussion on online communications in chapter 6, peer-to-peer file sharing software illustrates an attempt to form a sense of community among Internet music lovers. To the RIAA, that sense of community reflected little more than a loosely organized mob of thieves who performed the technical equivalent of breaking into a music store and looting the place under cover of darkness.

Using provisions of the Digital Millennium Copyright Act of 1998, the RIAA subpoenaed the records and contact information for prolific file sharers, including a 12-year-old girl whose mother was understandably shocked to find herself facing a lawsuit by a powerful association of music companies. Almost immediately, a public backlash followed, particularly in response to the suing of children, and the industry group began to offer settlements to avoid bruising court battles.

In coming months, their tactics fell under increasing scrutiny but the point remained clear. People who download music from Internet files without following up with a purchase may be branded criminals and hauled into court. In the wake of these cases and the many that followed, pay-for-play download stores like Apple's iTunes music store grew in popularity. Even so, the lawsuits and the furor that followed frustrated many people who never imagined that they'd done anything wrong. Quoted in the *San Francisco Chronicle*, school bus driver Nancy Davis sums up the confusion aptly: "I thought, if it's on the Internet, it must be OK" (Kopytoff, Yi, & Vargas, 2003).

Glossary

Anticipatory conformity: Adopting a docile and disciplined relationship to authority because of the potential rather than the practice of domination.

Cookies: Pieces of software downloaded from a computer network or Web site used to track your individual computing habits. Cookies are frequently used to generate customized browsing experiences on the World Wide Web.

Corporate convergence: The blurring of previously disparate industries. Convergence commonly occurs within and between communications, information, and computer industries. A recent example of corporate convergence is the creation of MSNBC—a blurring of information technology and a news and entertainment company. Goals of corporate convergence include cross-promotion and cross-media program development.

Cyberslacking: Using corporate information technology for personal ends.

Data mining: Process through which disparate pieces of information from multiple sources are gathered, stored, and sold to develop an evolving construct of a person's habits and personality.

Diffusion of innovations: Communication about new ideas through certain channels over time among members of a social system.

Disciplinary technology: A critical perspective on CMC that studies the ways in which machines serve to reflect and reinforce power relationships between individuals and groups.

Electronic communications monitoring: Storage and review of e-mail, recording and review of telephone conversations, storage and review of voice mail messages, storage and review of computer files, and video recording of employee job performance (definition adopted from American Management Association).

Electronic panopticon: An extension on the panopticon concept (see definition of panopticon) through which computer technology serves to deindividuate, isolate, and monitor the behaviors of persons, generally in a corporate context.

High-tech clusters: Concentrations of technological innovations such as Silicon Valley and Multimedia Gulch that generally depend on four factors to thrive: access to talent, proximity to other industries/support services, access to capital, and a high quality of life.

Information economy: An economy marked by an emphasis on knowledge and symbol manipulation, in contrast to an economy whose success is measured by the production of physical goods.

Information society: A broader term for a society whose cohesion may be traced to a dependence on standardization, bureaucracy, and national-scale advertising rather than oral traditions and regional ties.

Infotainment: An example of convergence: The blurring of information and entertainment.

Panopticon: Architectural notion of a humane penitentiary that disciplines prisoners through the constant use of surveillance and isolation rather than physical punishment.

Silicon Valley: Technology cluster in Palo Alto, Cupertino, and San Jose; headquarters of Apple Computer, Yahoo!, and eBay and location of Stanford University.

Topics for Discussion

1. Does the emergence of the information economy mandate an educational system different from the one that dominated during your parents' youth? Generate a list of the top five competencies required in today's workplace and propose ways in which modern schooling might better meet those needs.

2. In our discussion of the panopticon, we explored the roles of individuation and surveillance as tools to discipline the bodies of prisoners. Rank-order five examples of communication technology (e.g., voice mail, instant messaging) to determine which corporate tools contribute most to the construction of an electronic panopticon.

3. Data mining is a rapidly growing tool to determine a consumer's interests and habits. During a 24-hour period, keep a notepad with you and make a notation of every instance you feel that your personal information is being collected by someone else. Which occasions of data mining appear to be appropriate? When is data mining inappropriate?

4. In this chapter, we discussed the role of interaction and diversity in the diffusion of innovations. How might you employ communications technology such as the World Wide Web or instant messaging to increase one of these components of your workplace? In a paragraph, outline the specific approach you might take and anticipate problems you might face.

REFERENCES

American Management Association. (2003, May 28). *New survey on workplace e-mail reveals disasters in the making.* Retrieved from http://www.amanet.org/press/amanews/Email_Survey2003.htm

A. T. Kearney. (1999, June 21). *New study analyzes challenges to Silicon Valley's Internet industry leadership.* Retrieved from http://www.atkearney.com/about/press/072199.html

Barker, J. R., & Cheney, G. (1994). The concept and the practices of discipline in contemporary organizational life. *Communication Monographs, 61,* 19–43.

Belton, B. (1999). U.S. brings economy into information age. *USA Today,* p. B1.

Beniger, J. R. (1986). *The control revolution: Technological and economic origins of the information society.* Cambridge, MA: Harvard University Press.

Blackburn, N. (1999, January 19). Beware, your employer may be watching you. *Jerusalem Post,* p. E13.

Botan, C. (1996). Communication work and electronic surveillance: A model for predicting panoptic effects. *Communication Monographs, 63,* 293–313.

Bruckheimer, J. (Producer). Scott, T. (Director). (1998). *Enemy of the State* [Motion picture]. United States: Jerry Bruckheimer Films.

Chaplin, C. (Producer). Chaplin, C. (Director). (1936). *Modern times* [Motion picture]. United States: United Artists.

Coupland, D. (1994). *Microserfs.* New York: ReganBooks.

Fischer, C. S. (1991). "Touch someone": The telephone industry discovers sociability. In M. C. LaFollette & J. K. Stein's (Eds.), *Technology and choice* (pp. 87–116). Chicago: University of Chicago Press.

Foucault, M. (1979). *Discipline and punish: The birth of the prison.* New York: Vintage Books.

Gandy, O. H. (1989). The surveillance society: Information technology and bureaucratic social control. *Journal of Communication, 39*(3), 61–76.

Kopytoff, V., Yi, M., & Vargas, J. A. (2003, September 9). Music lawsuits snare 18 in Bay Area. *San Francisco Chronicle*, p. A1.

Lane, F. R. (2003). The naked employee: How technology is compromising workplace privacy. New York: AMACOM.

Lyon, D. (1994). *The electronic eye: The rise of surveillance society*. Minneapolis: University of Minnesota Press.

Marx, G. T. (1998). Ethics for the new surveillance. *The Information Society, 14,* 171–185.

Naughton, K. (1999, November 29). Cyberslacking. *Newsweek*, pp. 62–65.

Papa, M. J. (1990). Communication network patterns and employee performance with new technology. *Communication Research, 17,* 344–368.

Provenzo, E. F. (1992). The electronic Panopticon: Censorship, control, and indoctrination in post-typographic culture. In M. C. Tuman (Ed.), *Literacy online: The promise (and peril) of reading and writing with computers* (pp. 167–188). Pittsburgh: University of Pittsburgh Press.

Rogers, E. (1995). *Diffusion of innovations*. New York: Free Press.

Schiller, D. (1999). *Digital capitalism: Networking the global market system*. Cambridge, MA: MIT Press.

Wilbert, C. (2003, September 19). Media giant drops 'AOL' from name. *Atlanta Journal Constitution*, p. 1B.

Winner, L. (1999). Silicon Valley mystery house. In M. Sorkin (Ed.), *Variations on a theme park* (pp. 31–60). New York: Hill & Wang.

CHAPTER 8

ACCESSING THE MACHINE

The digital divide problem has been defined mainly in terms of access, but it needs to be defined more broadly as a matter of skill.
—Karen Mossberger (cited in Feder, 2003)

Grabbing a burger at your local McDonald's or sipping a latte down the road at Starbucks, you might find more than an inexpensive lunch or a caffeine jolt; you could also be able to download an mp3, update your blog, or check your e-mail. And you may be able to do it all for free. Inspired by the impressive rollout of by-the-hour wireless Internet access provided by Starbucks, fast food giant McDonald's has begun to experiment with wireless hubs so that customers can stay online even while grabbing a quick bite simply by opening their laptops or personal data assistants. However, two Chicago-area McDonald's franchisees have taken the next step: offering computer stations and Internet classes for their local communities. Why do they do it? One store-owner explains that his clientele, which includes a large number of economically disadvantaged folks, would otherwise lack access to the information and entertainment easily available to other populations in other regions. Without even having to purchase a small order of french fries, visitors waiting for the bus near Herb Bias' McDonald's can check out the World Wide Web just by signing up for a block of time at one of his store computer terminals: "People's time is precious. So why not give them the opportunity where they can have breakfast and do some computer work at the same time while they're in transit" (Jackson, 2003, p. 71)? Ideally, of course, patrons will sample the store's cuisine before logging off to hit the road, but even if they don't, McDonald's restaurants' experiments into free and (at other locations) low-cost Internet access will likely earn dividends in good will.

It is clear to many observers of Internet communication and commerce that this medium will have the same impact on national and global economy as the introduction of locomotives to the 19th-century world. Black (1999) quotes former Microsoft Chief Technology Officer Nathan Myhrvold: "E-commerce is an enormous equalizer .... It does not matter if you are in Dakar or Bombay. The Internet will be as important for the next 100 years as the railroad was for the last 100 years" (p. C2). Yet for many people, the Internet remains inaccessible.

Is access to information networks a human right, the same as access to food, clothing, and shelter? Many online activists say yes. Describing the work of groups such as Women Information and Technology, Spender (1998) illustrates an emerging goal: to increase **informacy** in the same manner as we seek to increase literacy, to ensure that all peoples—across the country and around the globe—enjoy the same opportunites to go online as most people reading this book.

In this chapter, we explore efforts by organizations and governments to increase access to Internet communication for disadvantaged and underrepresented groups—in short, we explore attempts to close the **digital divide**. The digital divide refers to a statistical difference in access to computer technology among various demographic groups. Initially, we analyze differing historical experiences of women and men on the Internet. We then explore the racial and economic dimensions of the digital divide. Following this discussion, we analyze critiques of the digital divide thesis, focusing on claims that advocates for federal involvement in the wiring of schools and communities overstate concerns about racial divisions online while ignoring regional divisions in high-speed Internet access. We conclude this chapter with comments about the global divide between information "haves" and "have-nots." Our purpose here is to continue a theme expressed throughout this text—to study the intersection of technology, identity, and culture within Internet communication. Even as the number of Internet users grows year by year, are some individuals and communities more likely than other to have access to online communication?

A CHICKEN IN EVERY POT AND AN INTERNET-CAPABLE COMPUTER IN EVERY HOME?

That certainly seems to be a goal of those who claim that access to computers and information networks has become a human rights issue for the new century. During the 1980s and early 1990s, many communication scholars concentrated on the differing levels of access to technology experienced by women and men (Baran, 1985; Jansen, 1989; Rakow, 1988; Rakow & Navarro, 1993). A common thesis to many of these works states that technology, although not necessarily the domain of man in an essentialist sense, has nonetheless been used to observe, limit, and control the movements of women in and out of the public sphere. Marvin (1988) provides an historical object lesson for this kind of study, describing the Electric Girl Lighting Company that in 1884 supplied "illuminated girls" for indoor occasions: "Women's bodies were . . . decorated with electric light, logically extending their conventional adornment and not less frequently their cultural objectification" (p. 137). Here, one imagines that women in the Victorian period could adorn themselves with electricity, but none could control the power.

As the United States industrialized in earnest during and after World War II, many technologies of work maintained their gendered natures—their appropriate uses defined by patriarchal assumptions. Toffler (1990) defines the industrial ideology that reinforced this state of affairs as "material-ismo" in which "the manufacture of goods—autos, radios, tractors, TV sets—was seen as 'male' or macho, and words like practical, realistic, or hardheaded were associated with it" (p. 79). Communication scholars would expand from Toffler's analysis to explore the metaphors and practices that serve to perpetuate this gendered notion of technology.

In the first years of popular Internet use, many women found that the same gender divide crippled their chances to enjoy equal access to the online medium. Kramarae (1998) noted:

> Looking at the programs and the discussions of computer technology, we see that women are in this cyberspace but in the same basic ways they have been in the rest of men's technology creations, not as primary decision makers but primarily as tools or concepts to be used in the creations of men. (p. 107)

Although it is difficult to fully account for the qualitative experiences of women online, it is possible to state that the numerical gender gap of Internet users has disappeared in general terms. A 1995 survey of Internet usage reported that the ratio of women and men Internet users as 30:70. By 2000, the ratio had evened at 50:50. It is important to remember that these numbers reflect U.S. Internet users. International numbers still diverge significantly. One should also remember that access to the Web does not mean the same thing to women and men. Intriguing research agendas await scholars who wish to pursue how subtle markers of gender continue to become inscribed in Internet communication. Moreover, it is important to realize that even as the digital divide has largely disappeared from a gendered perspective, it remains in other contexts.

Race, Class, and Internet Usage

During the past decade, the Department of Commerce has conducted research on the extent of Internet access throughout the United States. Their initial studies warned of a growing digital divide, particularly when the data factored in demographic variables such as race and income. Inspired by studies such as these, local, state, and national organizations emerged to close the gap, to ensure that most (if not all) Americans enjoy access to the Internet in the same manner as they do basic services such as water and electricity. What progress has been made since those earlier warnings? To answer that question the Commerce Department's National Telecommunications and Information Administration (NTIA), conducted a survey of about 57,000 households in September 2001, releasing their findings in 2002. Their results inspired many observers to conclude that efforts to close the digital divide have largely succeeded but that important work remains.

The report, entitled *A Nation Online: How Americans Are Expanding Their Use of the Internet*, argues that Internet access has become an essential component to public life for most Americans. Indeed, the Commerce Department found that in September 2001, 174 million Americans (two thirds of the population) were online. Moreover, during the time of their study, they found that roughly 2 million more Americans go online every month. Many of these new Internet users are children, the fastest-growing group in the study. Already, three fourths of all teenagers use the Internet for study, socializing, and entertainment. Just think, a mere decade ago, Internet usage was a rarity, a research tool for scientists or a plaything for the wealthy. Now the Net has wired itself into the fabric of our lives through stand-alone computers, personal data assistants, mobile phones, mall kiosks, and a growing number of other means that allow virtually anyone to go online from virtually anywhere.

That's the idea, anyway. However, the Commerce Department still found that certain populations within the United States continue to lag behind when it comes to Internet access, particularly when you consider income and race. Survey research indicates that only 25% of Americans making less than $15,000 use the Internet, compared to 80% of Americans making more than $75,000. The racial divide offers another critical dimension, given that roughly 60% of Whites, Asian Americans, and Pacific Islanders access the Internet, far more than African Americans and Hispanics (Table 8.1).

Here, one should remember that despite the continuing disparity between population groups, computer usage and Internet access have grown for all demographic categories. Indeed, since 1998, Internet usage by Americans earning $15,000 or less

Table 8.1
Approximate Percentage of Internet Usage

	2001	2000	1998
White non-Hispanics	60%	50%	38%
Black non-Hispanics	40%	29%	19%
Asian Americans and			
Pacific Islanders	60%	50%	37%
Hispanics	32%	24%	16%

Source: Adapted from U.S. Department of Commerce, Economics and Statistics Administration, National Telecommunications and Information Administration. *A nation online: How Americans are expanding their use of the Internet.* Retrieved from http://www.ntia.doc.gov/ntiahome/dn/nationonline_020502.htm.

increased by 25%, whereas Internet usage by Americans earning $75,000 or more increased 11%. Similarly, Internet use among African Americans and Hispanics increased at a higher level than it did for Whites, Asian Americans, and Pacific Islanders. Even so, given the explosion of computer ownership and Internet usage across demographic groups, the question remains: Why does an economic and racial divide remain among Internet users?

HYPERLINK: THE PEN AND ELECTRONIC DEMOCRACY

In 1989, the city of Santa Monica introduced a municipal computer network called **Public Electronic Network** (PEN) and almost immediately its online participants used the forum to comment on economic problems facing the city. Rheingold (1994) recalled that a PEN action group turned its attention to the city's homeless—several of whom participated in the dialogue—and the physical divides that kept them from becoming full-fledged members of the Santa Monica community.

As PEN participants discussed the issue, it became apparent that homeless members of the Santa Monica community had little chance of finding work because they had no place to prepare for interviews, clean their clothes, or store their belongings. Group members decided to advocate the formation of SHWASHLOCK, an acronym for SHowers, WASHing machines, LOCKers. Using PEN to hone their arguments, SHWASHLOCK advocates went to city hall and got funding for their project.

PEN provides a powerful example of how crossing the digital divide—by making computer access free and publicly available—can help reduce economic inequities. However, as Varley (1998) noted, the online community dealt with plenty of problems including hard core participants who tended to dominate the conference proceedings and online sexism. Even so, 10 years later, the city of Santa Monica celebrated its enduring experiment in electronic democracy.

There are no definitive answers to this question. But socioeconomic factors such as the presence of a computer at home—and the ability to afford access to an ISP—seem to be more significant indicators of the digital divide than any other factor, even race. Research indicates, for example, that the digital divide for Americans of all racial groups disappears beyond the income level of $75,000. Even so, the economic and racial divides between various demographic communities represent a significant concern in our increasingly computer-mediated society.

In this section, we have examined research that suggests that a persisting digital divide among racial and income groups has eclipsed the gender gap. For many advocates and researchers, the issue is more important than statistics or demographics. Reporting on their research on the introduction of Internet technology to disadvantaged people, Bier, Gallo, Nucklos, Sherblom, and Pennick (1997) report that closing the digital divide can empower individuals by providing them tools to manage and transform their lives. What remains to be studied are critiques of the digital divide thesis. Is there such a significant problem here?

CRITIQUING THE DIGITAL DIVIDE

Claims of a growing divide between information "haves" and "have-nots" understandably raise great concerns about inequalities hidden by the popular embrace of Internet communication. However, some critics have been effective in calling into question the existence and focus of digital divide concerns. We address two of these responses: the **snapshot critique** and the **place, not race, critique**.

Snapshot Critique: Have-Nows and Have-Laters

There are plenty of critics of the digital divide thesis. Some argue that it overstates the "racial ravine"; others claims that it misses the real gap. Boaz (1999), executive vice president of the libertarian Cato Institute, argues that the distinction between groups' access to the Internet should be defined not as "haves" and "have-nots" but, rather, as "haves" and "have-laters." He argues that the "digital divide" should be viewed as a snapshot of a rapidly changing environment.

To be sure, the time necessary for technological innovations to reach a critical mass of Americans has become shorter and shorter. Indeed, it took 4 years for the Internet to reach 50 million users, almost 10 times less than it took radio to reach the same number of people (see Fig. 8.1).

Boaz (1999) argues that initial statistics indicating a growing divide among Whites, African Americans, and Hispanics (except among the wealthy) obscured the overall growth in Internet access among all groups: "What is really happening is that computer ownership and Internet access are spreading rapidly through society, with richer households getting there first." Perhaps the divergence among African Americans, Hispanics, and Whites in Internet usage will become smaller, following the trend in other media.

Place, Not Race, Critique

There is another response to the digital divide thesis that suggests that the real problem is less a question of race or even income and more a matter of geography. Even today, downtown centers and edge cities with their high-density business parks enjoy

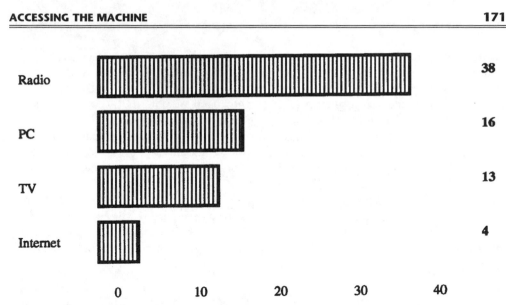

Fig. 8.1. Years to reach 50 million users for radio, PCs, TV, and the Internet. (Adapted from Commerce Department. Available online: http://www.esa.doc.gov/TheEmerging DigitalEconomy.cfm.)

much faster Internet connections than do small towns, rural areas, reservations, and inner-city neighborhoods.

Groups such as the Rural Broadband Coalition have begun to lobby Congress to provide more funding to small-town telecommunication companies to help wire

HYPERLINK: MAPPING THE NEW ECONOMY

Are there regions in the United States that are more likely to be wired than others? The Progressive Policy Institute, a Democratic Leadership Council think tank, decided to find out by creating a **New Economy Index:** a study that compares the states along five criteria:

1. The number and quality of "knowledge jobs"
2. The extent to which a state is involved in the global economy
3. The economic dynamism of state companies—epitomized by the number of **gazelle firms**, companies that thrive on rapid change
4. The degree to which its citizens are online
5. The amount of innovation generated by state companies

According to the Progressive Policy Institute (2002), the five states that have the highest numbers of people online are Alaska, Minnesota, New Hampshire, Wyoming, and Maryland. The five states with the lowest percentages of their populations online are Mississippi, Louisiana, Arkansas, Alabama, and West Virginia. On a regional basis, the hottest spots are on the Pacific Coast, along with the Mountain and Northeast states. The lowest rankings according to the New Economy Index are found in the Southern and Plains states.

communities that have been bypassed by the growth of Internet access in the past decade. Whereas dial-up connections have become virtually ubiquitous across the country, high-speed connections—aided by cable modems, digital subscriber lines, and similar technologies—remain beyond the reach of potentially 30% of Americans (Noguchi, 2003, p. E5). For many people who live on Native American tribal land, the numbers are even more striking. Entire communities continue to lack access to basic telecommunication services even today. Beyond demographic characteristics of race or class, geographical inequality of Internet access remains a daunting challenge.

Thus far, we have examined two critiques of the digital divide thesis: the snapshot critique and the place, not race, critique. What remains to be studied may be termed a third critique—the emphasis in the U.S. press on the domestic divide. Worldwide, researchers report that a more significant divide separates international haves and have-nots.

REDISCOVERING THE "WORLD" IN THE WORLD WIDE WEB

For many critics of the digital divide issue, the most obvious flaw in the argument concerns its focus: the United States. Although a fairly significant number of people living in the United States remain offline, most enjoy some access to the information economy, even if only through their proximity to a public library. When one considers the digital divide from a global standpoint, however, the gap turns into a chasm that will require decades to overcome. According to the Digital Opportunity Taskforce, a working group of the G8 industrialized nations, access to the Internet follows a much more fundamental set of problems:

> One third of the world population has never made a telephone call. Seventy percent of the world's poor live in rural and remote areas, where access to information and communications technologies, even to a telephone, is often scarce. Most of the information exchanged over global networks such as the Internet is in English, the language of less than ten percent of the world's population. (p. 6)

This statement illuminates a complicated range of problems. In many developing countries, the infrastructure necessary for the kind of telephony that most of us take for granted simply doesn't exist. Antiquated analog phone lines, exorbitant telephone tariffs, and similar challenges create seemingly insurmountable obstacles to the rollout of widespread Internet access in sub-Saharan Africa, South America, the Middle East, and other developing regions throughout the world. Thus the United Nations Conference on Trade and Development estimated in 2002 that although 655 million people use the Internet worldwide, the vast majority of them live in developed nations. Even so, change is coming.

Today, a third of all new Internet users throughout the world live in developing nations. Many rely on wireless "hot spots" sprouting up in places where telephone upgrades are simply not feasible. Many others access the Net through mobile phones and community centers set up by nongovernmental organizations. Thus, between 2000 and 2001, the number of "netizens" increased 43% in Africa and 36% in Latin

America, compared to the slower
gr~   ~es of 10% in North America
        ~re, 2002, p. 39). In many
        ~ns, the rise of Internet
            +~ governmen-
                ~~s quo.
                    ~ Re-
                    'ed

            ~ be
            ~e ques-
        ~ As we briefly
        tne three implica-
    ~nation networking around
    ~~d, consider this question: Does
~~ternet communication challenge or
merely mirror inequitable power relationships?

Decentralization Versus Recentralization

These terms refer to the relative control exerted by a "center" of power over those
people and institutions that surround it. To illustrate this point, consider the shifts in
power in U.S. society from the Washington, DC, beltway to states and cities—and back
from those institutions to the capital—through U.S. history. This process of expansion
and retraction might be defined as centralization versus recentralization. On a broader
stage, consider nation states.

Nation states are a relatively recent phenomenon. As you may recall from chapter 6, they might be considered a form of imagined community, woven together
through shared texts. However, the nation state is challenged by supranational organizations that use network communication (and a weak international legal structure) to cross borders and bypass local restrictions (Mathews, 1997). International
financiers can strengthen or crush national and regional economies through the
use of virtually instantaneous information and money transfers. The result is a simultaneous decentralization of government control and a tightening grip by newer
entities.

Fragmentation Versus Integration

Fragmentation and integration refer to the relative degree of cohesion, of closeness and
familiarity, experienced by ethnic, religious, racial, and social groups. Is the United
States truly one nation, or a patchwork quilt of many peoples? On the international
stage, it appears that a new tribalism composed of groups and organizations that
share no common geography or political structures—only a unifying set of principles,

interests, or aspirations—has begun to fragment traditional social networks. Global online communities challenge or simply ignore governments and national identities by using the Internet to communicate. In doing so, they enable the integration of closely knit interest groups on a global scale.

Diversity Versus Homogenization

These terms refer to the relative sameness of human experience shared by individuals and groups. If every member of a community watches the same television shows, reads the same newspapers, and laughs at the same jokes, it may be considered homogeneous. If, however, a society has many overlapping and contradictory notions of entertainment, news, and humor, it is diverse.

Just as media companies converge their interests and ownership until a relatively small number of conglomerates produces the same bland mix of news and entertainment, individuals and groups around the world have begun to exploit the

HYPERLINK: THE GREAT FIREWALL OF CHINA

The People's Republic of China is one nation that has struggled with these forces. Since the 1980s, China has attempted to reconcile its centralized communist political structure with its decentralized economy, which allows for relatively autonomous regions to compete in the global marketplace without the shackles of a command system. China has also witnessed cultural fragmentation as its young people have found countless types of media to contrast with the state-controlled press that seeks to maintain order. Finally, China's diverse languages and plethora of ethnicities limit the desires of its leaders to maintain the illusion of homogeneity. In 1989, these tensions erupted in the Tiananmen Square massacre and resulted in a government crackdown on information exchange and public debate. But no central planners or Beijing bureaucrats could anticipate the impact of Internet communication on the People's Republic. Almost at once, Chinese discovered uncensored accounts of China's internal policies and external relations they could never find in the state-controlled broadcast media.

Responding to this challenge, the Chinese government faces a conundrum. The Internet offers a world of information, the essential component for any economy seeking to compete in the global market. Yet news of the outside world threatens the social order its leadership seeks to maintain. In 2002, Beijing responded to this exigency by cutting off access to the Google search engine for 2 weeks and installing so-called "information purifiers" in the many Internet cafes sprouting up throughout the country. Even so, many Chinese have discovered ways to avoid government-controlled connections to the net, relying on servers based outside of the country. According to one observer, "the most popular phrase on search engines in China is 'proxy server'" (Snoddy, 2002, p. 20).

comparatively cheap communications infrastructure to craft and distribute ethnically diverse music, microlanguage news, and hyperspecific activism.

CHAPTER SUMMARY

In this chapter, we have examined recent research on the digital divide—focusing closely on dimensions of gender, race, and income. We concluded that, although the gender divide has largely disappeared in Internet access, work remains to be done on the digital divide when race, ethnicity, and class are considered. We also explored critiques of the digital divide thesis claiming that researchers are either too concerned about race or not nearly concerned enough about geography. Adding to these critiques, we concluded with a study of the global divide in information access. An appropriate next step for chapter 9 is an analysis of ways in which individuals and groups have begun to challenge the digital divide on their own terms. You may find that some of their tactics are quite surprising.

ONLINE COMMUNICATION AND THE LAW

The American Dream: your own home, maybe a yard, perhaps a nice porch— and a high-speed Internet connection? Increasingly throughout the United States, houses built with state funds must be wired to receive Internet access, preferably the high-speed variety you probably enjoy on campus. In many cities and states, using the power of the state to ensure that all citizens regardless of income have the potential to access the net from their homes represents the most tangible response to the digital divide. For example, the Kentucky Housing Corporation has mandated that homes and apartments financed with the aid of state funds for low-income housing must include the wiring that costs, on average, between $50 and $75 per unit. According to the president of a nonprofit organization that worked with Kentucky to ensure that each of its low-income housing units be wired for high-speed Internet access, the ability for residents to access a world of information far outweighs the relatively small price of the mandate: "The paradox of the digital age is that while technology expands opportunities for significant numbers of people, it can also divide us further by highlighting the difference between the haves and the have-nots" (Lyon, 2002, n.p.). Kentucky is the first state to embrace this initiative, but others will soon join the commonwealth. Nebraska, Oregon, and Wisconsin have begun to push homebuilders in their respective states to ensure that even low-income families can enjoy high-speed Internet access. Discussing the new policies in *Wired News*, Dustin Goot (2003) quotes an executive for the Chicago Housing Authority that has also begun experimenting with model home communities featuring fiber-optic connections: "It's a sensible policy . . . we're building homes for the 21st century" (n.p.). It remains to be seen whether Internet access will join electricity and clean running water as an essential component of all American homes, but the trend is clear. Across the country, cities and states are working to close the digital divide one front porch at a time.

Glossary

Digital divide: A statistical difference in access to computer technology among various demographic groups.

Gazelle firm: A fast-growing company, typically at a rate of 20% per year for 4 years.

Informacy: Extension of literacy, a universal right to information.

New Economy Index: Progressive Policy Institute index of states' relative transformation from traditional to contemporary growth strategies along five criteria: knowledge jobs, globalization, dynamism, online access, and innovation.

Place, not race, critique: Critique of the digital divide thesis claiming that disparities in geographical access to high-speed Internet access are a more significant measure of the digital divide than comparative access of demographic groups.

Public Electronic Network: An early experiment in online democracy pioneered by the city of Santa Monica. Noteworthy for its SHASHLOCK project designed to provide homeless persons access to showers, washing machines, and storage lockers.

Snapshot critique: Critique of the digital divide thesis responding that statistics used to prove a growing disparity in Internet access among demographic groups do not reflect historical trends.

Topics for Discussion

1. Many individuals and groups concerned about the digital divide have called for the federal government to increase its aid to states and organizations trying to get Internet access to disadvantaged and underrepresented groups. Generate a list of reasons for and against government activities to expand Internet access. What seems to be the trend in your responses?

2. Conduct a survey of local and private organizations that have set up Community Internet Access Centers near your college or hometown. Generate a set of suggestions for how your class might contribute knowledge and or labor to one of these centers.

3. Read the Commerce Department report on Internet Access online (http://www.ntia.doc.gov/ntiahome/dn/nationonline_020502.htm). Can you find a demographic category or group of persons not adequately addressed by the report findings? Be prepared to explain your answer.

4. Examine the Progressive Policy Institute New Economy Index (http://www.neweconomyindex.org/states/) and explore the position of your home state compared to others. What are three factors that explain your state's relative position?

5. Some international activists have begun to claim that information access is a human right on par with the right of free speech and religious expression. Do

you agree that access to online information should be included as a basic human right? Develop a 3-minute presentation for an imagined audience of folks opposed to the notion that information should be freely accessible. What strategies should you use?

REFERENCES

Baran, B. (1985). Office automation and women's work: The technological transformation of the insurance industry. In M. Castells (Ed.), *High technology, space, and society* (pp. 143–171). Beverly Hills, CA: Sage.

Bier, M., Gallo, M., Nucklos, E., Sherblom, S., & Pennick, M. (1997). Personal empowerment in the study of home Internet use by low-income families. *Journal of Research on Computing in Education, Winter,* 107–132.

Black, G. (1999, November 30). Sharing a goal to close the world's digital divide. *The Seattle Times,* p. C2.

Boaz, D. (1999). A snapshot view of the world. *CATO commentary.* Retrieved from http://www.cato.org/dailys/07-17-99.html

Digital Opportunity Task Force. *Digital opportunities for all: Meeting the challenge.* Retrieved from http://www.dotforce.org/reports/DOT_Force_Report_V_5.0h.pdf

Feder, B. J. (2003, July 8). Information on-ramp crosses a digital divide. *The New York Times,* p. C1.

Goot, D. (2003, February 11). A broadband hookup in every home. *Wired News.* Retrieved from http://www.wired.com/news/politics/0,1283,57249,00.html

Jackson, C. (2003). 2 Franchisees here already in cyberspace. *Chicago Sun-Times,* p. 71.

Jansen, S. C. (1989). Gender and the information society: A socially structured silence. *Journal of Communication, 39*(3), 196–215.

Kramarae, C. (1998). Feminist fictions of future technology. In S. Smith (Ed.), *Cybersociety 2.0: Revisiting computer-mediated communication and community* (pp. 100–128). Thousand Oaks, CA: Sage.

Lyon, K. (2002, October 1). New policy to connect more Kentucky families to the internet. *Press Release.* Retrieved from http://www.kyhousing.org/news/resources/PR10-01-02.pdf

Marvin, C. (1988). *When old technologies were new: Thinking about electric communication in the late nineteenth century.* New York: Oxford University Press.

Mathews, J. T. (1997). Power shift. *Foreign Affairs, 76*(1), 50–66.

Millions more use the internet. (2002). *Melbourne Australia Herald Sun,* p. 39.

Noguchi, Y. (2003, July 10). Bringing broadband to rural America. *Washington Post,* p. E5.

Progressive Policy Institute. (2002). *State new economy index.* Retrieved from http://www.neweconomyindex.org/states/2002/04_digital_02.html

Rakow, L. F. (1988). Gendered technology, gendered practice. *Critical Studies in Mass Communication, 5,* 57–70.

Rakow, L. F., & Navarro, V. (1993). Remote mothering and the parallel shift: Women meet the cellular telephone. *Critical Studies in Mass Communication, 10,* 144–157.

Rheingold, H. (1994). *The virtual community: Homesteading on the electronic frontier.* New York: HarperPerennial.

Snoddy, R. (2002, November 8). The great firewall of China. *The Times (London)*, pp. 2, 20.

Spender, D. (1998). Social policy for cyberspace. In R. Holton (Ed.), *Composing cyberspace: Identity, community, and knowledge in the electronic age* (pp. 266–269). Boston: McGraw-Hill.

Toffler, A. (1990). *Powershift: Knowledge, wealth, and violence at the edge of the 21st century*. New York: Bantam Books.

United Nations Development Program. (1999). *Human development report*. Retrieved from http://www.undp.org/hdro/99.htm

Varley, P. (1998). Electronic democracy: What's really happening in Santa Monica. In R. Holton (Ed.), *Composing cyberspace: Identity, community, and knowledge in the electronic age* (pp. 244–252). Boston: McGraw-Hill.

CHAPTER

CARVING ALTERNATIVE SPACES

This is not the age of pamphleteers. It is the age of the engineers. The spark-gap is mightier than the pen.

—Lancelot Hogben

Do you agree with the above quotation? Before you decide, consider this case. In 2003, as the United States prepared to go to war in Iraq for the second time in little more than a decade, billions of people around the world awaited news of the first strikes. As aircraft streaked through the skies and troops hurtled across miles of desert, the attack inspired countless responses and personal reflections. Was the war morally justified? Would the Iraqis respond with chemical weapons? What was going on in Baghdad? In previous conflicts, most people would wait for traditional news media to sift through questions such as these, crafting their responses to second-hand accounts from events shrouded in the "fog of war." In the Internet Age, however, we did not depend on formal journalists to provide our only account of the war. The short attention spans of broadcast news programs and limited space of newspapers, even those promising to report "all the news fit to print," began to compete with self-styled journalists who used blogs to offer alternative views of the war.

In Baghdad, a 29-year-old blogger nicknamed Salam Pax challenged the assumption communicated by the Bush administration that Iraqi citizens would throng American troops immediately on their arrival, celebrating their liberation from the dictatorial regime of Saddam Hussein. Larsen (2003) quotes him as writing, "There are no waving masses of people welcoming the Americans nor are they surrendering by the thousands. . . . People are doing what all of us are, sitting in their homes hoping that a bomb doesn't fall on them" (p. 26). Begun as an extended conversation with friends from architecture school, Salam Pax's blog became transformed into a vivid account of life in the crosshairs. Branded a tool of the CIA, pursued by the Iraqi secret police, Pax become an international sensation because of his ability to use the Internet to share his voice and reflect on his anger at both sides of the conflict. Recently, he has published a book of his missives and attained a striking degree of fame for his witty and acerbic blog. Suddenly, the scared and angry fellow hiding in his parent's house has become an author with a place for his words in bookstores around the world.

And Salam Pax is not alone. Today across the globe, activists who might have been shut out of the public arena have found a powerful tool in the Internet (Coombs, 1998). Certainly, this network of networks can be blocked by various means. Many companies protect themselves with **firewalls**—software and hardware barriers that restrict access to and from their internal networks. Many parents, schools, libraries, and workplaces employ **filtering software** designed to restrict access to certain Web sites. Many national governments regulate their citizens' use of the Internet, fearing that their cultural and political harmony (and control) might be thwarted by foreign ideas. However, as discussed earlier, the Internet is not like any other communications medium. It is designed to regulate itself with little governance from a central location. When you think about CBS, *The New York Times*, or your favorite radio station, you can probably imagine a specific anchor person, building, or broadcasting tower. Internet communication, in contrast, pulses through many conduits. Close one, and it finds another.

In this chapter, we examine ways in which individuals and organizations have used Internet communication to carve alternative spaces for themselves in an increasingly global and centralized world. Much of this chapter focuses on the manner in which disparate groups, marginalized by small size, are forming communities of like-minded people to confront problems on the global stage (Warf & Grimes, 1997). In many ways, this chapter serves to bookend chapter 8. Chapter 8 outlined some critics' concerns that a digital divide separates information "haves" from "have-nots." Considering that so many communications networks are merging and growing, it may appear that this process is irreversible. We respond to this sense by outlining a notion of discursive resistance that emerges when individuals and groups use technology to create spaces of community and protest. Second, we analyze two specific rhetorics employed to shape these spaces: agonistic and utopian discourse. Finally, we evaluate a dangerous intersection of agonistic and utopian rhetoric online, the use of computer networks to disseminate hate speech.

DISCURSIVE RESISTANCE: CRAFTING ALTERNATIVE SPACES WITHIN DOMINANT PLACES

Discursive resistance is a process through which text, oral, nonverbal communication, and other forms of meaning-making are employed to imagine alternatives to dominant power structures. This definition rests on a conception of discourse—communication that shapes or influences human relationships. A bit vague? Consider the discourse of being a student. There are rules, practices, and habits that one learns to adopt. There are also things that one may say and other things that one best not utter in a classroom. Is it OK to answer a question, or 10 questions? Is it OK to share your political views? Your family background? Your prejudices? Discourse contains all of these components. It is not what you say; it contains the rules for what may be said. Of course, all communication may be considered discursive to some degree; some are just more obvious than others. Discursive resistance may confront and reject those structures, but it seldom attacks them directly. Ironically, current trends reveal that the Internet may be an unlikely site of discursive resistance.

For some observers, the Internet will inevitably become ubiquitous and indistinguishable from other social institutions. Rather than maintain its cultural mystique as a lawless frontier where anybody can put down a homestead, the Internet will become domesticated, controlled, and part of disciplined society. David Plotnikoff (1999) writes in the *San Jose Mercury News* that the Internet will become a "ubiquitous component of the economic and social landscape (or, to look at it another way, as economic and social affairs become part of the Net's landscape) all this technology will recede to the back of our consciousness and seem utterly unremarkable." If Plotnikoff is right, will there be room left in this medium for individuals and groups who resist dominant society?

To answer this question, we first outline our notion of alternative spaces online as discursive resistance against dominant culture. These forms of resistance may not enjoy wide popular support; they may not even be successful in literal terms. However, they succeed insofar as they enable some form of critique against powerful places that might otherwise obstruct or even eliminate any form of dialogue. Hopefully, at this point, you have noticed that we use "space" and "place" somewhat specifically. These concepts are examined more carefully next.

Places of Control: Spaces of Resistance

Place works to formalize, authorize, and make permanent the processes through which dominant interests maintain their influence. We approach this definition from the perspective outlined by de Certeau (1984), who studied the way in which abstract institutional power—architectural drawings, maps, census data, and the like—is rendered concrete in places. When you think of a place, think of a shopping mall whose architectural design serves a singular purpose—to consume. You can think of other uses of the mall, but the place—its laws, habits, and organization—works hard to limit your choices. Toulmin (1990) further described the power of modern places to affirm "universal, timeless concepts" (p. 75). Places justify ideology and power by attaching a sense of permanence to them. When Blair, Jeppeson, and Pucci (1991) describe the modernism as a process through which dominant powers maintain their identities by invoking comprehensiveness of purpose and intent, we imagine place as a site where that process occurs.

Space, in contrast, is a localized, particular, momentary response to place. Space is a set of options for the individuals and groups who struggle to find meaning and identity within (and despite) physical places. For de Certeau (1984), space is a profoundly personal and fluid experience: "The [place called 'street' is] geometrically defined by urban planning [yet] transformed into a space by walkers" (p. 117). Within that space, ideally, the places that surround us might be transformed. Here is an example: Imagine that you live in a country where any sign of protest would be met with violent police response. If you enter the public square and hoist banners and placards, you might be harmed or killed. But what if you enter that square and merely stand your ground—making no obvious protest? That's what the Mothers of Plaza de Mayo did when they occupied public arenas in silent protest of the military and economic brutality of an Argentinean dictatorship during the 1970s. Their construction of a rhetorical space through the astute manipulation of an architectural place blurred the distinctions between public and private. Their inner pains were revealed, but not spoken. The space of their stance in public locales made it possible for disenfranchised women to seize the public sphere, even if only for a moment (Fabj, 1993). As Lefebvre (1991) reminded us, "Space is becoming the principle stake of goal-directed actions and struggles" (p. 410). Place and space might best be related in this manner: Places constrain and affect the movements of people who construct spaces in response. When we speak of Internet communication "carving alternative spaces," we refer to the use of computer networks to construct discursive resistance to dominant forces—to build alternative paths, hiding spaces, impromptu monuments, and unauthorized meeting places online.

We approach this notion from an historical and theoretical perspective that posits that technological innovation has long served to challenge existing social orders. This does not mean that technology is the single engine of social change, only that technology plays a critical role in shaping changes in society. Consider the introduction of the printing press to Western society. Historians such as Lewis Mumford argue that movable type is second only to the clock in its impact on our culture and worldview. With mass production of the written word, access to new ideas becomes available to all people. Control over the press, literacy, and the public forum where the written word may be displayed and archived remained a critical factor that limited the potential of this technology to significantly affect human relationships. Thus, it should come as no surprise that the Protestant Reformation began when Martin Luther posted his 95 Theses in the public forum of a church door.

In the last 35 years alone, the technology of communication served to challenge cultures of control. In the 1970s, tape recorders carried illegal speeches by Iranian holy men who rejected their nation's government. In the 1980s the fax machine became a critical tool of anti-Communist leaders in the former Soviet Union. In the 1990s, the Internet carried appeals by the Zapatista insurgency for global attention to their stand against the Mexican government. In each case, individuals and groups shaped discursive spaces that acted to resist dominant places in their societies.

How might studies of space and place sharpen your analysis of online communication? Consider cyberspace as a site where individuals and groups craft alternatives to dominant places that shape their interaction. These spaces may be individual Web sites or constellations of sites located on servers around the world. Some of these sites enable discursive resistance by advocating direct action: Some ask you to join boycotts against oil companies, purchase locally grown fruits, or support charitable causes. As discussed later, some advocate far more radical responses to perceived moral decay of a people.

However, as we also discover, not all alternative spaces work so publicly. Some sites achieve some measure of success merely by providing a location where intentional and ad hoc communities may form. **Intentional communities** are those comprised of persons who elect to join one another for a specific cause. Typically, they are unified by some shared geography, language, or cultural practice. These sustain themselves long enough to accomplish some goal—even when the goal is continued interaction.

Ad hoc communities are those groups that form spontaneously, often in response to a traumatic or threatening event. Online, these communities may be composed of strangers who may never meet face to face. Bereaved family members and friends who fashion virtual shrines after a disaster (such as the many web pages created to commemorate the lives of victims of the September 11th attacks) may be defined as ad hoc communities. In many important ways, this type of community serves as a site and means of protest.

Thus far, the discussion has focused on the site of Internet protest. The language of space and place provides a metaphoric means to identify how alternative and contradictory messages may possess the same discourse. As a student of communication, you might examine local examples in which individuals and groups craft an alternative space within a dominant place. What we need to examine at this point, however, is the process through which those resistant discourses are shaped. Do they seek to redeem a failed institution by confronting its limitations? Or, perhaps, do they concentrate their appeal to the evocation of an ideal social order that can be realized online, if not in the real world? Here we turn to agonistic and utopian rhetorics.

When the Mexican government stormed the Chiapas rain forests in 1995 to wipe out the ragtag Zapatista insurgency, the rebels knew they couldn't survive the onslaught. What started as a revolt against the signing of the Free Trade Agreement and its threatened exploitation of indigenous peoples turned into a bloodbath as the government poured troops and tanks into the region. Outnumbered and outgunned, Zapatistas appealed for help in e-mail messages forwarded around the world.

They accused the Mexican government of pillaging the poor state and brutalizing its people during the crackdown. Almost immediately, the government backed down and began peace talks. They had been beaten by the written word that connected guerillas to academics, journalists, and peace activists around the globe. Cleaver (1995; also see Cleaver, 1998), an economist at The University of Texas at Austin compared the Zapatista revolt online to postcolonial revolts in the second half of the 20th century:

> In cyberspace just as in the geographical frontiers of the Americas (the North American West, the South American Pampas or Rainforests) there has been a dynamic struggle between the pioneers and the profiteers. Just as mountain men, gauchos and poor farmers have sought independence through the flight to and colonization of new lands, so cyberspace pioneers have carved out new spaces and filled them with their own activity.

By 2004, you could find more than 50 Web sites dedicated to the Zapatista cause (see, e.g., http://www.ezln.org/). The Zapatista leader known as Subcommander Marcos explains how these sites can alter the balance of power between a government and its opponents. Social control can no longer be maintained by force: "What governments should really fear...is a communications expert" (Watson, 1995, p. 36).

But, remember, redemption and idealism do not necessarily mean the same thing to all peoples. Some of the most troubling discourse seeks to create a better world.

AGONISTIC AND UTOPIAN RHETORIC ONLINE

Communication theorists have long debated the role of confrontation in public discourse. Ancient teachers (and critics) of rhetoric argued that the speaker's primary goal is to evoke and embody the goals and ideals of the audience. Confronting socially accepted and culturally embedded assumptions would surely result in rhetorical failure—indifference. The speaker would be rendered silent through force or some other mechanism and the audience would depart the scene unmoved. However, in times of social crisis, theorists of rhetoric tend to rethink the assumption that confrontational speech is counterproductive. After all, where can change take root but from the fields of conflict as values are placed in contest?

Perhaps confrontation may be defined as the rejection of a contemporary order of things and simultaneous invocation of a better worldview. Describing this process, Cathcart (1978) includes agonistic rhetoric in his study of human behavior. **Agonistic rhetoric** includes those forms of discourse that produce or invoke ritualized conflict with an established order. An example of agonistic rhetoric would be for you to upload a web page explaining why AOL is an awful ISP and demanding a change in its habits. Cathcart drew from literary critic Kenneth Burke to explain how this confrontation—reordering rather than reforming a broken system—attempts to inspire a sense of guilt that is either accepted by the speaker (and audience) or cast onto another person, group, or entity. The goal of agonistic rhetoric is to achieve redemption—to replace a faulty and disordered hierarchy of values and institutional power with a more perfect order.

This form of confrontation—where a communicator either accepts the role of mortified victim of some evil and admits guilt or blames an exterior force for the introduction of that evil onto an otherwise perfected hierarchy—can be used to explain the power of some forms of Internet communication to resist and rebuke contemporary systems and established order. In carving out alternative spaces of interaction, some communicators seek redress for perceived personal limitations or reaction to external failings of a system they cannot control.

Consider the example of a web page entitled "Sam Walton is the Anti-Christ." Harsh words! The site's creator, Alyssa Warrick, created this satiric web page in response to her concerns that the discount retailer has harmed the social order of small-town life by putting the owners of "Mom and Pop" hardware

---

Ethical Inquiry

Many so-called "hactivists" have employed their craft to attack corporate and governmental Internet resources they deem to be unethical, claiming that their actions accomplish a greater good than any potential cost suffered by their victims. As an issue of law or policy, the matter of hactivism can be rendered clear-cut. But the ethical quandary remains. Is it right to do harm to a person's or group's computer system if one feels that their actions merit such rebuke? Immanual Kant might remind us of a Categorical Imperative that makes deeds wrong in all cases. A more contextual ethicist could reply that the situation defines one's action as good or bad. Now, the matter is yours to contemplate. Can you imagine a case in which hacking would be ethical, even necessary?

stores out of business. Her page argues that Wal-Mart's founder, Sam Walton, is very likely the embodiment of evil imagined by the image of the Anti-Christ. Her "proof" includes some clever numerology that associates the discounter with the "mark of the beast," 666. She also notes that Wal-Mart was incorporated on Halloween—obviously proof of its demonic intentions. Finally (with the aid of some digital manipulation), Alyssa offers a "photograph" of Sam in Hell: "still up to no good." Obviously, "Sam Walton is the Anti-Christ" is a joke; Alyssa makes this clear. She does not intend to prove a case but rather to make a point through absurdity. Hers is, nonetheless, an example of agonistic rhetoric in which she places the blame for the decline of "Mom and Pop" America squarely at Sam's cloven feet.

To this point, we have studied a definition of confrontation online that is agonistic—the conflict is a ritualized response to the perceived failures of a dominant group or social order. However, confrontation that provides no alternatives can hardly be expected to succeed in doing more than destroying the existing system. Thus, as a necessary corollary to agonistic discourse, many Internet communicators evoke a form of rhetoric that is best described as utopian.

Utopian rhetoric is that which seeks to redress contemporary problems with the social system by invoking an ideal form of human interaction distant from the audience in time, space, or both. This form of communication was coined by Sir Thomas More, who wrote *Utopia* as a response to the perceived injustices of English society in the 16th century (Fig. 9.1).

Utopian rhetoric is more than the redemption imagined by Burke and enhanced by Cathcart's agonistic rhetoric. The power of utopia is its lack of accessible position. Indeed, the word *utopia* stems from an ironic relationship between Greek words for "no" and "place." In other words, it is a place that cannot exist; it signifies a perfect order that can never be achieved. As a corollary, utopian rhetoric creates an unassailable site from which one may protest with relative safety.

Internet protest might be regarded as utopian because the "sites" from which this discourse emerges are not physical—they are not "places" one can visit in a literal

Fig. 9.1. Sir Thomas More, author of *Utopia*.

manner. They are collections of text, pictures, and sounds. This is their limitation and their strength. Consider the notion of the "virtual nation": Some cyberactivists envision the construction of virtual nations in an attempt to gather like-minded folks seeking a better way of life than found in their own countries. For several years, Zoran Bacic inspired such a dream with his Virtual Yugoslavia: an attempt to recreate what had been destroyed through years of ethnic clashes and the implosion of the Milosevic regime in Belgrade. His nation would not be defined by blood or language; one would need only to "feel Yugoslav" to gain a passport. For a time, he imagined that his virtual country would gain admission to the United Nations, the physical land large enough only to hold the computer server that housed the national Web site. But, like the real country, his vision could not endure. One wonders, however, if the future of nationality—the potential for postnationality—awaits in the online realm.

What are some of the components of utopian rhetoric online? As we have seen, *absurdity* is one powerful tool of protest. To reveal imperfections in the dominant system, many online communicators respond with comical rebukes that, through their humor, reveal a deeper pathos. Utopian protest also draws from the notion that *community* invokes a powerful response to entrenched power. Most utopian fictions attend carefully to the details of community maintenance, if only because the gathering and keeping of potential utopians is so difficult. Third, utopian communication rests on a firm foundation of *social order*, even when the apparent relationships between individuals appear to be free of government control. The most extreme example of utopia might be defined as anarchy, the removal of government from human affairs. However, even in a true state of anarchy, some moral order of prescribed human relations exists in the absence of the "state." Without some moral order, utopia is often replaced by its opposite, **dystopia** (bad place).

The social order evoked in online utopias seldom resembles the orders that we inhabit. The order of utopia is typically a radical alternative that reveals, through its difference and distance from the contemporary world, the corruption of the dominant worldview. In this sense, every basic term and referent that shapes our daily lives becomes a site of potential conflict.

Throughout our discussion of agonistic and utopian rhetorics, we have run the risk of confusing protest with analysis. Protest seeks to change an existing social system, whereas analysis merely works to make sense out of the world. Many observers seeking to make sense of the Internet (and we may occasionally fall into this camp) run the risk of obscuring careful analysis with utopian rhetoric.

Kling (1996) responds to the perceived excesses in utopian and antiutopian writings about computerization in our society by arguing that students of Internet communication should adopt a posture of social realism. According to Kling, **social realism** employs empirical data to examine computerization as it is actually practiced and experienced. The question of whether realism simply obscures a particular worldview is interesting, but beside the point. Critics of any worldview do not stop with analysis; they employ agonistic and utopian discourses to change it. In Web sites and other electronic modes of communication, these messages benefit from a potentially global audience. However, as hinted earlier, the intersection of agonistic and utopian rhetoric is not necessarily positive.

In the section that follows, we explore ways in which individuals and groups have attempted to subvert existing power structures by invoking ideal communities that you might very well find to be troubling. Some of the ideas and statements uttered in this section have been selected because of their controversial nature. Their inclusion does not signify acceptance by us but, rather, our belief that the most frightening ideals found on the Internet should be recognized, not ignored.

HYPERLINK: KATHY DALIBERTI'S CYBER-QUILT

In March 1995, David Daliberti and Bill Barloon, U.S. civilians, were imprisoned by the Iraqi government after they inadvertently entered the country. David's wife, Kathy, waited at home for news from the State Department concerning the whereabouts of her husband, for some word that her government was acting to free the prisoners.

Home, ordinarily a site of comfort and safety, only reminded Kathy of her inability to act on her husband's behalf. In response to her growing frustration as the government failed to secure her husband's release, she created a home page called Yellow Ribbon. The Yellow Ribbon site worked on several levels to create an alternative space by recrafting the "home" as a public intersection of people and ideas, not a private and lonely abode. The home page featured press releases, archived e-mail by visitors, and links where friends and concerned observers could send messages to government officials. Most intriguingly, however, was the site's depiction of the date and time in Baghdad. This device created a dual location of the home page; it mirrored to some extent Kathy's home in Jacksonville, but it also symbolized David's temporary "home" in Iraq. In many ways, this conduit between Daliberti and her well-wishers was more than a cry for help. It was a protest against two governments.

The nature of this protest might remind you of early American quilts. Although homey and comforting, the selection of patches often served political purposes. Sometimes, those purposes were obscured by their simple design and lack of public display, but they served to provide voices to individuals kept from the public sphere: Freed from the isolating and controlling constraints of the structure, the quilt grows and connects, creating places of community on the very margins of power. Those who participate in its cocreation, even through the simple act of viewing, construct an alternative world—like the patches of the quilt that serve to recall distant times and places (Wood & Adams, 1998). Looking back on our discussion of discursive resistance, which rhetorical approach did Kathy Daliberti take: Agonistic? Utopian? Perhaps a combination of the two?

THE RHETORIC OF HATE ONLINE

Every January, the media go into a kind of almost spastic frenzy of adulation for the so-called "Reverend Doctor Martin Luther King, Jr." King has even had a national holiday declared in his honor, an

> honor accorded to no other American, not Washington,
> not Jefferson, not Lincoln. (Washington and Lincoln
> no longer have holidays---they share the
> generic-sounding "President's Day.") A liberal judge
> has sealed the FBI files on King until the year 2027.
> What are they hiding? Let's take a look at this
> modern-day plastic god.

Before the emergence of electronic networks, the only place you might find a screed like the one above would be on a hastily mimeographed flyer handed out in a crowd or posted on a telephone pole. However, in 2004, this message was available to anyone with an Internet connection. More alarmingly, it was posted on a Web site called Martinlutherking.org—a page operated by a hate group called Stormfront—advertised specifically for children seeking to do school reports on the civil rights leader (Fig. 9.2). As you might imagine, this message—not a specific threat or provocation against a person or group, simply a hateful post on a Web site—is protected by the First Amendment. However, there are other messages online that are far more dangerous, other forms of discourse that have forced antihate groups to refashion themselves as Internet watchdogs.

You may be surprised to learn that antihate groups like the NAACP and the Anti-Defamation League are purchasing Web addresses that feature some of the most insulting epithets for persons and groups imaginable—so that no one can use them (Leibovich, 1999). Think of the worst word for a person that you can imagine, and you will likely find that it has been purchased as a domain name by some individual or entity. For some observers of Internet communication, this is the Internet's dark side: its growing use as a platform for hate speech.

What is a **hate site**? According to *Tolerance.org*, a community of volunteer activists who monitor the emergence of Internet resources employed by antisocial groups to disseminate their messages, a hate site

> advocates violence against or unreasonable hostility toward those persons or organizations identified by their race, religion, national origin, sexual orientation, gender or disability. [This definition also includes] organizations or individuals that disseminate historically inaccurate information with regards to these persons or organizations for the purpose of vilification.

Fig. 9.2. White Pride logo found at Stormfront.org Web site.

What makes hate sites worth our attention is their potential ability to incite violence in ways that cannot be mirrored by traditional hate speech (Zickmund, 1997).

According to the Anti-Defamation League, Internet communication provides five advantages to individuals and groups seeking to transmit messages of hate: community, anonymity, outreach, commerce, and information. Throughout this analysis, you might wish to draw from your knowledge of agonistic and utopian rhetoric because it appears that both are at play at these kind of sites.

Community

Many hate groups use Internet communication to create or enhance a sense of community. Early in the 20th century, it was common—even fashionable—to be a public bigot in the United States. Many local communities and state governments included members of hate groups such as the Ku Klux Klan. Many historians argue that Klan messages found sympathetic ears in the federal government as well. Since the civil rights struggles of the 1960s, hate speech has become much less acceptable to most Americans. In the 1990s, the trend appeared to shift from established groups with sophisticated doctrines toward bedroom-based haters—individuals and small groups who had difficulty finding an audience for their messages. With the advent of the Internet, however, these cliques or cells of haters have discovered an ability to network among themselves—to fashion a sense, if not a reality, that they are not alone. Doing so, they craft a community that resists most people's notions of public life while seeking to construct a peculiar utopia.

Anonymity

Hate communities who find themselves isolated by popular opinion and legislation maintain their ties through the anonymity provided by Internet communication. Certainly, any message posted online can potentially be tracked to its originator. However, it is a far less dangerous act to e-mail a hateful message or view a racist Web site from a public computer than to stand in the middle of a town square in a white robe and pointy hood.

This component of Internet communication appears to support the conclusion made by some scholars that a virtual community of strangers is more likely to spawn and tolerate radical voices than a physical community of intimates. A necessary aspect to online anonymity is the ability for hate-site originators to move from service provider to service provider. Visit any list of hate sites and you will find that more than half do not function. Like mushrooms that grow after a hard rain, radical Internet hate sites that appear to advocate violence seldom last for long. However, their creators do not necessarily cease their communication; they just find a new site on which to post their messages.

Outreach

Some hate groups have begun using the Internet to seek new members often by crafting subtle appeals whose implications are difficult to discern. Remember the example of students doing research on Martin Luther King. They might be intrigued by a Web site entitled "Martin Luther King Jr.: A Historical Perspective." Its Web address (http://www.martinlutherking.org/) appears to be legitimate—maybe even owned by the King family or an institute dedicated to his memory. The first page includes an image of Dr. King in a thoughtful pose with children sitting nearby. However, closer examination of this site reveals its true intent. Its "Truth about Dr. King" section derides the civil rights activist as "a sexual degenerate, an America-hating Communist, and a criminal betrayer." The site's "Recommended Books" section features a biography of David Duke, a notorious "White rights" advocate and former Klan leader.

Commerce

Like most organizations, hate groups thrive on some level of commerce—if only to maintain access to ISPs, print newsletters, and purchase attire that marks their particular brand of community. Mail order centers and backroom shops hardly provide the customer base necessary to sustain a group of individuals whose views are shared by a minuscule percentage of the local population. However, Internet storefronts offering music, posters, books, and other paraphernalia may exploit a market of millions. The National Alliance (http://www.natall.com/) online store, for example, features 600 items, including a poster depicting a blond-haired, blue-eyed family as "Earth's Most Endangered Species." Commerce is essential to the body of hate groups around the world; Internet communication is an important artery.

Information

The most potentially significant component of Internet communication embraced by hate groups is the proliferation of bomb-making information available to anyone with access to Web sites. In their report, "Poisoning the Web: Hatred Online," the Anti-Defamation League (1999) reported, "For those inclined to violence, the Net offers a wealth of information—from instructions on building an ammonium nitrate bomb to methods for converting semi-automatics to fully automatic weapons—that can be accessed in minutes" (n.p.).

There are relatively few hate sites available online. Yet observers of radical rhetoric are concerned about their potential to spread their messages beyond a hard core following of social misfits. Many of these sites—most notably Stormfront—include "kids-only" pages, with games, stories, and illustrations designed to teach children a disturbing view of racial identity. They attempt to accomplish their goal through a combination of agonistic and utopian rhetoric—rejecting social order and, simultaneously, envisioning a new one that horrifies most people. Perhaps, most importantly, the five advantages gained by hate groups that have turned to the Internet to communicate their messages—community, anonymity, outreach, commerce, and information—are unlikely to be overcome by regulation or legislation. For many observers of this phenomenon, the only way to overcome bad speech is to confront it with good speech. Of course, in a democratic society, the definitions of those terms can never be fixed for long.

CHAPTER SUMMARY

In this chapter, we have described a process of discursive resistance that emerges when disenfranchised individuals or groups seize or fashion spaces of tactical response to places of dominant discipline. We found that these sorts of communication may be defined as agonistic or utopian. Agonistic rhetoric refers to those sorts of discourse that confront a perceived failing in the social order through a dramatic and ritualized display that seeks purification through either an admission of guilt or casting of blame. The goal of agonistic rhetoric is a form of redemption of the corrupted place. Utopian rhetoric, in contrast, focuses its attention on alternative spaces—often by ignoring or demeaning the importance of "real places." By existing "no place," this form of discursive resistance does not face the same risk of confrontation. However, it does not ensure a high probability of success in a traditional sense. Finally, we turned to the dark side of Internet protest by examining the emergence of hate groups online. Although their numbers are small, their impact is felt throughout society.

ONLINE COMMUNICATION AND THE LAW

In the wake of the September 11 attacks, the federal government acted quickly to propose new laws that would extend the power of intelligence gathering agencies to search for telltale signs of a future attack. While smoke hung in the air over New York City, while rescue personnel scoured the Pentagon for survivors, while strangers met at the field in Pennsylvania where Flight 93 made its final descent, Attorney General John Ashcroft spearheaded the USA Patriot Act, which would empower the government to search business records for clues of the plans and whereabouts of potential terrorists. As a result, an ISP could be compelled by the government to detail a person's online activities but be required by law not to reveal this to anyone. To critics of the Act and its subsequent revisions, the government has expanded its reach with the use of secret courts and broad interpretations of the standards by which a person's civil rights may be curtailed. To advocates, the Act reflects the reality of the post-9/11 world, in which people who hate the United States are willing and able to inflict catastrophic damage on its cities, landmarks, and population.

While *Online Communication* was in press, various provisions of the Patriot Act had begun to face congressional scrutiny, and a potential showdown in the Supreme Court seemed inevitable. Proponents and critics of the Act would marshal claims that these enhanced government powers either defend the Constitution in a fundamental way or trample its fundamental principles. Regardless of the decisions that would follow, the case is clear according to Ashcroft: "Sept. 11 taught us that terrorists had outflanked law enforcement in technology, communications and information. . . . So we fought for the tools necessary to protect the lives and liberty of the American people" (quoted in Lochhead, 2003, p. A4).

Glossary

Ad hoc communities: Communities of individuals brought together by an unforeseen event.

Agonistic communication: Discourse that produces or invokes ritualized conflict with an established order.

Discursive resistance: A process through which text, oral, nonverbal communication, and other forms of meaning-making are employed to imagine alternatives to dominant power structures.

Dystopia: Opposite of utopia; a "bad place."

Filtering software: Software that limits access to certain Internet sites, often by comparing Web addresses requested by users against a directory of domains.

Firewall: Software and hardware barriers that regulate access between networks.

Hate site: Web site that advocates violence against or unreasonable hostility toward those persons or organizations identified by their race, religion, national origin, sexual orientation, gender, or disability.

Intentional communities: Planned organizations of individuals to accomplish some goal or maintain some lifestyle.

Place: A location that formalizes, authorizes, and renders permanent the processes through which dominant interests maintain their influence over individuals and groups.

Social realism: The use of empirical data to examine computerization as it is actually practiced and experienced.

Space: A tactical response to a place through individual or group rearticulation of its intended use.

Utopian rhetoric: Discourse that imagines an ideal world that is distant from the real world in time and/or place in order to critique the contemporary social order.

Topics for Discussion

1. Conduct a Yahoo! search to find an insurgency group similar to the Zapatistas. Can you identify images or phrases that illustrate components of utopian rhetoric (absurdity, community, and social order)?

2. What are the necessary components of an effective online parody site? Visit one of the several Yahoo! parody sites available on the Web (such as "Yankovic!" at http://www.Yankovic.org). Which site seems to make its point most memorably? Write a one-paragraph statement that identifies your criteria for effective online parody.

3. Should online hate sites be banned by the federal government? Craft a one-page essay to support your answer. Draw from constitutional arguments, historical parallels, and a clearly stated ethical stance. Indicate which body of government, if any, should regulate online hate.

4. Of the five components of online hate sites described in this chapter (community, anonymity, outreach, commerce, and information), which one is most important to sustain a hate site?

REFERENCES

Anti-Defamation League. (1999). *Poisoning the web: Hatred online*. Retrieved from http://www.adl.org/poisoning_web/

Blair, C., Jeppeson, M. S., & Pucci, E. P., Jr. (1991). Public memorializing in postmodernity: The Vietnam veterans memorial as prototype. *Quarterly Journal of Speech, 77,* 263–288.

Cathcart, R. S. (1978). Movements: Confrontation as rhetorical form. *Southern Speech Communication Journal, 43*(3), 223–247.

Cleaver, H. M. (1995). *The zapatistas and the electronic fabric of struggle.* Retrieved from http://www.eco.utexas.edu/faculty/Cleaver/zaps.html

Cleaver, H. M. (1998). The zapatista effect: The Internet and the rise of an alternative political fabric. *Journal of International Affairs, 51,* 621–636.

Coombs, W. T. (1998). The Internet as potential equalizer: New leverage for confronting social responsibility. *Public Relations Review, 24,* 289–305.

de Certeau, M. (1984). *The practice of everyday life* (S. Rendall, Trans.). Berkeley: University of California Press.

Fabj, V. (1993). Motherhood as political voice: The rhetoric of the mothers of Plaza de Mayo. *Communication Studies, 44,* 1–18.

Kling, R. (1996, February 1). Hopes and horrors: Technological utopianism and anti-utopianism in narratives of computerization. *CMC Magazine.* Retrieved from http://www.december.com/cmc/mag/1996/feb/kling.html

Larsen, P. T. (2003, March 29). Bloggers take the war on Iraq on a journey into cyberspace. *Financial Times (London).* (First section), p. 26.

Lefebvre, H. (1991). *The production of space* (D. Nicholson-Smith, Trans.). Oxford: Basil Blackwell.

Leibovich, M. (1999, December 15). A new domain for hate speech. *The Washington Post,* p. A1.

Lochhead, C. (2003, September 25). Democrats seek rollback of the Patriot Act. *San Francisco Chronicle,* p. A4.

Plotnikoff, D. (1999, December 4). The closing of the Internet frontier is closer than you think. *San Jose Mercury News* [online]. http://www.mercurycenter.com/svtech/columns/modemdriver/docs/dp120599.html

Toulmin, S. (1990). *Cosmopolis: The hidden agenda of modernity.* Chicago: University of Chicago Press.

Warf, B., & Grimes, J. (1997). Counterhegemonic discourses and the Internet. *Geographical Review, 87,* 259–274.

Watson, R. (1995, February 27). When words are the best weapon. *Newsweek,* p. 36.

Wood, A., & Adams, T. (1998). Embracing the machine: Quilt and quilting as community-building architecture. In B. Ebo (Ed.), *Cyberghetto or cybertopia? Race, class, and gender on the Internet.* Westport, CT: Praeger.

Zickmund, S. (1997). Approaching the radical other: The discursive culture of cyberhate. In S. Jones (Ed.), *Virtual culture: Identity and communication in cybersociety* (pp. 185–205). Thousand Oaks, CA: Sage.

CHAPTER 10

POP CULTURE AND ONLINE EXPRESSION

> *The robot is going to lose. Not by much. But when the final score is tallied, flesh and blood is going to beat the damn monster.*
>
> —Adam Smith

> **Marge:** What exactly is it your company does again?
> **Homer:** This industry moves so fast it's really hard to tell. That's why I need a name that's cutting-edge, like CutCo, EdgeCom, Interslice.... Come on, Marge, you're good at these! Help me out!
> **Marge:** How about...CompuGlobalHyperMegaNet?

"CompuGlobalHyperMegaNet," a fictional company created by Homer Simpson in his attempts to cash in on the supposed Internet bonanza, illustrates the degree to which Internet communication has begun to saturate popular culture. Indeed The Simpsons Archive, the Web's most comprehensive resource dedicated to America's favorite cartoon family, lists dozens of Internet and computer references that have appeared on the show, including an episode in which Lisa, seeking to learn about badgers, visits the Web site whatbadgerseat.com. Anticipating the millions of people who might visit the site, Fox created an actual Web site that offers advice on feeding badgers. Reality following art, we find popular culture's embrace of online communication a sign of things to come.

In a way, this chapter's topic culminates the purpose of this book. It is important that we evaluate more than the technology of Internet communication. We seek to explain ways in which people interpret this technology, using it to make sense of identities and cultures in a changing world. In this manner, this chapter explores the **popular culture** that shapes our understanding of Internet communication. As Brummett (1994) explains, "Popular culture refers to those systems or artifacts that most people share and that most people know about" (p. 21). **Artifacts** are bits and pieces of human sense-making: books, magazines, movies, advertisements, comics, and the like. Popular culture research is certainly controversial (Jacobson, 1999). The study of *The Simpsons*, after all, can hardly be compared to the study of Shakespeare or Hemingway—can it?

We propose that the distinction between high and low culture implicit in that comparison is not nearly as important as this question: How do most people reading this book make sense of Internet communication? Theories and research projects offer useful and refined insights to answer that question. Historical and journalistic efforts further help us contextualize that question. But we are certain that *most* people trying to interpret the changes that sweep through our society in this so-called Internet Age are more likely to make use of pop culture than any social scientific tools available. The stories we tell about ourselves and the changes we recognize in our culture, inspired by deep-rooted myths and images of human community, often take the form of throwaway communication—a movie that you might have seen to pass the time, a book that kept you company while suntanning at the beach, a song whose lyrics you can't quite recall. Each of these artifacts is formed and re-formed each time we attempt to interpret the social world around us. Thus, we end this book with an analysis of some key themes that seem to shape popular conceptions of the Internet.

We begin by discussing the role of literature in shaping a response to the role of technology in our lives. In this section, we explore the relationship of two key themes in American literature that illustrate the complicated role played by technology within our lives. Following this overview, we examine cyberpunk fiction and its examination of the manner in which humans and machines have become blurred in contemporary society. Drawing primarily from the fiction of William Gibson and Donna Haraway's notion of the "cyborg," we explore a world that looks vaguely like the future but actually serves to warn us about the present. Following a discussion of cyberpunk's ambivalent relationship to "the future," we outline three common themes to this literary form: rejection of flesh, fear of multinational corporations, and obsession with speed. Turning to film in popular culture, we focus our attention on several "Internet-era" movies: *2001: A Space Odyssey*, *Tron*, *WarGames*, *Blade Runner*, *AI (Artificial Intelligence)*, and *The Matrix Trilogy*. A process that begins to unfold in these films, a collapse of human abilities to control their machines, seems to end with the obsolescence of humans altogether. However, as the latter two movies indicate, popular culture artifacts have not given up on humanity's ability to control its machines quite yet. Ultimately, this chapter seeks to explore ways in which Internet communication is situated in a larger cultural discourse about an increasingly technological society.

LITERARY DEPICTIONS OF TECHNOLOGY

Studying the impact of Internet communication on popular culture requires a brief discussion of the role of technology in literature (Dunn & Erlich, 1982). After all, popular literature is a central location where our cultural myths and assumptions are shaped. Literary efforts to make sense of technology often struggle to define the meaning of progress. As with many notions of public life, we seek a single and coherent view—a final answer to the question, "What is progress?" According to Joel Garreau's (1991) chapter, "The Machine, the Garden, and Paradise," progress is less a thing and more of a process through which fundamental debates over public life are fought. In other words, the improvement of a city street to accommodate businesses and homes may, to you, be progress. To your neighbor, that very same process may represent the decay of nature. Garreau turns to Leo Marx to illustrate this process through which American public life may be defined by a struggle between two objectives of progress: the **machine** and the **garden**.

Leo Marx describes the **machine**—epitomized by the locomotive that cuts a sharp path through the landscape—as the metaphor for industrialization in America. In a

1988 interview with Judith Lee, Marx wrote, "The general faith...was that things were going to get better and better—not only materially but also morally, politically, and socially—and this predominant view assumed that advancing technology was a sufficient basis for that progress" (p. 35). For many lovers of the machine, particularly after the 18th century, this notion of progress led to the potential to reduce the role of deity in our lives. To illustrate, consider the autobiographical *Education of Henry Adams*, in which Adams (writing in third person) illustrates the almost-spiritual power of progress. In this passage, Adams (1918) describes a dynamo he discovers at the 1900 Paris Exposition:

> To Adams the dynamo became a symbol of infinity. As he grew accustomed to the great gallery of machines, he began to feel the forty-foot dynamos as a moral force, much as the early Christians felt the Cross. The planet itself seemed less impressive, in its old-fashioned, deliberate, annual or daily revolution, than this huge wheel revolving within arm's reach at some vertiginous speeds, and barely murmuring— scarcely humming an audible warning to stand a hair's-breadth further for respond of power. (p. 380)

Leo Marx describes the **garden**—epitomized by the Elysian Fields of ancient Greek myth, not to mention the biblical Garden of Eden—as a site of pastoral fields and cool breezes, a place of spiritualism and simplicity. The literary garden often appears to eschew technology for plainer work by human hands. When you imagine the garden, you might envision an Amish barn-raising, in which families gather to aid one another to build structures for their community without the aid of technology, only the power of muscle and sweat. Of course, we find the garden even in the midst of our cities. Consider the baseball stadium, a pastoral setting where young men (often called "The Boys of Summer") perform feats of sacrifice and physical prowess. Scholars such as Roger Aden (1999) write that the baseball field, with its green pasture and cyclical promise of a return home, illustrates the pastoral ideal in public life. Already, you might have noticed some room for contradiction. Technology, the extension of human power beyond bodily limits, resides in the garden, even if it emerges only in the simple pulley used by workers to lift a heavy board. And the baseball field, of course, demands a fantastically complex array of technological aids to function. Indeed, the green grass of the field often isn't grass at all! Here, puzzle presents itself. How might the machine, the use of technology to enhance human ability, reside within the garden? In literature and film, this puzzle frequently presents itself as a conflict between humans as technology, particularly when the difference between the two seems to blur more every day.

In the past two centuries, authors have attempted to make sense of the blurring of machine and garden, the growing role of technology in everyday life. Some, like H. G. Wells, proposed optimistic accounts of the potential for technology to resolve human problems and eliminate human weaknesses. However, many science fiction novelists offer a critique of that thesis. In the 19th century, Mary Shelley's *Frankenstein* warned of the risks that follow our use of technology to attain godlike powers. Ultimately, she demonstrates, we create monstrosities. Nathaniel Hawthorne's "Celestial Railroad" demonstrates how the use of technology, in this case a train on its way to heaven, provides us only illusory power and ultimately jeopardizes our very souls. Early in the 20th century, even our illusory powers over the machine began to be stripped away in literature such as E. M. Forster's "The Machine Stops," Karel Capek's *R.U.R.* (Rossum's Universal Robots), and Fredric Brown's "The Answer."

A group of authors who launched a movement called *cyberpunk* have been quite successful in shaping our public concepts of technology and culture over the past two decades (Balsamo, 1995). Cyberpunk refers to a literary movement that took hold among many science fiction writers in the 1980s–its primary theme is the blurring distinction between humans and machines. As discussed later, some critics hold that cyberpunk no longer offers a coherent philosophy or critique in contemporary times. However, the question asked by cyberpunk authors remains critical in our day: What happens when our society gets all the things promised by pulp comics and Flash Gordon serials and science fiction novels?

Answering this question, cyberpunk authors took a somewhat dim view of the future, given that the present—yesterday's tomorrow—appears to have become a dehumanizing and dangerous time. They no doubt recalled the ringing promises of earlier visionaries who imagined 10-lane superhighways and nuclear-powered cities. Gleaming towers like the Emerald City of Oz were indeed depicted in popular advertisements for products as basic as automobile tires and life insurance in the 1930s and 1940s. The problem with these marvelous futures isn't that they were an illusion; the problem is that they actually came true! Today, we face the consequences of those technological utopias: snarled traffic jams and environmental hazards. In a short story called the "**Gernsback Continuum**," Gibson (1981) writes:

> Dialta had said that the Future had come to America first, but had finally passed it by. But not here, in the heart of the Dream. Here, we'd gone on and on, in a dream logic that knew nothing of pollution, the finite bounds of fossil fuel, or foreign wars it was possible to lose. . . . Behind me, the illuminated city: searchlights swept the sky for the sheer joy of it. I imagined them thronging the plazas of white marble, orderly and alert, their bright eyes shining with enthusiasm for their floodlit avenues and silver cars. It had all the sinister fruitiness of Hitler propaganda. (p. 88)

In this piece, Gibson reveals a dangerous dimension to the technologically perfect world of tomorrow: The machines necessary to build that utopia have a nasty tendency of reprogramming the people who built them.

As discussed in chapter 9, Internet communication is frequently idealized as a utopian promise that ensures equal access to an **Encyclopedia Humanus**—a universal collection of all the knowledge generated by humankind. Cyberpunk is a critical response to the assumption that CMC is a humanizing influence on our society. "Cyber" refers to the impact of technology in its many forms on the human condition. The 1970s show, *The Six Million Dollar Man*, illustrates this dimension by depicting an astronaut who crashes his experimental aircraft and almost loses his life. Medical science is his only hope: "We can rebuild him. We can make him better than he was before. . . ." Thanks to modern technology, he is rebuilt as a **cyborg**—part human and part machine, or as Haraway (1996) puts it, "a fusion of the organic and the technical forged in particular, historical, cultural practices" (p. 51). The cyborg–astronaut can run faster, see farther, and jump higher than any other other man alive. However, the question emerges, Is the astronaut a man or a machine?

Although the show rarely delved into the psychological and social implications of that conundrum (focusing, instead, on Steve Austin vs. Big Foot and similar episodes), the question resonates in an age when human physiology seems to be similar to a Swiss Army knife—one piece goes bad, replace it with a new one. At what point does the knife (or person) cease to be what it was before? To put it a slightly different way, borrowing from a popular slogan a few years back: "Is it live or is it Memorex?"

The second part of "cyberpunk" is, of course, *punk*. Punk refers to a range of antisocial movements in music, fashion, and literature. Grossberg (1986) describes how punk included a range of behaviors designed to challenge dominant assumptions about power by demystifying its trappings. Instead of looking sharp toward a glittering future, punk bands such as the Sex Pistols inspired youth to cut up their corporate logo T-shirts and mock their elders' sanctimonious statements about doing it "my way." Punks responded: "We're the future. Your future!"

Of course, the notion of the antiestablishment gadfly flaunting tradition and questioning authority is not so new. Socrates drank hemlock for challenging the city fathers of Athens 25 centuries ago. However, cyberpunks appeared to address a contemporary problem that had not been imagined before: What happens when the far-fetched promises of science fiction stories about the power of technology to change the human condition become possible? How can we confront the impact of a computer-mediated society whose members seem increasingly more alienated from each other? In this form of literature, punks respond as outlaws, hackers, castaways, and victims might; they use the system for their own purposes. They make do in a world not of their making.

Cyberpunk, therefore, is an ironic response to contemporary life—a play on the notion that a computerized society is necessarily a better one. No one story can adequately incorporate all of the themes suggested by this literary movement. Cyberpunk, like its musical punk predecessors, is at first a style rather than a coherent message. As Sterling (1986) observes, "The work of the cyberpunks is paralleled throughout Eighties pop culture: in rock video; in the hacker underground; in the jarring street tech of hip-hop and scratch music; in the synthesizer rock of London and Tokyo" (pp. xi–xii). The lyrics or the moves are dissimilar, but the attitude is uncanny. Knarf (1998) maintains the alt.cyberpunk FAQ file that defines cyberpunk style:

> The setting is urban; the mood is dark and pessimistic. Concepts are thrown at the reader without explanation, much like new developments are thrown at us in our everyday lives. There is often a sense of moral ambiguity; simply fighting "the system" (to topple it or just to stay alive) does not make the main characters "heroes" or "good" in the traditional sense.

Some historians of the movement claim that cyberpunk began in 1983 with Bruce Bethke's (2004) short story of the same name. Most agree that its most prolific and well-known contributors were Gibson and Sterling. The irony is that few authors would actually classify themselves as being cyberpunk. This makes sense given a fundamental antiauthoritarianism that animates so much of their writing.

Some critics respond that cyberpunk died with the 1995 release of the film *Johnny Mnemonic* (Ahrenberg et al., 1995; a disappointing film version of the William Gibson short story). The demise of the cyberpunk "movement" might be traced back 2 years earlier, when "punk rocker" Billy Idol released his homage to computer-mediated rebellion, "Cyberpunk." Either way, Kroker and Kroker (1996) write that cyberpunk, once the literary hideout for social outcasts bent on revealing the contradictions of techno-utopia, sold itself out with the release of bland and soulless entertainment that seemingly perpetuated everything contested by "the movement." Predictably, "real" hackers have responded that plenty of rebels remain to resist dominant culture, no matter what the critics say.

Why talk about cyberpunk today? For the same reason that one explores any literary form, even when written decades or centuries ago—cyberpunk is worth our attention because of its contemporary nature. Unlike traditional science fiction and fantasy, which wraps its intended critique of dominant culture in a narrative isolated in distant space or time, cyberpunk fiction attempted to locate its people and technology in the near present. Its rhetoric lay in a rejection of some distant future where social problems are magically resolved.

What specifically were cyberpunks rejecting? Think back to reruns of Gene Roddenbury's *Star Trek*. Set in the 23rd century, the show revealed an optimistic future. How the people of Earth formed a cooperative world government and began to explore the stars is occasionally referenced, but never in much detail. In contrast, cyberpunk places its audience in the near-future or what might be termed the hyperpresent: a contemporary time that seems a bit faster than our own experience—as the *Max Headroom* television series puts it: "20 minutes into the future" (Warner Brothers Virtual Lot, 1999). In his essay, "The Future? You Don't Want to Know," Sterling (1995) claims that cyberpunk authors fear dating "the future" because so much of it has already come to pass—much faster than we ever could have anticipated.

> If we can't control the future—if we can't make it do what we want—what is there left to say or do about it? We're all hip to nonlinearity now—anyone with two brain cells knows that the future is unpredictable, even in principle. Science fiction writers still like to jabber about it, and they are more reckless than a lot of other basement prophets because they have so very little to lose. But why say anything? The crystal ball's as cracked and clouded as the ozone layer. Who are we kidding? (Sterling, 1995, p. 152).

Almost 15 years after this piece was written, our collective faith in the future seems no more solid than it did in the 1980s or 1990s. Worse, it seems that we can longer keep up with the present, much less anticipate tomorrow. As Jurek (1991) writes, "Velocity can be calculated, the pliability of entrails cannot" (p. 85). Some of the more radical visions of cyberpunk authors remain in the realm of fiction or in the future. But several themes remain significant to our understanding of the role of computer technology in popular culture.

We propose three common themes to cyberpunk fiction and provide some examples from Gibson's (1991) *Neuromancer* to illustrate them. It is hard to overestimate the impact of this award-winning book on popular culture. Authors striving to make sense out of computer technology return to this literary totem in search of guidance. Moreover, as Conklin (1987) notes, *Neuromancer* may be responsible for our contemporary notions of hypertext, the underlying principle of the World Wide Web. The novel (part of a trilogy of cyberpunk literature) follows the attempts by Case, a hacker who has been cut from the net of computerized information and hunts desperately for a way back in—only to discover that the matrix of information might be a conscious entity with its own agenda. *Neuromancer* demonstrates primary themes of cyberpunk literature: (a) human flesh is weak in comparison to computer technology, (b) corporate dominance of social life is enabled by computer technology, and (c) the pace of human life is increasing beyond our ability to adapt.

The Weakness of Human Flesh

The constant refrain in cyberpunk fiction is the sense that human beings cannot possibly continue to exist as we do in a world dominated by machines. We have two choices: We become outlaws who slip through the digital cracks and live our lives on the run from various forms of surveillance, or we integrate machines into our flesh and thinking processes. Choosing that path, we discover that human flesh is a poor substitute for pure machinery. One scene from *Neuromancer* first illustrates this concept:

> Ratz was tending bar, his prosthetic arm jerking monotonously as he filled a tray of glasses with draft Kirin. He saw Case and smiled, his teeth a webwork of East European steel and brown decay.... His ugliness was the stuff of legend. In an age of affordable beauty, there was something heraldic about his lack of it. The antique arm whined as he reached for another mug. It was a Russian military prosthesis, a seven-function force-feedback manipulator, cased in grubby pink plastic. (Gibson, 1991, p. 65)

A corollary to this literary rejection of the flesh is its cyberspatial counterpart, the glorification of noncorporeal existence. Losing access to this virtual paradise results in an almost-biblical punishment:

> For Case, who'd lived for the bodiless exultation of cyberspace, it was the Fall. In the bars he'd frequented as a cowboy hotshot, the elite stance involved a certain relaxed contempt for the flesh. The body was meat. Case fell into the prison of his own flesh. (p. 67)

In *Neuromancer*, as in many cyberpunk fictions, CMC is more than a way to access data; it is freedom from social constraint and power to act in a world of powerful forces. Therefore, it is not surprising that Case's experience of the matrix is shaped explicitly by corporations.

The Power of the Wired Corporation

As discussed in chapter 7, corporations of all types find their interests converging and the abilities to impact our daily lives increasing, thanks to the integration of computer technology into homes and businesses. Cyberpunk fiction offers a stinging rebuke to this trend by frequently painting multinational corporations and their "artificial intelligence" agents as enjoying privileges to transgress or simply ignore laws that bind persons of lower socioeconomic class. One quotation from *Neuromancer* suffices:

> Now he slept in the cheapest coffins, the ones nearest the port, beneath the quartz-halogen floods that lit the docks all night like vast stages; where you couldn't see the lights of Tokyo for the glare of the television sky, not even the towering hologram logo of the Fuji Electric Company, and Tokyo Bay was a black expanse where gulls wheeled above drifting shoals of white styrofoam. Behind the port lay the city, factory domes dominated by the vast cubes of corporate arcologies. (Gibson, 1991, p. 68)

The punk aesthetic of this literary form is to reveal the broad range of corporate control manifested by vast buildings, huge expanses, and endless cyberspace. One imagines the digital Las Vegas of computer-generated buildings representing "lattices of logic," but their shapes and colors are strictly copyrighted—their accumulated knowledge jealously guarded. As discussed in the next section, at least one corporation finds insight from this notion of mediated dominance. However, we first turn to a third theme of cyberpunk literature: the computer-mediated acceleration of human experience.

The Pace of Human Life

It is a timeless complaint; the times are changing faster than our ability to adapt. Futurist Alvin Toffler (1971) coined the term **futureshock** to account for an increasingly common sense that technological change is accelerating at a revolutionary, and potentially dangerous, pace. More recently, Bertman (1998) and Gleick (1999) returned to this argument with more contemporary evidence. In *Neuromancer*, we see this theme most powerfully:

> Night City was like a deranged experiment in social Darwinism designed by a bored researcher who kept one thumb permanently on the fast-forward button. Stop hustling and you sank without a trace, but move a little too swiftly and you'd break the fragile surface tension of the black market; either way, you were gone, with nothing left of you but some vague memory.... (Gibson, 1991, pp. 68–69)

The pace of life in a computer-mediated—and -dominated—society appears in cyberpunk literature as a prime cause of the disembodiment of humankind and the rise of corporate structures and artificial intelligence. As shown in the forthcoming section, this transition appears frequently in popular film.

Visions of computer technology in literature have historically struggled to strike a balance between utopianism and dystopianism. However, with the apparent increase in state and corporate influence over our daily lives, rebellious movements like cyberpunk warned of a near-future in which our bodies might be devalued by machines, our lives controlled by wired corporations, and our lives overwhelmed by accelerating change. In this way, popular culture provides a site where Internet communication is reinterpreted within historical and political contexts. However, fewer and fewer people appear to gain their cultural identities in literature.

That doesn't mean that people have stopped reading: only that, for most contemporary readers, Scott Adams' *Dilbert* cartoon resonates more clearly than any story or novel. As Aden (1999) notes, *Dilbert* provides a therapeutic response to millions of cubical dwellers literally and technologically isolated from their colleagues yet under constant surveillance by their bosses. How might these corporate drones climb the walls of their cubicles? And, if they do, can only a vestige of humane society be found? Adams offers a humorous but ultimately pessimistic view. In one strip that ran in February 2000, Asok the intern announces that he's created a "prison Morse code" so that he and Wally can communicate. Tapping on the cubical wall, Wally responds, "I sent you e-mail": an example of pop culture literature at its most transitory, Dilbert illustrates the power of throwaway communication to mock a computer-mediated society.

Of course, popular film offers an even more powerful way to define and contest images of computer technology. Sitting in darkened theaters (more than in our living rooms) film can overwhelm our senses with striking images that affix themselves long after the popcorn is gone. Despite the advent of cable and the promise of high-definition television, cinematic approaches toward our rapidly computerized society maintain their central role in popular culture.

POPULAR FILM AND TECHNOLOGY

With the introduction of cinema to popular culture, we find another medium through which society confronts a growing sense that computer technology contains both utopian and dystopian implications. In this section, we focus on "Internet-Age" films—movies released since the advent of the Internet. We cheat a bit by discussing in more detail Stanley Kubrick's *2001* (which appeared months before the construction of the first Internet in 1969) before outlining the impact of *Tron*, *WarGames*, *Blade Runner*, *AI (Artificial Intelligence)*, and *The Matrix Trilogy* on popular conceptions of technology. Other films (and, in some cases, more popular films) could be argued to deserve inclusion in this list: *Johnny Mnemonic*, *The Lawnmower Man*, *The Net*, *Hackers*, and *Enemy of the State*. But we have chosen those movies whose technology themes were the most significant in their time. Notice that although virtually every film involves a theme of humans and their use of technology—either to explore the universe or to control other people—each film raises the troubling question of whether our machines actually control us.

> **Ethical Inquiry**
>
> A surprisingly large number of students surveyed in one of your textbook author's classes agreed that downloading films "ripped" from DVDs or copied from video cameras stashed inside the coats of moviegoers is more than a clever way to avoid paying 10 bucks for a theater ticket. Many said that downloading "pirated" videos is ethical. Their reasons included the growing costs of entertainment, the declining quality of today's movies, and the naked fact that so many people do it. Issues of fair remuneration for artists' creative efforts and the basic notion that theft is wrong seem to blur when the medium of the matter is digital. A useful exercise may be to develop an ethical standard that permits this kind of activity, the downloading of digital entertainment without purchase, while clarifying what kind of theft remains unethical. How might you craft such a compromise. If one cannot be found, what ethical standard compels you to conclude your inquiry in this way?

2001: A Space Odyssey—Confronting Technology

Since its release in 1968, Stanley Kubrick's *2001: A Space Odyssey* has confounded its viewers. As some critics have noted, *2001* is a Rorschach film blot; when you stare at it closely, you end up studying your own assumptions about the world. The film illustrates the role of computer technology in the transformation (or potential obsolescence) of humankind. Starting with the depiction of how an alien monolith is responsible for the evolution of humans from their prehistoric ancestors, *2001* narrates in stark detail (and even starker acting) the voyage of the Discovery spacecraft to Jupiter's moons, where another monolith awaits. On the way, the ship's crew confronts its own computer, HAL 9000, which apparently has other plans. When Mission Commander Dave Bowman leaves the ship to recover the body of his colleague who is killed by HAL, a central crisis to the film ensues:

  Dave: Open the pod bay doors, HAL.
  HAL: I'm sorry, Dave, I'm afraid I can't do that.
  Dave: What's the problem?
  HAL: I think you know what the problem is just as well as I do.

Dave: What are you talking about, HAL?
HAL: This mission is too important for me to allow you to jeopardize it.
Dave: I don't know what you're talking about, HAL.
HAL: I know that you and Frank were planning to disconnect me, and I'm
         afraid that's something I cannot allow to happen.

Bowman's ingenuity allows him to overcome HAL. But he cannot overcome the voiceless and inscrutable monolith, an alien technology infinitely more advanced than humankind's feeble machinery or intellect. When Bowman attempts to land on the device, he falls into a sort of intergalactic "Grand Central Station" where he winds up on his own deathbed, only to be reborn as a "star child." *2001* matters because of its depiction of computer technology as simultaneously an engine of human growth and an obstacle to human expression. Its conclusion, confusing to most viewers, is designed to suggest that humanity has ultimately triumphed over its machines, but only by becoming something more than human. As shown here, even this bleak narrative appears to be optimistic compared to some later films.

Tron: Taking on the Master Control Program

Disney's foray into computer animation resulted in *Tron* (Ellenshaw, Kushner, & Miller, 1982), a significant advance in the use of computer technology to make movies. The plot, such as it is, features a computer program designer, Kevin Flynn, trapped in a parallel-digital universe where computer programs take human form. In this pseudo-cyberspace, the malevolent Master Control Program forces his fellow software agents to forgo allegiance to their human masters ("users") or risk destruction ("de-rezzing") in various forms of gladiatorial combat. In haste to escape this digital underground and free the subjugated programs, Flynn and his virtual friend, Yori, discover a security program, Tron:

Kevin Flynn: It's time I level with you. I'm what you guys call a "user."
      Yori: You're a user?
Kevin Flynn: I took a wrong turn somewhere.
      Tron: If you ARE a user, then everything you've done has been
              according to a plan, right?
Kevin Flynn: Ha, ha, ha, you WISH! Well, you guys know what it's like. You
              just keep doing what it looks like you're supposed to be doing
              no matter how crazy it seems.
      Tron: That's the way it is for programs, yes.
Kevin Flynn: I hate to disappoint you, pal, but that's the way it is for users,
              too.
      Tron: Stranger and stranger . . .

Tron's blurring of human and machine occurs on multiple levels. Most directly, Flynn is seized by the Master Control Program, digitized, and dropped into the computer network. More importantly, computer programs are said to possess the same emotions and drives as people. It's not a giant leap from that supposition to claim that humans might act like machines from time to time. However, to researchers such as Lippert (1996), *Tron* represents more than a journey into the workings of a machine; the film represents "dominant culture"—a vision of social forces that shape our lives yet cannot be altered: "absolute Cartesian space divided by abstract linear coordinates, or irradiated light neither reflected nor blocked by anything solid" (p. 266). Chances are that *Tron*'s target audience viewed the film as a pleasant diversion and could hardly be expected to adopt Lippert's perspective. However, the power of the film to introduce a cultural notion of unchecked computer power is hard to deny. *Tron* matters because it retells the common story of human versus machine in a new way. This time, in order to beat the program, one must *become* a program.

HYPERLINK: "INVASION OF THE DOTS"

Black spheres fall from the sky, crashing into the street, setting cars aflame, sending business-suit clad victims fleeing for their lives. It's not an alien invasion or the setting of the next Stephen King novel—it's "Invasion of the Dots," a clever advertisement run by Sun Microsystems, whose slogan was once, "We're the dot in .com." Leaf through any mass market magazine and you'll find dozens of advertisements for computers, peripherals, or Internet services. Not too surprisingly, few of these ads offer a critique of the new economy. But some, like this one, play on a culturally shared fear that computer technology is somehow growing faster than we'd like. Like the film, *Tron*, these images depict a machine that is no longer under our control. An excerpt from the copy: "LOOK, UP IN THE SKY. It's a whole new dot-conomy! It's an INVASION OF INGENUITY, powered by technology that seems OTHERWORLDLY. . . ." Designed like a 1950s monster movie, the Sun ad plays on shared fears about the power of technology to alter our lives even as it sells its computer product.

In 1984, Apple was less ambivalent about its role in contemporary society. In a classic advertisement directed by *Blade Runner*'s Ridley Scott, Apple Computer (1984) portrayed IBM computer users as corporate drones under the watchful eye of a "big brother"-like character. In the midst of this oppressive environment, a woman runs toward the telescreen and smashes it with a hammer. The voiceover announces: "On January 24th, Apple Computer will introduce the Macintosh. And you'll see why 1984 won't be like *1984*."

The ad aired only once, during Super Bowl XVIII. But its impact was unmistakable. Real-life "corporate drones" recognized themselves in that ad and wished they could trade places with the lithe runner who smashed the system. The fact that she was merely selling another kind of computer (albeit, a computer "for the rest of us") was elegantly understated. We do not include this discussion because advertisements are a site where popular culture routinely and obviously works out its contradictions. Rather, we point your attention to artifacts like magazine ads precisely because they attempt to *eliminate* traces of the ideological clash so explicitly stated in other forms of human expression—but can't quite succeed in doing so. As you thumb through a magazine, try to look between the images and slogans to discern the subtle messages about technology in popular culture. They may be hidden, but they're out there.

WarGames: Is It a Game or Is It Real?

As the tagline reads, *WarGames* (Goldberg, Hashimoto, & Schneider, 1983) focuses on the struggle for individuals to convince a computer network to abandon its plans to start World War III. *WarGames* introduced most people to the image of the computer hacker, capable of controlling machines through clever phone tricks. Although the actual habits (and capabilities) of hackers are portrayed none too literally in the film, a generation of computer enthusiasts traces their obsession with software and net-working technology, at least in part, to this groundbreaking film. The main character, David Lightman, initiates the movie's crisis by tapping into a defense department supercomputer. Innocently asking it to play a "game" of thermonuclear war, David is shocked to discover that the machine believes his commands are real. Setting the countdown for doomsday, David and his girlfriend race to stop the machine, which clearly has little regard for human decision making. "You want a war, I'll give you a war," the machine seems to decide.

> **David Lightman:** Is this a game or is it real?
> **Joshua (the computer):** What's the difference?

WarGames contributes to the evolving cinematic depiction of computer technology by switching the roles between computers and machines. Mirroring literary uses of this theme by such authors as Isaac Asimov ("The Evitable Conflict") and Arthur C. Clarke ("The Nine Billion Names of God"), *WarGames* depicts most of its human characters as hopelessly foolish. Only the machine can discern the lesson of this deadly game: "The only winning move is not to play." Tragically for cinematic humanity, the machine isn't so humane in *Terminator 3: Rise of the Machines* (2003) when the military computer network, "SkyNet," kills 3 billion people. However, a common theme remains: Computer technology in film has begun to dispense with human decision making. Machines now act like people, exhibiting childlike wisdom in the case of *WarGames* or willful self-preservation in the case of *Terminator*. The result: the obsolescence of human beings.

Blade Runner: More Human than Human

Where cyberpunk fiction and popular film converged most impressively was in Ridley Scott's 1982 film noir classic, *Blade Runner* (Deeley et al., 1982). The film features a sparse plot set in Los Angeles of the near-future, a site where "replicants" have escaped an "off-world colony" to seek their maker, Dr. Eldon Tyrell. Although his corporation's motto is "More human than human," Tyrell's replicants are hobbled by a 4-year life span. The film, with its gritty depiction of near-future urban life, focuses on a somewhat pedestrian series of chases and close encounters as Rick Deckard, the Blade Runner, is dispatched to "retire" the replicants. However, the film gains significance when one of these machine–humans, Roy Batty, confronts Tyrell.

> **Tyrell:** I'm surprised you didn't come here sooner.
> **Roy:** It's not an easy thing to meet your maker.
> **Tyrell:** What could he do for you?
> **Roy:** Can the maker repair what he makes?

As the movie settles into its inevitable struggle between the replicant and the Blade Runner, the plot careens toward an unexpected outcome: Perhaps Deckard *himself* is a replicant—the ultimate shadow identity. The notion of machines stalking machines in a world in which most humans could easily be confused for animals may not be so far-fetched. Davis (1999) described the "high-tech police death squads" of 2029 Los Angeles as "not fantasies, but merely extrapolations from the present" (p. 155). But the most troubling question for humanity remains:

> **Rachael:** "Have you ever retired a human by mistake?"
> **Deckard:** "No."
> **Rachael:** "But in your position that is a risk, isn't it?"

Ridley Scott's *Blade Runner*, loosely based on Philip K. Dick's novel, *Do Androids Dream of Electric Sheep?*, challenges the viewer to confront a society in which machines and people have blurred to such an extent that neither can truly be considered human by traditional standards.

AI: Artificial Intelligence: His Love Is Real. But He Is Not

Steven Spielberg's *AI* (Curtis, Harlan, Kennedy, Parkes, & Spielberg, 2001) offered a tantalizing view of an imminent future in which "mechas" play an increasingly significant role in the lives of people and, yet, are feared for their abilities to replace humanity. As one character, Gigolo Joe, notes, "They made us too smart, too quick, and too many. We are suffering for the mistakes they made because when the end comes, all that will be left . . . is us." The film asks challenging questions of its audience (one of the reasons for its relatively low success as a moneymaker). Most intriguingly, can machines be taught to love—not merely to emulate the physical behaviors associated with the emotion, but to actually *feel*? Moreover, if machines can be trained or created to love humans, do we have a responsibility toward them? One can imagine no more harrowing way to play this quandary out than to introduce a mechanical child into a family that has lost a flesh-and-blood son. At what point does the machine cease to be a novelty or a pet and to become a family member? This challenge ties back to notions of technology as more than a set of inanimate objects, technology as more than an extension of human will, to the idea of technology as a reflection of the human soul.

The Matrix Trilogy: Ghosts in the Machine

Andy Wachowski and Larry Wachowski's *Matrix Trilogy* (Berman et al., 1999) captured the public imagination with its clever effects and optimistic view of humanity's ability to overcome computer technology. The films depict all of humankind as being stuck in a "matrix"—an artificial world shaped by a computer network—designed to lull them into submission. In the first film, Neo, the protagonist, struggles to come to grips with the fact that his entire life is merely a digital prison. However, after being freed from the Matrix and taught to manipulate its power, Neo prepares to strike back against the machine:

> I know you're out there. I can feel you now. I know that you're afraid—afraid of us. You're afraid of change. I don't know the future. I didn't come here to tell you how this is going to end. I came here to tell how it's going to begin. I'm going to

hang up this phone, and then show these people what you don't want them to see. I'm going to show them a world without you. A world without rules or controls, borders or boundaries. A world where anything is possible. Where we go from there is a choice I leave to you.

Recognized for its state-of-the-art effects and eclectic references to religious and philosophical texts, the Matrix spawned two sequels, a series of animated shorts, a video game, and a seemingly endless number of late-night conversations about the meaning of reality. The second film, *Reloaded*, expanded on the computerized nature of the Matrix reality, proposing that all forces that appear to be natural reflect a sort of cosmic program. At one point, The Oracle explains:

Look, see those birds? At some point a program was written to govern them. A program was written to watch over the trees, and the wind, the sunrise, and sunset. There are programs running all over the place. The ones doing their job, doing what they were meant to do, are invisible. You'd never even know they were here.

HYPERLINK: WHAT ABOUT VIRTUAL REALITY?

Doesn't virtual reality (VR) provide a setting to reinterpret the role of computer technology in our lives? For years, scholars have argued that VR will allow us to immerse ourselves in cyberrealities and expand our ability to experience artificial worlds (Hayles, 1993; Lanier & Biocca, 1992). However, the fully interactive worlds that whet the appetites of computerphiles have yet to emerge except in the form of expensive video games and high-tech experimentation—and, of course, *The Matrix*. For the rest of us, VR is a more figurative than literal experience. Even so, some video games are increasingly effective in crafting environments that draw players into their digital realms. Anyone who has lost a weekend playing a simulation game knows how immersive these games can be.

Games like *SimCity 4000* and *The Sims*, both created by Maxis, enable players to vicariously play the roles of mayors of their own towns—or, more intriguingly, become virtual deities who shape the lives of human beings. Laying virtual water lines, zoning artificial airports, or instructing a digital person to take a shower may not seem to have much cultural impact. Indeed, these games might merely represent an isolated activity through which persons create worlds rather than inhabit their own "real" lives. However, as the popularity of these computer simulations continues to grow, we might discover that these cybercommunities provide a therapeutic response to our increasingly technological society. As with books, films, and television shows that depict fictional struggles between humans and machines, VR games—both real and conceptual—provide the opportunity for people to "play" with machines and, perhaps, rediscover the sense that although they cannot fully control technology, technology doesn't fully control them either.

The film ends with the suggestion that even the "real world," the one outside of the computerized Matrix, is itself another computer program, that "God" is merely an architect, a computer programmer. The third film, *Revolutions*, reveals the truth of the computer program and its purpose. Throughout, questions of human choice resonate beyond the cool special effects. If all human experience can be replicated by software and if all human choices can be shaped by computer programs, how can an individual act as if his or her choice matters? The grit and determination of a hardy band of survivors offer an optimistic conclusion to the trilogy, but reality may offer a far different future as we find our choices shaped by the tools we use. As always, we find within the playful texts of popular culture the seeds of any number of potential futures.

Arching from Kubrick's bleak *2001* to the Wachowski brothers' *Matrix Trilogy*, it is hard to discern whether film provides any conclusion about the role of computers in contemporary society. But it is certain that these movies provide cultural totems where many people attempt to make sense out of the emerging wired-world.

CHAPTER SUMMARY

In this chapter, we've "gone meta." Going meta refers to the notion of **metacommunication**: communication about communication. In other words, we haven't limited our analysis to the functional uses of CMC to facilitate or hinder human expression and sense-making. We've turned our analytical gaze onto computers as texts that demand interpretation and invite rereadings. Rather than simply accepting the common notion that computer technology is changing popular culture—perhaps for better, maybe for worse—we've attempted to discern the themes that animate various forms of popular response to this technology. Books, films, and television shows are all challenged by this channel of discourse in some way. The fact that you can download a novel, view a DVD movie on your computer, and get CNN headlines on a digital assistant surely indicates that traditional media must accommodate Internet communication. But as we've seen, they also provide the means to articulate and interrogate common assumptions about computer technology.

Throughout our journey, a common question has emerged: How might popular culture shape our understanding and articulation of computer technology? Today's software engineers grew up on *Tron* and *Blade Runner* and William Gibson. The images and notions inspired by these artifacts of popular culture have infiltrated themselves into commercials, magazine advertisements, musical styles, and clothing accessories. Trying to build and update a world-girdling communications network is not simply a matter of physics or mathematics or even engineering. Computer technology is, at heart, an attempt to manipulate abstract data with physical tools. In a way similar to our use of a graphical user interface to move bits from sector to sector, popular manifestations of the machine inform the ways in which designers make sense out of their own work and articulate future innovations. For that reason, we challenge you to read popular culture closely—for the visions of computer technology you find there may indeed come to pass.

ONLINE COMMUNICATION AND THE LAW

Artifacts of popular culture like the film and literature examples cited in this chapter help us to interpret the world around us. We have already discussed how this function is performed in helping us deal with misgivings that we share about the role of technology in our lives. However, we should also remember that the same technology has a tremendous impact on popular culture. As Scott Bowles (2003) notes, "superfans" have long created Web sites to celebrate and criticize films, even those that have not yet been released. The most influential, Harry Knowles's AintItCoolNews.com, began as a diversion while Harry recovered from a spinal cord injury. Today, his collection of fan reactions to film prescreenings and even purloined script information that provides "spoilers" that will not be released for months has entered the pantheon of industry forces that can make or break a film. Ask Joel Schumacher. Hollywood observers routinely cite the negative response generated by AintItCool about Schumacher's Batman films as a primary reason why fans abandoned the franchise. As a positive force, however, superfan sites provide an essential way for the television and film producers to gain invaluable feedback from the folks who buy tickets and generate buzz. As a result, whereas "unofficial" sites once garnered legal cease and desist orders, they are now often considered part of an extended advertising campaign. Universal Studios, for example, created a web master program for fans of the film *The Hulk* to use trademarked images on their Web sites. As one movie executive writes, "I thought it was just a place where people stole our products. But I see how influential these fans can be when they build a consensus, which is what we seek. I now consider them filmmaking partners" (p. 1A).

Glossary

Artifacts: Bits and pieces of human sense-making: books, magazines, movies, posters, comics, and the like.

Cyberpunk: 1980s literary movement whose primary theme is the blurring distinction between humans and machines.

Cyborg: Mechanical blurring of human and machine, illustrated by the 1970s show, *The Six Million Dollar Man*.

Encyclopedia Humanus: A universal collection of all the knowledge generated by humankind.

Futureshock: Term coined by Alvin Toffler to describe the results of excessive innovation and social change.

Garden: Metaphor for a return to organic life marked by simplicity and consistency.

Gernsback Continuum: An alternative universe that exists alongside our own—and occasionally intersects with our "real" world through artifacts such as comics, novels, films, and other forms of human communication.

Machine: Metaphor for industrial life that perpetuates human progress.
Metacommunication: Communication about communication.
Popular culture: System of artifacts that shape our common understanding of the world.
Punk: A range of antisocial movements in music, fashion, and literature.

Topics for Discussion

1. Join a small group of film buffs in your class and view Fritz Lang's (1926) *Metropolis* and H. G. Wells' (1936) *Things to Come*. Construct a list of themes about the role of computers and machines in our daily lives. Which film seems more similar to our contemporary experiences of public life?

2. Go to your library and pick up (or request) a copy of Sterling's (1986) *Mirrorshades: The Cyberpunk Anthology* and read William Gibson's (1981) "The Gernsback Continuum"—an ironic response to technological optimists. Then take a walk through your downtown. Can you find artifacts of the America-that-never-was as described by Gibson?

3. Go to the Dilbert Zone (available online at http://www.dilbert.com/) and examine 2 weeks of Scott Adams' comic strip about corporate life. Generate a list of themes or motifs related to technology appearing in *Dilbert*. Does Adams' contribution to pop culture provide any means of resistance to the computer-mediated workplace?

4. View the director's cut of Ridley Scott's (1982) *Blade Runner*. Beyond the director's vision for this film there continues to be debate within the fan community about whether Rick Deckard is indeed a replicant. Search for clues to indicate his true nature and write a paragraph outlining why you think he is either a man or a machine.

5. Although they offer vastly different qualities of writing and execution, *Tron* and *The Matrix* provide strikingly similar plots: A group of outcasts searches for a chosen one (a security program in *Tron* and Neo in *The Matrix*) to free them of a malevolent computer program. Which film's depiction of cyberspace is most compelling to you? Write a paragraph to explain your point of view.

REFERENCES

Adams, H. (1918). *The education of Henry Adams: An autobiography*. Boston, New York: Houghton Mifflin.
Aden, R. (1999). *Popular stories and promised lands: Fan cultures and symbolic pilgrimages*. Tuscaloosa: University of Alabama Press.
Ahrenberg, S., Carmody, D., Desormeaux, J., Hamburg, V., Lantos, R., & Rack, B. J. (Producers). Longo, R. (Director). (1995). *Johnny Mnemonic* [Motion picture]. United States: TriStar Pictures.
Apple Computer. (1984). http://www.apple-history.com/history.html

Balsamo, A. (1995). Signal to noise: On the meaning of cyberpunk subculture. In F. Biocca & M. R. Levy (Eds.), *Communication in the age of virtual reality* (pp. 347–368). Hillsdale, NJ: Lawrence Erlbaum Associates.

Berman, B., Cracchiolo, D., Hughes, C., Mason, A., Mirisch, R., Osborne, B. M., Silver, J., Stoff, E., Wachowski, A., & Wachowski, L. (Producers). Wachowski, A., & Wachowski, L. (Directors). (1999). *The matrix* [Motion picture]. United States: Silver Pictures.

Bertman, S. (1998). *Hyperculture: The human cost of speed*. Westport, CT: Greenwood.

Bethke, B. (2004). Cyberpunk. Retrieved from infinity plus http://www.infinityplus.co.uk/stories/cpunk.htm

Bowles, S. (2003, June 20). Fans use their muscle to shape the movie. *USA Today*, p. 1A.

Brummett, B. (1994). *Rhetoric in popular culture*. New York: St. Martin's Press.

Conklin, E. J. (1987). Hypertext: An introduction and survey. *IEEE Computer, 20*, 17–41.

Curtis, B., Harlan, J., Kennedy, K., Parkes, W. F., & Spielberg, S. (Producers). Spielberg, S. (Director). (2001). *Artificial intelligence: AI* [Motion picture]. Warner Brothers.

Davis, M. (1999). Fortress Los Angeles: The militarization of urban space. In M. Sorkin (Ed.), *Variation on a theme park: The new American city and the end of public space* (pp. 154–180). New York: Hill & Wang.

Deeley, M., Fancher, H., Kelly, B., Perenchio, J., Powell, I., Scott, R., Shaw, R., & Yorkin, B. (Producers). Scott, R. (Director). (1982). *Blade runner* [Motion picture]. United States: The Ladd Company.

Dunn, T. P., & Erlich, R. D. (1982). *The mechanical god, machines in science fiction*. Westport, CT: Greenwood.

Ellenshaw, H., Kushner, D., & Miller, R. (Producers). Lisberger, S. (Director). (1982). *Tron* [Motion picture]. United States: Walt Disney Productions.

Garreau, J. (1991). *Edge city: Life on the new frontier*. New York: Doubleday.

Gibson, W. (1991). Neuromancer. In L. McCaffery (Ed.), *Storming the reality studio: A casebook of cyberpunk and postmodern science fiction* (pp. 65–74). Durham, NC: Duke University Press.

Gibson, W. (1981). The gernsback continuum. In T. Carr (Ed.), *Universe 11* (pp. 81–90). Garden City, NY: Doubleday.

Gleick, J. (1999). *Faster: The acceleration of just about everything*. New York: Random House.

Goldberg, L., Hashimoto, R., & Schneider, H. (Producers)., Badham, J. (Director). (1983). *WarGames* [Motion picture]. United States: Metro–Goldwyn–Mayer.

Grossberg, L. (1986). Is there rock after punk? *Critical Studies in Mass Communication, 3*, 50–74.

Haraway, D. J. (1996). *Modest_witness@second_millennium*. New York, London: Routledge.

Hayles, N. K. (1993). The seductions of cyberspace. In. V. A. Conley (Ed.), *Rethinking technologies* (pp. 173–190). Minneapolis: University of Minnesota.

Jacobson, D. (1999, March 5). Pop culture studies turns 25. *Salon*. Retrieved from http://www.salon.com/it/feature/1999/03/05feature.html

Jurek, T. (1991). Straight fiction. In L. McCaffery (Ed.), *Storming the reality studio: A casebook of cyberpunk and postmodern science fiction* (pp. 85–86). Durham, NC: Duke University Press.

Knarf, F. (1998). *Frequently asked questions alt.cyberpunk*. Retrieved from http://www.knarf.demon.co.uk/alt-cp.html

Kroker, A., & Kroker, M. (1996). *Hacking the future*. New York: St. Martin's Press.

Kubrick, S. (Producer). Kubrick, S. (Director). (1968). *2001: A space odyssey* [Motion picture]. United States: Metro–Goldwyn–Mayer.

Lanier, J., & Biocca, F. (1992). An insider's view of the future of virtual reality. *Journal of Communication, 42*, 150–172.

Lee, J. Y. (1988). Paradise limited: An interview with Leo Marx by Judith Yaross Lee. *Invention & Technology*, Vol. 4, pp. 34–39.

Lippert, P. (1996). Cinematic representations of cyberspace. In L. Strate, R. Jacobson, & S. B. Gibson (Eds.), *Communication and cyberspace: Social interaction in an electronic environment*. Cresskill, NJ: Hampton Press.

Sterling, B. (1986). *Mirrorshades: The cyberpunk anthology*. New York: Ace Books.

Sterling, B. (1995). The future? You don't want to know. *Wired, 3*(11), 152.

Toffler, A. (1971). *Futureshock*. New York: Bantam Doubleday Dell.

Warner Brothers Virtual Lot. (1999). *Max Headroom*. Retrieved from http://www.virtuallot.com/cmp/vault/classic/cl01.html

APPENDIX A

INTRODUCTION TO HYPERTEXT MARKUP LANGUAGE

In this appendix, we offer a brief overview of some of the technical components to building a web page. In this effort, we recognize that keeping up with the changing standards and protocols for Web site design is impossible. The World Wide Web (WWW) changes constantly, and so do the means to contribute to this "docuverse." Nonetheless, we offer this brief overview to provide some guidance as you develop your first contributions to the Web. We begin with an overview of hypertext markup language (HTML) before describing some key hypertext "tags." We conclude with a note on uploading and downloading files.

HTML is really a form of word processing. Hypertext refers to the ability of documents placed on the WWW to be read in more than two dimensions. In other words, rather than having the choice of reading a document from top to bottom or left to right—or in any other set of directions on a flat sheet of paper—hypertext allows the author to craft pages in three or (theoretically) more dimensions. Imagine several sheets of paper stacked on top of one another. Typically, the reader will progress through each page in linear fashion, one after another. In hypertext, the reader has that option. But he or she also has the option of moving from concept to concept, page to page, through the pages. As Fig. A.1 illustrates, the reader and/or page author is free to choose a piece of information and then create a link between that information and some text on another page.

This concept of hypertext is similar to "hyperspace" as demonstrated in the film, *Star Wars*. In hyperspace, our heroes were able to evade the evil empire by creating "holes" in space from which they could "jump" from one location to another with ease, instantaneously. Hypertext allows people to consume texts in any order, "jumping" from idea to idea as they wish. Authors of hypertext documents shape this experience somewhat by placing links in their pages, suggesting connections between documents that may not be so apparent from a traditional linear order. As discussed in chapter 2, this hypertext business raises serious questions about the power of authorship and the responsibilities of readership. But our purpose here is to explore the ways in which you can craft textual spaces that enable the reader to discover connections across, between, and beyond your words.

So far, we've figured out the "hypertext" in hypertext markup language; now let's tackle the "markup" part. Markup refers to the traditional editing practice in which the author takes a pen and literally "marks up" the page with extra notations to indicate specifically how the page should appear when it is complete. Here is an example: You

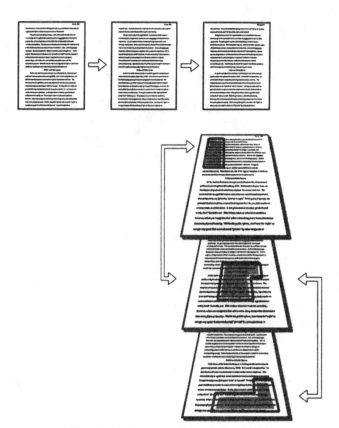

Fig. A.1. Linear versus hypertext.

might manually place an underline beneath a word to emphasize that the word should be underlined or italicized in the final draft of your document. HTML works the same way. This language adds notations called tags to tell browsers how to display the documents they have downloaded from the server. Thus, an HTML document is no different from any word-processing document you create. In fact, you can write a Web-ready document using any kind of Notepad software. The only difference is that you add tags to the document to make it readable by browsers. What is a browser? A browser is like a pair of glasses. We often wear glasses to see the world more clearly. We use a browser to access information more easily. A browser—such as Apple's Safari or Microsoft Explorer—helps you "see" the information on the Web; it also helps you select which information you wish to see and which information you wish to ignore. A browser "reads" a web page when you use a computer to access files in another computer called a server, a machine that stores information. You maintain your files in a "public folder" on your server. The files can be as simple as a school lunch menu or as complicated as a virtual world complete with three-dimensional images and stereo sound. The principle in accessing files on the Web is pretty much the same.

So, what actually happens when you browse a web page? When your browser accesses a document on the Web, it takes a copy of the information you seek and places it in your hard drive, the location in your computer where its files are saved. The Internet connection (phone lines and a modem, ethernet connection, or some other way of accessing this information) is necessary to get the Web document. The browser is necessary to "read" the document by translating HTML tags.

What can tags do? That answer is evolving. During the infancy of the WWW, tags were utilitarian. They centered text, added italics, and facilitated other simple tasks. Nowadays, tags allow page authors to lay their documents out with precision that rivals that of a magazine designer. For our purposes, however, it is necessary only to speak of a handful of tags. Once you know how to use these tags, you will be able to create documents that can be read by any browser in the world. At this point, you might wonder, "Why learn HTML tags" when there are plenty of software packages that can create web pages—no HTML required? The authors of this book believe that you should first learn the nuts and bolts of HTML, its theory and its functions, before playing with software packages like Dreamweaver and Frontpage. Moreover, if you learn basic HTML code, you're more likely to craft documents that can be read on any browser; code created by packages can sometimes create havoc on browsers.

The first tags you should know are those that are essential for your page to be read. When a browser "reads" a page, it looks for these tags first.

```
<html>
<head>
<title>
Note: Your page title appears here.
</title>
</head>
<body>
Body of your page appears here.
</body>
</html>
```

Let's discuss them in turn.

- <html> is generally the first tag that should appear on your page. It tells the browser, "Read this document as a hypertext-markup-language document."
- <head> tells the browser, "The information from this part onward (until I indicate otherwise) is for you to organize this document in relation to others." An HTML document is composed of a "head" and a "body." Information at the head will not appear in the browser window (with one exception, which is explained later). It is information used by the browser and the server. In the example we have provided, the only information in the head is a "title." But some heads include special key words designed to help automated search engines locate your documents more easily.
- <title> tells the browser, "The information from this part onward (until I indicate otherwise) will appear in the 'title' section of the browser." The title is generally found at the very top of your browser, above the buttons. If someone chooses to bookmark your page, the title is the name his or her browser will give to that link.

- </title> tells the browser, "I've stopped naming the title." Notice how the slash (/) is the browser's cue to stop some function. Almost all tags work in this manner. Thus, <title> says, "Start title here." </title> says, "stop title now. " The information between these tags (above, we wrote "Note: Your page title appears here") is usually a descriptive word or phrase such as "my home page." **Remember**: The title is not the same as a headline that might appear in the body section of your web page. It only appears at the very top of your browser. Also, you should never put other tags in the title section; they will appear as the title.
- </head> tells the browser, "I've stopped creating the head. Everything from here onward is the body." **Remember**: You have to use the slash to tell the browser, "Stop reading the document in this manner."
- <body> tells the browser, "The information from this part onward (until I indicate otherwise) will appear in the "body" section of the browser." This section is the "page" we've been talking about. The page can include words, pictures, and other media. In theory, you don't need any tags in the body section; the browser will display your words without them. However, certain tags are necessary to ensure that your words will be displayed in a reader-friendly manner.
- </body> tells the browser, "I've stopped creating the body. Nothing from here onward should appear on my page."
- </html> tells the browser, "My HTML document is complete." This tag is not technically essential, but some browsers get cranky without it.

SOME COMMON TAGS

At this point, we've learned that on any page, regardless of its complexity, you will find the same set of tags. They are fairly basic to use, but not so easy to remember when you're first developing pages. To save time, we recommend that you create a page with those tags to serve as a template. Then, when you wish to start a new HTML page, open the template and save it under a different name. Let's explore some more tags you can use to lay out your pages.

These first tags are exceptions to the rule that states that each tag must come paired with another one containing a slash (Remember <tag> and </tag>?). These tags are useful when you want to avoid excessive "gray" on your pages. They create hard returns and line breaks. "Wait a second," you might say. "Don't we use key strokes to do that?" Yes, but browsers aren't terribly discriminating. They read text but don't care about keyboard niceties like hard returns. Browsers do read the single space-bar strokes that separate words, but they ignore strokes beyond that.

Thus, "Web design is   fun." would read, "Web design is fun." Moreover, a text document laid out in this manner:

> Web design
> is fun.

would read on a browser, "Web design is fun."

Fortunately, we have tags that can tell the browser, "I want the line to stop. I want you to create a hard return."

<P>   The "P" tag works as a hard return and a space between lines. It won't provide more than one hard return at a time, however. In other words, <P><P><P> only gives you one empty line.

                   The "BR" tag works as a simple line break. For example, to tell the browser to break text up into stanzas, you'd code as follows:

                       Gone, gone, sold and gone
To the rice swamp dank and lone
From Virginia hills and waters—
Woe is me, my stolen daughters!

Your browser would display the text in this manner:

    Gone, gone, sold and gone
    To the rice swamp dank and lone
    From Virginia hills and waters—
    Woe is me, my stolen daughters!

Remember: The browser doesn't care if you use hard returns to separate the text. It only looks for commands within these keys: < and >.

<H>   Use this tag to control the size and boldness of headers and subheaders. This command requires a number to tell the browser how large the text should be. The command also requires a closing tag (with a slash) to tell the browser, "Stop formatting the text this way. Go to standard size." There are six options—<h1> through <h6>. The lower the number, the larger the font. For example:

                       <h1>This is text</h1> would display This is text

                       <h6>This is text</h6> would display This is text

<font size>   Use this tag to control large sections of text. <font size=+1> tells the browser, "Add one unit of size to the size of font." <font size=−1> tells the browser, "Subtract one unit of size from the size of the font." At the end of the text you are resizing, place the tag </font> to tell the browser, "Go back to the normal font size."

                       <font size=+1>Look at the large font</font> that is available

Look at the large font that is available

Remember: You don't need to use the font size tag unless you want to alter the font size. Browsers have a default size that's fairly readable.

<a href=" "></a> This is a set of complicated but powerful tags. They allow you to link to other documents within and beyond your pages. When a

browser sees the tag <a href=", it looks for the quotation marks. Within those quotes, you will place the Web address of the site to which you are linking. The browser will then look for the > symbol. After that symbol—and before the < symbol, any text you place will be highlighted. The text becomes a hypertext link that, when clicked, downloads the file addressed within those quotes. The </a> tag is absolutely essential. It tells the browser, "Don't turn any text beyond this point into hypertext unless I start a new link."

Here's an example. To link to one of the authors' home pages, you'd tag as follows:

Here's a link to
<a href="http://www.sjsu.edu/faculty/wooda">
Dr. Andrew Wood</a>'s home page.

Note: Within the quotation marks, you place the full address of Dr. Wood's page. Between the > and the <, you tell the browser what word (or words) to highlight. After the </a>, you instruct the browser to stop highlighting. The result is this:

Here's a link to **Dr. Andrew Wood**'s home page.

Note: The boldfaced words, when selected by clicking, tell the browser to link to the address within the quotes.

You can also link to other pages within your own server space (we'll talk more about placing files in your server later). This is useful to break up long pages. Instead, you can provide several short pages and allow readers to choose the direction they will follow. When linking to a file within your public folder, you don't need the full address—just the name of the document will do.

<center> This tag centers a piece of text. In fact, all text below it will be centered until you employ the </center> tag. For example:

This text is not centered.
<P>
This text is.
<P>
This text is not centered.

A browser would display the coded text in this manner.

This text is not centered.

This text is.

This text is not centered.

<B> This tag allows you to set pieces of text in boldface. To do so, place the <B> before the text you wish to boldface and a </B> after the text you wish to make boldface. Thus:

This text is <B>bold</B>.
This text is **bold**.

<I>   This tag allows you to set pieces of text in italics. To do so, place the
                  <I> before the text to be italicized and </I> after the text you wish to
                  italicize. Thus:

> This text is <I>italicized</I>.
> This text is *italicized*.

<U>   This tag allows you to underline pieces of text. To do so, place the <U>
                  before the text to be underlined and a </U> after the text you wish to
                  underline. Thus:

> This text is <U>underlined</U>.
> This text is <u>underlined.</u>

DISPLAYING IMAGES

Using the <IMG> tag, you can display images on your web page. The <IMG> tag acts
sort of like a linking tag. It instructs the browser to locate a document and display
its contents. In this case, the document is an image. On the Internet, most images
end with either .gif or .jpeg as their suffix. What's the difference between .gif and
.jpeg? Image type .gif generally is used for images with flat color (cartoons, for example). The suffix .jpeg is saved for more complicated images with rich gradients
of color (photographs, for example). .gif images almost always take up less memory
than .jpeg images. Linking to an image requires a tag with the following attributes:
<IMG SRC>
   This tag tells the browser, "Look for an image at the following location and display
it." The location of that image is a web address, placed within the quotation marks.
Here's an example:

> <IMG SRC="http://www.sjsu.edu/faculty/wooda/homeguy3.jpeg">

Note: There must be no spaces within the quotation marks, just the Web address.
   The address should provide the browser enough information to find the image.
If you are displaying an image that is not in your public folder, provide the entire
address (see earlier example). If, however, you are displaying an image in the same
public folder as the html document, you need only place the name of the image
(including suffix) in your tag. Example:

> <IMG SRC="logo.gif">

OTHER IMG ATTRIBUTES

Within the tag you may add other attributes such as ALT, HEIGHT, and WIDTH.
ALT is used to display text while the image is downloading to provide users a sense
of what they'll see. ALT is particularly useful for text-only browsers (such as those
used by the visually impaired). HEIGHT and WIDTH can be placed in the IMG tag
to tell the browser the dimensions of the image. These attributes are useful if you
have many images along with your text on a page. There are some browsers that
require so much effort to process those images that they won't display the text for
several seconds or longer, forcing the user to wait for anything to appear on the

screen. With the HEIGHT and WIDTH tags, the browser can calculate the approximate dimensions of the images and display the text first. Then, while the user reads the text, the browser works to display the images. Here's an example of a tag using all of these attributes:

```
<IMG HEIGHT=38 WIDTH=30 ALT="image description"
SRC="logo.gif">
```

UPLOADING AND DOWNLOADING FILES

Accessing the WWW is really just a process of uploading and downloading information between your computer and a server that maintains files. We know that browsers search for documents in our public folders and download them, based on the addresses they are sent. The question remains, How do we upload files to our folders? For many web page maintainers, the answer is a free piece of software that enables a process called File Transfer Protocol (FTP). FTP does pretty much what its name signifies. It transfers files according to a common protocol so that their contents remain unaltered, even as they cruise in digital format through multiple telephone wires.

Although each piece of FTP software works in a slightly different way, the process is similar. You select a file or files on your hard drive and indicate—through either pressing a button or "dragging"—that you wish to move a copy of that file to a location on a remote server. All types of FTP software need four pieces of information to transfer your files. They need a server, a path, a user name, and a password.

- The server is the address where the computer that stores your files is situated on the Internet. Frequently, the address for this site is unlike the location of a document on the WWW.
- The path is a set of nested folders that indicates specifically where your public folder is located. Again, this address is unlike your Web address. It is composed of locations that are specific to the server.
- The user name is pretty simple. It's the name you use to access your account with the university or your ISP.
- The password is also pretty self-explanatory. It's the word (generally a combination of letters and numbers) that ensures that only you can alter files in your public folder. By keeping your password secure, other people can look at your public files, but only you can alter them.

Once you have established a connection to the server through FTP software, you move the documents in the manner indicated by the specific program you're using. The process is fairly simple either way. For instance, if you are using a piece of software called Fetch to FTP your files, you will see a window filled with the documents in your public folder. Using the mouse, you select the document on your hard drive and drag that document into the server window. Depending on the speed of the Internet connection, the file transfer can range from being instantaneous to being mind-numbingly slow. The only other consideration is to ensure that you are using the correct protocol for your document type. If you are given the option to choose, select "text" for HTML documents and "binary" for images (in either .gif or .jpeg format). This is not a rule; it is advice after trial and error on several systems.

Learning how to get online and develop web pages takes practice and patience, but the result is worth the effort. There's a world of ideas floating between computer servers and bouncing off the satellites. We hope that this appendix has helped you get closer to entering that world.

RESEARCHING THE INTERNET EXPERIENCE

If you've read parts of *Online Communication* or completed the whole book to this point, then you have some appreciation for how academics are striving to understand the online experience. As you've probably noticed in your reading, researchers from communication, composition, computer science, law, psychology, and sociology, to name but a few disciplines, are working to interpret the human-to-human interactions mediated by computer technology. As you know, the introduction of the Internet into our lives has raised a host of issues, including questions about self, relationships, addiction, communities, commerce, privacy, and censorship, among others. The answers to these questions rest in careful investigation into Internet phenomena.

As an appendix to this book, we suggest some of the considerations scholars have taken as they have sought explanations for online phenomena. In particular, this appendix defines two types of scholarship into mediating technologies and reviews guidelines for conducting ethical research initiatives. It is our hope that these points will assist you as you evaluate the research of others and plan research projects of your own. As you have read in the previous chapters, the results of such investigations have yielded a growing body of literature that helps us make sense of the communicating online, and your contribution could be one that furthers our knowledge that much more.

RESEARCH INTO THE TECHNICAL OR SOCIAL ASPECTS OF CMC

In *Doing Internet Research*, James Costigan (1999) states that CMC literature can be divided into two categories. The first category involves research into how information is stored and retrieved from the Internet. This research seems to focus on the technological aspects of the computer and its software and the implications for how humans manage them. Such a technological perspective is evident in the following two relevant works of communication scholarship.

In the first, Greg Elmer (1997) examines how the indexing capabilities of the Internet function. One form of indexing that many of us encounter is through search engines on the World Wide Web. These engines draw particular sites to our attention, but also draw attention to us. As Elmer notes, a number of sites, notably those of a commercial nature, are seeking to index us by soliciting our personal information for marketing purposes. His research calls to our attention the double-edged sword of the Internet indexing functions. Another scholarly contribution in terms of understanding how humans manage the Internet comes from Steve Whittaker and Candace Sidner (1997). They looked at how people manage "e-mail overload," which is when one gets too many messages to cope with all of them efficiently. Their research reveals some of the ways in which people flooded with so much communication practice the reading, filing, and overlooking of and the responding to messages. (Other examples of this kind of research are found throughout the text, with a notable amount appearing in chapter 7.)

In addition to aspects of technology management, Costigan (1999) cites a second body of research that has emerged, this one dealing with the social aspects of the Internet. This is the kind of research that covers human interaction in forums like newsgroups, chat rooms, and MUDs. As he notes, "Research on these topics is truly unique to the Internet. There is no existing parallel social construct, and in many ways, the Internet creates wholly new social constructs" (p. xix). Much of the material in the previous chapters draws on this type of research. (Chapter 4 is particularly rich with this kind of research.)

In pursuing knowledge about the social aspects of the Internet, scholars have adopted a number of methods to explore questions they have about these "new social constructs." Some have "gone native," participated with the various forms of CMC, and then written ethnographies of their experiences. A good deal of work on software designed for group decision making involved experiments where the responses of a group exposed to online interaction were compared to those of a control group of people who interacted without mediation. Other researchers have performed surveys in order to solicit the feedback of other users. Still others adopt a more critical perspective and have analyzed examples of communication as artifacts from a rhetorical perspective. Certainly these and many more of the research methodologies scholars use to investigate human interaction in other contexts have been, or have the potential to be, used in online research as well.

As you move forward in your studies of CMC, it is likely that you too will have questions about the nature of social phenomena online. As you consider how to come up with answers to these questions, you too will need to consider what type of phenomenon you will be examining and what scholarly methods will provide you with a greater understanding of it. As you do, however, it is important that you keep in mind certain ethical principles to guide your investigation.

Hyperlink: Reading up on Internet Research

If you are about to explore some question that you have about the social phenomenon of the Internet, there's a good chance that related research on the topic may already have been published. In order to track down these sources, you may have to review a number of indexes and databases. Kevin Kawamoto (2003) has collected a list of periodicals that frequently publish research articles focusing on online communication. Among others, his list includes the following publications:

Computers in Human Behavior
Convergence
Cybersociology
Electronic Journal of Communication
First Monday
International Journal of Human-Computer Studies
Journal of Computer-Mediated Communication
Journal of Online Behavior
New Media & Society

Kawamoto (2003) also recommends that researchers consult the resources of sites that specialize in Internet research, including the following.

The Association for Internet Researchers (http://www.aoir.org)
The Internet Studies Center (http://www.isc.umn.edu)
Resource Center for Cyberculture Studies
   (http://www.com.washington.edu/rccs/)

Other good starting points for finding literature on a particular topic include consulting an existing bibliography (such as the lists of references found at the end of each chapter in this and other books) as well as conferring with a qualified research librarian for assistance.

PRACTICING ETHICS IN ONLINE RESEARCH

Hand-in-hand with what you want to learn about online interaction is how you go about investigating it. Advocates for an ethical approach to Internet research argue that a code of ethics should guide our inquiries whenever human beings are voluntarily contributing to our efforts, in real life or virtual life (Hamilton, 1999; Suler, 2000). Even as researchers who use student volunteers in their experiments or distribute survey questionnaires to mass lecture courses must protect their subjects from harm, so too must those who conduct research online keep their contributors safe.

Traditionally, a plan for research involving human subjects has taken into account three crucial factors. John Suler (2000) explains that these factors are:

1. Obtaining "informed consent" from the participants, such that they are aware of the fact that research is being done and the ends to which information collected about them will be put.
2. Ensuring the privacy of those involved, so that confidentiality is maintained and no discernible harm can come to them as a result of participating in the study.
3. Consulting with knowledgeable colleagues about the ethical issues involved in the study and, consequently, adjusting the method to minimize the potential for harm to the participants.

In search of meeting those criteria, we can look to James Hamilton (1999), who recommends that researchers indeed construct a careful plan for conducting their efforts and submit it to the members of the **Institutional Review Board (IRB).** At universities, an IRB helps to ensure that research involving human or animal test subjects is conducted in an ethical manner. However, because online research is a relatively recent phenomenon, IRBs may not as yet have established guidelines for what qualifies as ethical research on the Internet. Moreover, some smaller institutions may not have such an overseeing body to provide guidance, and thus Hamilton has suggested minimal guidelines to facilitate such research.

The researcher should provide...

- A way (e-mail, address, or phone number) for participants to contact the researcher.
- A means for obtaining participants' fully informed consent.
- Full disclosure of any risks to the participants' confidentiality.
- A postexperimental debriefing page.
- A way for the participants to learn about the results of the study. (adapted from Hamilton, 1999)

Hamilton's five minimal guidelines emphasize that researchers have a responsibility to provide their subjects with as much information as possible, beginning with who the researcher is and continuing through the completion of the project. First, identifying oneself and one's professional affiliation is a good idea, if only because it serves to distinguish one's legitimate research efforts from those of commercial or parody efforts. Second, respondents should be provided with a form for acknowledging that they are aware of the research and its purpose. If you have ever participated in a research project on campus, you might recall signing an informed consent form prior to your participation. In like manner, online participants should be told what they are getting into and have a channel to acknowledge their agreement to have the information they provide used for research-specific purposes. Implicit in the third checklist item are the steps that the researcher should take to protect the identity of any respondent. Letting people know the degree to which their information is secure from the prying eyes of a hacker, especially if the information is sensitive, is a fair disclosure in helping a person decide whether or not to contribute to the research. Fourth, following the completed experiment, respondents should be directed to a debriefing page, which provides them with a full explanation of the study and, as indicated by the fifth criterion, a reference for how to learn the results of the research initiative (such as a Web site or other publication they can eventually turn to).

Hamilton is concerned that researchers using the Internet may not be treating people online with the same safeguards as they would people in real life. If you have questions about online communication that you are looking forward to having answered using online surveys or experiments, keep in mind that behind every tally and comment there is a person who should enjoy the same privacy that you would expect as a participant yourself.

Certainly, there is a lot yet to be explored when it comes to understanding and managing online interaction. We hope that our introduction to the issues raised and research conducted up to this writing will help you in your own further explorations into the nature and processes of CMC.

REFERENCES

Costigan, J. T. (1999). Introduction: Forests, trees, and Internet research. In S. Jones (Ed.), *Doing Internet research: Critical issues and methods for examining the net* (pp. xvii–xxiv). Thousand Oaks, CA: Sage.

Elmer, G. (1997). Spaces of surveillance: Indexicality and solicitation on the Internet. *Critical Studies in Mass Communication, 14*, 182–191.

Hamilton, J. C. (1999, December 3). The ethics of conducting social-science research on the Internet. *The Chronicle of Higher Education,* pp. B6–B7.

Kawamoto, K. (2003). *Media and society in the digital age.* Boston: Allyn & Bacon.

Suler, J. C. (2000). Ethics in cyberspace research: Consent, privacy, and contribution. In *The psychology of cyberspace* [Online]. Available: http://www.rider.edu/suler/psycyber/psycyber.html

Whittaker, S., & Sidner, C. (1997). Email overload: Exploring personal information management of email. In S. Kiesler (Ed.), *Culture of the Internet* (pp. 277–295). Mahwah, NJ: Lawrence Erlbaum Associates.

GLOSSARY

ACE model: A theoretical explanation for the allure of the Internet that suggests that the qualities of accessibility, control, and excitement lead to IAD.

Ad hoc communities: Communities of individuals brought together by an unforeseen event.

Agonistic communication: Discourse that produces or invokes ritualized conflict with an established order.

Agora: An open meeting space within the Greek city of Athens, commonly used for transacting all kinds of social exchanges.

Analytical engine: A 19th-century concept that serves as the predecessor to the modern computer.

Anonymity: Communication without one's identity being apparent.

Anticipatory conformity: Adopting a docile and disciplined relationship to authority because of the potential rather than the practice of domination.

Apa: Amateur press association, an imagined community sustained by members who distribute self-published periodicals to one another.

ARPANET: Early computer network designed for the U.S. Defense Department.

Artifacts: Bits and pieces of human sense-making: books, magazines, movies, posters, comics, and the like.

Asynchronous communication: The exchange of messages with significant lag time between them.

Avatar: An incarnation of oneself in a virtual environment.

Bandwidth: The resources (including others' patience) consumed by messages in online forums; originally bandwidth referenced the carrying capacity of media delivery systems, such as a cable line.

Blog: A journal-like Web site where authors regularly post new contributions of prose, poetry, hypertext links, and other materials for readers.

Browser: A software program that interprets information from the Internet and displays it as text, images, animation, and sounds (e.g., Mosaic, Netscape Navigator, Microsoft Explorer).

Bulletin board system (BBS): A publicly accessible collection of organized messages posted by various contributors.

Chronemics: The use of time as a nonverbal channel for communicating qualities such as liking or dominance.

Command and control: The channeling of information to ensure that individuals act efficiently as a unit.

Computer anxiety: Fear of using or considering using computer technology.

Computer-assisted therapy (CAT) programs: Software that provides an interactive, conversational experience with alleged mental health benefits (e.g., ELIZA).

Computer-mediated communication (CMC): The ways in which human behaviors are maintained or altered by exchange of information through machines.

Cookies: Pieces of software downloaded from a computer network or Web site used to track your individual computing habits. Cookies are frequently used to generate customized browsing experiences on the World Wide Web.

Copyright: A property right over intangible materials such as books, musical compositions, and films.

Corporate convergence: The blurring of previously disparate industries. Convergence commonly occurs within and between communications, information, and computer industries. A recent example of corporate convergence is the creation of MSNBC—a blurring of information technology and a news and entertainment company. Goals of corporate convergence include cross-promotion and cross-media program development.

Cues-filtered-out approach: A perspective on CMC that says the Internet is inferior as a channel for communication because of a lack of nonverbal cues.

Cyberaffair: A perceived infidelity that occurs when one partner in a real-life relationship maintains a romantic relationship with a different partner online.

Cyberbalkanization: The fragmentation of virtual communities into potentially intolerant interest groups.

Cybernetics: The science of automatic control systems.

Cyberpunk: 1980s literary movement whose primary theme is the blurring distinction between humans and machines.

Cybersex: Textual descriptions of sexual behavior exchanged between two partners in an online encounter.

Cyberslacking: Using corporate information technology for personal ends.

Cyberspace: The consensual, conceptual space where online interaction occurs.

Cybersquatter: An entrepreneur who registers for a domain name and then sells the rights to use that domain name to another person or corporate entity for a profit.

Cyberstalking: The repeated sending of harassing or threatening electronic communications.

Cyborg: Mechanical blurring of human and machine, illustrated by the 1970s show, *The Six Million Dollar Man*.

Data mining: Process through which disparate pieces of information from multiple sources are gathered, stored, and sold to develop an evolving construct of a person's habits and personality.

Deindividuation: The psychological process of surrendering personal identity in favor of the dominant social identity; the so-called mob mentality.

Dépaysement: Process of seeing the familiar through different eyes.

Diffusion of innovations: Communication about new ideas through certain channels over time among members of a social system.

Digital divide: A statistical difference in access to computer technology among various demographic groups.

Disciplinary technology: A critical perspective on CMC that studies the ways in which machines serve to reflect and reinforce power relationships between individuals and groups.

Discursive resistance: A process through which text, oral, nonverbal communication, and other forms of meaning-making are employed to imagine alternatives to dominant power structures.

Domain name: A recognizable URL, or address on the World Wide Web, typically used by corporations and individuals to distinguish themselves through a popular term or trademark (e.g., www.mcdonalds.com).

Dystopia: Opposite of utopia; a "bad place."

Electronic communications monitoring: Storage and review of e-mail, recording and review of telephone conversations, storage and review of voice mail messages, storage and review of computer files, and video recording of employee job performance (definition adopted from American Management Association).

Electronic panopticon: An extension on the panopticon concept (see definition of panopticon) through which computer technology serves to deindividuate, isolate, and monitor the behaviors of persons, generally in a corporate context.

Emoticons: Text-based cues designed to reveal the emotional intent of a message.

Encyclopedia Humanus: A universal collection of all the knowledge generated by humankind.

Face-work: Effort invested in maintaining a role.

Filtering software: Software that limits access to certain Internet sites, often by comparing Web addresses requested by users against a directory of domains.

Firewall: Software and hardware barriers that regulate access between networks.

Flaming: The practice of sending intended or perceived hostile messages in mediated contexts.

Functional alternatives: A perception that one channel accomplishes the same task just as well as another.

Futureshock: Term coined by Alvin Toffler to describe the results of excessive innovation and social change.

Garden: Metaphor for a return to organic life marked by simplicity and consistency.

Gazelle firm: A fast-growing company, typically at a rate of 20% per year for 4 years.

Gemeinschaft: A sense of community based on identification with the group.

Gender-swapping: The adoption of a gender other than one's own in presenting oneself in mediated contexts.

Gernsback Continuum: An alternative universe that exists alongside our own—and occasionally intersects with our "real" world through artifacts such as comics, novels, films, and other forms of human communication.

Gesellschaft: A community based on proximity and circumstance.

Handle: A pseudonym on CB radio.

Hate site: Web site that advocates violence against or unreasonable hostility toward those persons or organizations identified by their race, religion, national origin, sexual orientation, gender, or disability.

High-tech clusters: Concentrations of technological innovations such as Silicon Valley and Multimedia Gulch that generally depend on four factors to thrive: access to talent, proximity to other industries/support services, access to capital, and a high quality of life.

Hyperlink: Selected words or images that connect to other sections of a document or other documents in a hypertext environment like the World Wide Web.

Hyperpersonal communication: A perspective on mediated communication suggesting that greater control over self-presentation by the sender, overestimations by the receiver, the asynchronicity of the channel, and confirming messages offered through feedback allow some people to express themselves better in mediated rather than in face-to-face interactions.

Hypertext: A form of nonsequential writing that composes a text out of smaller bits of material that exist in relation to one another in a multilinear, decentralized network.

Identity: A construct formed by the interaction of the self with the social environment.

Identity fraud: A criminal's misuse of another individual's personal information (e.g., credit card number) to make unauthorized purchases or commit crimes using the victim's name.

Imagined communities: Aggregates of people who, thanks to forms of mediated communication, perceive themselves as part of a common social unit despite the geographic distances among them.

Immediate communication: "Live," face-to-face human interaction.

Informacy: Extension of literacy, a universal right to information.

Information: An exchange of data necessary for one system to influence the behavior of another system.

Information economy: An economy marked by an emphasis on knowledge and symbol manipulation, in contrast to an economy whose success is measured by the production of physical goods.

Information society: A broader term for a society whose cohesion may be traced to a dependence on standardization, bureaucracy, and national-scale advertising rather than oral traditions and regional ties.

Infotainment: An example of convergence: The blurring of information and entertainment.

Intentional communities: Planned organizations of individuals to accomplish some goal or maintain some lifestyle.

Internet: A network of computers that allows for the transmission of data for multiple purposes through a common set of protocols according to a global address system.

Interactivity: The quality of telepresence that measures a person's ability to manipulate the content of the medium.

Internet addiction disorder (IAD): A psychological condition associated with Internet use that leads to adverse effects on one's psychological, physical, or social well-being.

Internet relay chat (IRC): Synchronous exchanges of primarily text-based messages through an online channel.

Jacquard loom: A device that allows a weaver to mass-produce patterns of cloth by following the patterns of punch cards.

Lexia: A chunk of material in hypertext.

Listservs: A type of e-mail in which one posts messages to and receives messages from others through a program that delivers to all those who subscribe to it.

Lurkers: People who observe but make no contribution to a virtual community.

Machine: Metaphor for industrial life that perpetuates human progress.

Mediated communication: Human interaction that is aided by some exterior technology such as print, radio, or the Internet.

Memex: A theoretical machine for the storage and retrieval of information linked together by hypertext.

Metacommunication: Communication about communication.

AUTHOR INDEX

Page numbers in *italics* denote full bibliographic references.

A

A. T. Kearney (Consulting Firm) 160, *164*
Adams, H., 196, *210*
Adams, T. L., 113, *121*, 187, *193*
Aden, R., 196, 201, *210*
Ahrenberg, S., 198, *210*
Alighieri, D., 21
Allison, C., 96, *99*
Alstyne, M. V., 138, *142*
American Management Association, 152, *164*
American Psychological Association, 110, 115, *118*
Anderson, B., 125, *142*
Anselmo, J. C., 139, *142*
Anti-Defamation League, 189, *192*
Apple Computer, 204, *210*

B

Badham, J., *211*
Balsamo, A., 197, *211*
Baran, B., 167, *177*
Bargh, J. A., 60, *75*
Barker, J. R., 150, *164*
Barlow, J. P., 21, *26*, 78
Baym, N. K., 12, *26*, 129–131, *142*
Beard, K. W, 108, *118*
Bechar-Israeli, H., 65, *75*
Belton, B., 148, *164*
Benedikt, M., 21, *26*
Beniger, J. R., 148, *164*
Bennahum, 35, *47*
Berman, B., 206, *211*
Bernhardt, J. M., 115, *118*
Bertman, S., 201, *211*
Bethke, B., 198, *211*
Bier, M., 170, *177*
Bilstad, B. T., 105, *118*
Binik, Y. M., 110, 114, *118*
Biocca, F., 207, *212*
Birdwhistle, R. L., 79, *98*

Birnie, S. A., 88, *98*
Birsch , D., 105, *118*
Black, G., 166, *177*
Blackburn, N., 151, *164*
Blair, C., 181, *193*
Boaz, D., 170, *177*
Bornstein, K., 61, *75*
Bosky, B., 125, *142*
Botan, C., 152, *164*
Bowles, S., 209, *211*
Boyd, J., 123, *142*
Brasher, B. E., 20, *27*
Bressand, A., 78
Bricking, T., 102, *119*
Bromberg, H., 19, *26*
Brown, A., 101
Bruckheimer, J., 150, *164*
Bruckman, A., 58, 61, *75*
Brummett, B., 194, *211*
Brynjolfsson, E., 138, *142*
Bugeja, M. J., 7, *26*
Bush, V, 35, *47*
Buten, J., 61, *75*

C

Cantor, J., 110, 114, *118*
Carmody, D., *210*
Cathcart, R. S., 184–185, *193*
Chandler, D., 66, *75*
Chang, G., 102, *121*
Chaplin, C., 147, *164*
Cheney, G., 150, *164*
Chester, A., 66, *75*
Christie, B., 80, *99*
Clark, L. S., 93–94, *98*
Cleaver, H. M., 183, *193*
Cody, M. J., 16, *26*
Cole, J. I., 108, *119*
Conklin, E. J., 199, *211*
Coombs, W. T., 179, *193*
Cornelliussen, R. A., 86, *99*
Costigan, J. T., 222–223, *226*

Page numbers in *italics* denote terms appearing in glossaries.